Revisiting *Divisions of Labour*

Manchester University Press

Revisiting *Divisions of Labour*

The impacts and legacies of a modern sociological classic

Edited by
GRAHAM CROW AND JAIMIE ELLIS

Manchester University Press

Published by Manchester University Press
Altrincham Street, Manchester M1 7JA

www.manchesteruniversitypress.co.uk

British Library Cataloguing-in-Publication Data
A catalogue record for this book is available from the British Library

Library of Congress Cataloging-in-Publication Data applied for

ISBN 978 1 5261 0743 5 hardback
ISBN 978 1 5261 0744 2 paperback

First published 2017

Typeset in 10.5/12.5pt Sabon by
Servis Filmsetting Ltd, Stockport, Cheshire
Printed in Great Britain
by CPI Group (UK) Ltd, Croydon, CR0 4YY

The book is dedicated to the memory of Ray Pahl (1935–2011)

Contents

Images

Photo section: Sheppey today

All photos in this section Mike Smith, 2015

Figures

Contributors

Graham Crow is Professor of Sociology and Methodology at the University of Edinburgh.

Jane Elliott is Chief Executive of the Economic and Social Research Council.

Jaimie Ellis is a research fellow in Health Sciences at the University of Southampton.

Jonathan Gershuny is Professor of Sociology at Nuffield College, Oxford.

John Holmwood is Professor of Sociology at the University of Nottingham.

Jon Lawrence is Reader in Modern British History at Emmanuel College, Cambridge.

Dawn Lyon is Senior Lecturer in Sociology at the University of Kent.

Mike Savage is Professor of Sociology at the London School of Economics.

Tim Strangleman is Professor of Sociology at the University of Kent.

Claire Wallace is Professor of Sociology at the University of Aberdeen.

Acknowledgements

This book evolved from Ray Pahl's idea of bringing out a second edition of *Divisions of Labour*, for which he had recovered the copyright from the publishers Wiley-Blackwell. A new edition based on comprehensive updating of the original fieldwork was obviously out of the question given the number of researcher years that would be required to achieve that, so instead the present book took shape. The contributors were approached with the invitation to write something on their views of what accounted for the success of *Divisions of Labour* in the period since its publication in 1984, and then to collaborate by sharing drafts among the group. A bequest from Ray Pahl's will enabled the group to meet up at this stage (November 2015), on the Isle of Sheppey. The Blue Town Heritage Centre kindly hosted this gathering, and Jenny Hurkett and her team deserve our thanks for facilitating a very productive and enjoyable visit. Our debt to Jenny runs deeper than this one event, because without her support many of the things reported in this book would not have been possible; as a community partner in our revisiting of the Isle of Sheppey and its people she has been stalwart in her support. Long may her enthusiasm for Sheppey and its people past and present continue to rub off on all those who meet her.

We are also grateful to Michael Smith for taking the photographs of present-day Sheppey. The original *Divisions of Labour* was given an added dimension through the inclusion of photographs, and we have sought to continue that here. The publisher's anonymous readers must be thanked for their careful reading of the draft manuscript and their helpful suggestions for improvements to the book as it now appears. Garry Runciman kindly commented on a draft of the Introduction in which we draw on his ideas in an effort to identify what made his friend Ray Pahl's work stand out. At Manchester University Press, Thomas Dark and Robert Byron have facilitated the process of getting published with a calm professionalism and supportiveness to us as editors for which we are very appreciative. And as editors we are also mindful of the supportiveness of our respective partners, Rose and Richard, who have over several years lived with our talk about the project to the point at which either could offer Sheppey as a *Mastermind* specialist subject. Sheppey and its people can have a captivating effect, as they evidently did for Ray Pahl, and because this book would not have been possible without that we dedicate it to him and his memory.

Graham Crow and Jaimie Ellis, July 2016

Introduction

Graham Crow and Jaimie Ellis

This is a book about another book, *Divisions of Labour*, written by R. E. (Ray) Pahl in 1984. There are several good reasons for returning to that book. First, it contains themes of enduring interest. It is about ordinary people and how they get by in difficult economic and social circumstances. It shows what can be learned about people's everyday lives when ordinary activity is investigated in an imaginative and sustained way. Second, it has been an extraordinarily influential book in British sociology and in countries and disciplines beyond. The path-breaking arguments that it contains meant that it became, and remains, a significant reference point in the sociological sub-fields of work, households, gender, class and stratification, community and social history, while also providing numerous insights into broader theoretical debates. Healthy citation rates of a book well into its second quarter century since publication are unusual and thus indicate something special. The book tells us numerous things about how a particular piece of research can come to stand out as extraordinary. Third, we have a methodological interest. We have returned to this book because of what it reveals about the craft of conceiving, planning, undertaking and presenting research. Ray Pahl was more frank than most social and economic investigators either then or now about research practice. The book provides an account of serious mistakes made and how these problematic situations were retrieved. It is a story of a research project, warts and all, but not only warts; the book also includes gems that help to set it apart from other research monographs. Together, these three elements persuaded us to revisit *Divisions of Labour* following the death of its author in 2011. Our task has not been to bring out a new edition of the book, although we have done that in part through selective excerpts which are intended to give a sense of the style and content of the original. The more important purpose has been to explore from a variety of angles what has gone into making the book a modern sociological classic.

We have undertaken this task as a collaborative project because the book's significance is acknowledged by many different people for a variety of reasons. One powerful rationale for revisiting it is to explore how it provided a springboard for subsequent debates through its sheer audacity and provocativeness. Its themes are certainly ambitious. Pahl was looking to do nothing less than to re-think what we understand by 'work'. In doing so he was bound to upset not only common-sense perspectives but also analytical frameworks that had been evolved and invested in by scholars, commentators and policy-makers over previous decades. By the mid-1970s it was increasingly apparent that these established frameworks were failing in both theory and practice. In the UK and other advanced industrial societies unemployment returned to levels not seen for more than a generation, to widespread surprise and dismay. At the same time the lack of attention to unpaid work, owing to a concentration on formal employment, was being questioned by feminists concerned with the issues of housework and family care, and by other social scientists with an interest in informality in the spheres of production and exchange broadly conceived. Together, these changes around not just paid work but divisions of labour in all processes of getting things done (at home as well as in the public sphere) struck Pahl as being potentially as significant as anything since the development of modern industrial societies. He was prompted to speculate that: 'It is just possible that the remaining two decades of the twentieth century will be a period of revolution in everyday life' (Pahl 1980: 17–18) while also noting that existing understandings appeared to stand in the way of the appreciation of this unfolding transformation. Mindful that the profundity of the changes wrought on families and households by the industrial revolution was not fully appreciated at the time that those changes unfolded, Pahl was wondering aloud whether a shift of similar historical proportions was afoot. Subsequently, others have pursued the idea that the third quarter of the twentieth century was distinctly favoured (Hobsbawm 1994), and that the 1970s witnessed a pivotal 'great transformation' (Blyth 2002) in economic thinking and institutional practice that led to a new and less comfortable set of arrangements.

Pahl's preparedness to re-think the various configurations of 'work' was coupled with unconventionality and inventiveness in research design. He saw the possibilities of following in the tradition of community studies or of conducting a policy-driven project as others around him were doing in the context of rising unemployment and social connections coming under corresponding strain. He opted to do neither, and chose instead to follow a more ambitious (and by implication more risky) route. Pahl was clear that he was not undertaking a conventional community study, a genre that had been critiqued as 'atheoretical and uncumulative' (Pahl 1980: 1). Of the six topics that were the core interests of Robert and Helen Lynd in 'Middletown' and which set the agenda for community studies, work and home figure prominently in *Divisions of Labour*, but education and leisure are mentioned only sporadically, while religion and community action are, by and large, absent. As a result the book is not an exploration of how the various constituent parts of community fit together on the Isle of Sheppey in Kent, the selected fieldwork site. The study was to be narrower than that, but also much wider as Pahl sought to place changing divisions of labour in broader historical, geographical and philosophical contexts. This concern to develop a far-reaching comparative perspective meant that the questions that interested Pahl went beyond the search for policy solutions to the immediate situation on the ground, important though he recognised that was. The project combined wide-ranging reviewing of several literatures (that it took the first third of the book to report upon) with a pioneering combination of fieldwork methods that included ethnographic observation, qualitative interviews, a large-scale formal survey, analysis of historical documents, oral history, essay-writing and photography. The research design that underpins the book was characterised by methodological innovation long before that term came into vogue.

Ray Pahl's route to Sheppey

The full extent of the book's ambitious methodological and theoretical agenda can be conveyed by tracing the book's gestation within the context of Pahl's unfolding career. This is summarised in the timeline of Pahl's life included at the end of this Introduction. Obituaries (e.g., Harloe 2011; Wallace 2011), career histories (e.g., Crow and Takeda 2011), and interviews with Pahl such as that in the Pioneers of Social Research collection (http://discover.ukdataservice.ac.uk/catalogue/?sn=6226) confirm that he was already a well-established mid-career academic by the mid-1970s when the ideas that formed the basis for a decade of research on Sheppey started to crystallise. They did so around the question of how people were getting by in the unfamiliar and challenging context of rates of unemployment that had been unknown for a generation, occurring at the same time as unprecedented rates of inflation. The conventional wisdom of the time, known as the Phillips curve, was that the reduction of either unemployment or inflation came at the cost of an increase in the other, so the simultaneous increase in unemployment and inflation was an indication of having entered a new and more perplexing era.

These changes threw into doubt the previous certainties following the Second World War settlement, namely secure employment (at least for male heads of households) and steadily rising living standards. All watershed moments, turning points and reversals of long-term trends are a challenge to contemporary observers who seek to understand them as they unfold (Abbott 2001b: chapter 8), so we should not expect it to have been immediately apparent at a time when the sustained move towards the reduction of social inequality in the UK that had been a product of the development of the welfare state was going into reverse. There were, even so, sufficient straws in the wind to suggest that some fundamental shift was occurring. By the 1970s the post-war settlement was clearly 'in trouble', and although it was less clear that the changes would be the precursors of 'Thatcherism at work' (MacInnes 1987: 26), it was apparent that the 'long boom' of the post-war decades had come to an end (Glyn and Sutcliffe 1972: 98). These developments were thrown into sharp relief not only by the break with past experience but also by being at odds with popular predictions of the direction of social change.

The American sociologist Daniel Bell's influential book *The Coming of Post-Industrial Society* (1973) was careful not to endorse the idea of the end of scarcity which had some currency at the time, but it nevertheless embodied a discordantly optimistic tone in mid-1970s Britain in which the word 'crisis' appeared more appropriate (Turner 2008). Bell had already focused attention on what might be expected by the end of the century in his and Stephen Graubard's *Toward the Year 2000* (1997 [1967]). When they returned to this project in 1997, Bell and Graubard conceded that although many of their predictions had been correct, they had 'failed to deal with the changing role of women' (Bell and Graubard 1997: xvii), particularly in the workplace. By the early 1970s the issue of gender and work had already attracted Pahl's attention in his and Jan Pahl's 1971 book *Managers and their Wives* in which the tensions around wives' opportunities for careers were noted. At the same time, Pahl was aware of significant changes occurring in both the housing and labour markets. Owner-occupation was becoming established as the majority tenure, and the benefits of property ownership relative to renting in an inflationary context meant that owner-occupiers 'may gain more from the housing market in a few years than would be possible from savings from a lifetime of earnings' (Pahl 1975: 291). In such circumstances, existing thinking about social class divisions as well as gender relations would be bound to need reassessment.

Like all good social scientists (indeed, all scientists), Pahl had an inquiring mind. He was curious about what was happening in the world around him, including things that were, for one reason or another, hidden from public view (something reflected in his interest in the writings of Erving Goffman (Pahl 1973)). His curiosity was coupled with a relaxed approach to speculation about what research might find, incorporating a certain frisson about the possibility of discovering something unexpected or troubling to existing ways of thinking and acting. It was a favoured maxim of Pahl's that researchers should 'always begin with history', and this concern to locate research in its appropriate historical context was complemented by his preparedness to speculate about emergent social trends. This speculative tendency was expressed in initial position statements that preceded his empirical investigation into the meaning of contemporary friendship (Pahl 2000; Spencer and Pahl 2006), for example. Here he pondered the idea that relations between friends were becoming 'an increasingly important form of social glue' (Pahl 2000: 1) as conventional family and place-based community relationships went into relative decline. The possibility that ideas put forward speculatively might turn out to be wrong was for Pahl an occupational hazard with which he was already acquainted by the time of the Sheppey project. One of the things for which he was best-known in his pre-Sheppey career was his writing on urban managerialism, but he was unabashed to acknowledge in a 1975 essay reconsidering this work that his approach of only a few years previously 'lacks both practical policy implications and theoretical substance'; it was wanting because: 'It ignores the constraints of capitalism' (Pahl 1975: 265, 268). This self-criticism is on a par with his earlier demolition of the rural–urban continuum in one telling sentence: 'Any attempt to tie particular patterns of social relationships to specific geographical milieux is a singularly fruitless exercise' (Pahl 1968: 293). The quest for truth requires unsparing criticism, including (where appropriate) self-criticism.

In the case of the Sheppey research, there are several expressions of speculative ideas that were formulated and published early on, including in his article with Jonathan Gershuny, 'Work outside employment: Some preliminary speculations' (Gershuny and Pahl 1981), which had first appeared in the *New Universities Quarterly* in the winter of 1979/80. The timing of this article is important because it pre-dates the great bulk of the Sheppey research, and it came out before he was prepared to disclose the location of his fieldwork (Pahl 1980: 2, fn. 1). This did not constrain Pahl from claiming that he, like Gershuny, had 'undertaken studies in urban areas which reveal buoyant communities coping with job losses through informal economic activity' (Gershuny and Pahl 1981: 83). This was a preliminary conclusion that Pahl would later concede was overly optimistic about the situation on Sheppey which the fuller investigation reported on in *Divisions of Labour* revealed to be a long way from 'buoyant'. His justification would have been that he and his co-author were setting a research agenda. Indeed, they declared the development of a better understanding of work outside of employment as 'the most urgent priority for research in the social sciences' (1981: 88), and were led to this conclusion by their speculations about the profundity of the changes unfolding around them.

Already in this piece are the key questions that underpinned *Divisions of Labour*, namely '*Which* work? in *which* economy? for *which* member of the household? for *how long*?' (1981: 87, emphases in original). In posing these questions they were prepared to look beyond the certainties of the post-war corporatist settlement that had promised full employment and general improvements to wellbeing but which was showing unmistakeable signs of being unable to continue to deliver them. Such a scenario required radically different fresh thinking, and Gershuny and Pahl's speculations about redefining 'work' and the possibilities for developing flexible patterns of sharing that work certainly fitted that bill. A pithy expression of these ideas in the journal *New Society* saw Gershuny and Pahl express the view that: 'We need new concepts as well as more detailed ethnography. The scale of adjustment in intellectual frameworks is enormous' (Gershuny and Pahl 1980: 9). They also argued that while some scenarios associated with the move away from the formal economy were 'grim', a more 'pleasant' one was also available in which the move from formal to informal economic activity could be seen as 're-skilling' rather than the more fashionable idea of 'de-skilling' (1980: 8), and linked to the potential to 'extend the range of genuine options open to people' (1980: 9).

In a similar vein, Pahl's 1980 article 'Employment, work and the domestic division of labour', published in the *International Journal of Urban and Regional*

Research, buzzed with speculative ideas. In a particularly provocative statement, he proposed that 'unemployment could, under certain specified conditions, be a positive benefit'. The logic of this argument was that the conditions of work as an employee can sometimes be 'bad', and that formal employment is only one of several ways in which people with skills can gain access to the necessities of life and affirmation as a worker. Income may be generated and the identity of a worker achieved through informal work. This may be remunerated by undocumented payments (undeclared to the tax authorities), or recompensed in kind. People may also produce things for themselves, which Pahl makes much of in *Divisions of Labour* as 'self-provisioning'. In these and other cases, unemployment pay may also be available, and this can also contribute to an individual who does not have formal employment nevertheless not being 'in such a vulnerable positon' (1980: 5) as classic accounts of unemployment would lead us to believe. Pahl acknowledged that his thinking was open to challenge as mere 'travellers' tales' (1980: 2), that it included anecdotes and trivial examples, and that: 'The criticism that I am basing my argument on a handful of cases in one labour market is inevitably correct' (1980: 16). His defence was that there was at least something that needed to be explained about the material that he (and, by the time he wrote the article, Claire Wallace) had started to collect, which suggested that fundamental changes were unfolding.

Adopting the device of presenting case studies of two contrasting couples that would work so effectively in the stories of Linda and Jim and Beryl and George in chapter 11 of *Divisions of Labour*, Pahl devoted a significant part of the article to describing the contrasting patterns of relationships to work (in all its forms) that the Simpson and the Parsons households had. This discussion included the suggestion that Mr Simpson had turned away from the world of formal employment and 'reverted to a pre-industrial pattern of hunter and gatherer' (1980: 13), for example by bartering wild duck that he had shot on the marshes. Pahl's argument then rowed back to the more cautious statement that: 'It is unlikely that my theme constitutes a paradigmatic shift … despite the confident assertions of some of the authorities I cite' (1980: 191). This step in his argument emphasised his role as the empirical investigator, obliged to explore the more outlandish speculations of others, even though he had elsewhere in the article engaged in just such speculation himself.

The contrasts between these early speculative pieces of writing and the more fully formed analyses put forward in *Divisions of Labour* are striking. In the book Pahl acknowledged that as the research proceeded and robust data were collected and analysed, the initial hypotheses had needed to be discarded. The book refuted the 1980 article (Pahl 1984: 11 fn. 23). He conceded that: 'my ideas in 1980 were, I was told, plausible, sociologically interesting and challenging. I have since had to modify them substantially' (1984: 13). His disarmingly upbeat assessment of this reversal of his position was captured in the remark, 'I am as delighted that I have been proved wrong as I would have been if I had been proved right. Perhaps more so' (1984: 200). This tells us several things. First, it confirms the narrative of his study of Sheppey that Pahl provided in the Introduction to the book. There was not one overarching plan at the outset, but a succession of research projects that grew seemingly exponentially from small beginnings as hunches. The acorn out of which the oak tree that is *Divisions of Labour* grew was a period of research leave in 1977 in which Pahl read extraordinarily widely, thought imaginatively, talked and argued with colleagues a lot, and undertook some very preliminary fieldwork in the nearby Medway towns, where the idea of 'urban pirates' gave early expression to the speculative position described in the 1980 article that the informal economy opened up opportunities for people to get by without formal employment.

The focus on the Isle of Sheppey resulted from the practical considerations which the funding body (the Nuffield Foundation) required as a condition of their support for two years' pilot research. Commencing in 1978 this included further ethnographic interviews and observations by Pahl and also Wallace, and 141 essays written by 16-year-olds about to leave full-time education for inauspicious employment prospects (Pahl 1978). Additional projects followed, including an ambitious survey of one in nine Sheppey households conducted by Social and Community Planning Research, a historical analysis of the Admiralty dockyard and the rise and fall of the occupational community that grew up around it (Buck 1981), a survey of local employers' attitudes, and other researchers and research students pursuing further issues. This research team grew sufficiently large to warrant Pahl buying a property in the fieldwork site, thereby following in the footsteps of other social scientists, such as Erving Goffman on Unst and Herbert Gans in 'Levittown'.

Had there been an overarching plan of work at the outset, *Divisions of Labour* would have been a very different book. Arguably, what holds the book together is the engagement by Pahl and his team with things thrown up by the fieldwork that do not quite fit established ways of thinking. Sheppey was neither straightforwardly urban nor rural but 'a curious mixture' (Pahl 1980: 14) of the two. Middle-class visitors would see it as 'an ugly and polluted industrial wasteland' (1980: 16), but the geographical space was treated with some affection by its inhabitants. And despite the constrained nature of their situation, people on the margins of the formal labour market could be seen to be responding pragmatically (Pahl 1982) and with 'a different rationality' (1984: 200), not a lack of rationality. Certainly, Pahl was under no illusions about the research process being neat and tidy. He was a contributor to the path-breaking book *Doing Sociological Research* (Bell and Newby 1977) which set out to de-bunk the sanitised narratives of methods 'cook books' whose recipes misled readers by leaving out the personal dimension of research. Pahl was setting the research agenda according to what struck him as curious and interesting. A key prompt in this respect was the presence of 'a disjunction between … [people's] personal experience' (Pahl 1984: 5) and inherited sociological wisdom. Murray Davis's aphorism that 'interesting ideas are novel because they externally contradict a conventional baseline' (Davis 2000: 113) is pertinent here. Pahl's sense was that established divisions of labour were breaking down. Informal ways of working were developing as a more flexible alternative to formal practices, and gendered norms associated with different types of work were coming under strain from both economic and cultural pressures to change. In short, existing arrangements were losing their capacity to convince in a time of endings and new beginnings. At such a moment of crisis, experimentation with speculative ideas carried more appeal than the reproduction of established agendas.

Pahl's speculations, which he acknowledged were presented in a 'polemical' (1984: 247) style, certainly captured people's attention. He recounted how the 1980 article was disseminated widely including through translation, and prompted many invitations to speak abroad as well as in the UK (1984: 10). He wondered whether it may have generated interest because it provided the sort of good news story that people at a time of difficulty wanted to hear (1984: 11). As a result, the publication of the book was eagerly awaited, to see whether the evidence supported the challenging idea of an unfolding revolution in everyday life that took people 'beyond employment', to use the title of one of the books in which findings from the Sheppey project were published (Redclift and Mingione 1985). It was the point at which 'empirical research caught up with theoretical speculation' (Edgell 2006: 145).

For a book of its size and scope, it was written and put into the public domain remarkably quickly (Pahl 1984: viii). Given the amount of material collected on Sheppey, the publication could have stretched to several volumes and Pahl had been happy to countenance this, but his publishers and his university were keen to see speedy publication. Numerous reviews appeared, commending Pahl's willingness to challenge sociological wisdom and his engaging and accessible writing style. It was 'sociology at its penetrating best' (Marshall 1985: 450). For Peter Saunders, the subject matter made for 'bleak reading', but the book was nevertheless 'delightfully well written' (1985: 645, 646). Linda McDowell called it 'an interesting and provocative book' in which Pahl managed 'to not only produce a masterly synthesis of existing debates but also to extend the ideas in an exciting and scholarly way' (McDowell 1986: 182). David Morgan also used the word 'provocative' to describe the book, along with 'informative' (1985: 615), while Michael Harloe found it 'absorbing and stimulating' because of its development of an approach 'at variance with much recent sociology' (Harloe 1985: 273). Damaris Rose described it as 'a bold attempt to tackle an important and neglected set of themes' (1986: 335). Following its publication, *Divisions of Labour* quickly generated widespread interest and comment, and this has continued down to the present.

Considering *Divisions of Labour* as a modern sociological classic

Citations provide one indication of a book's prominence. According to A. H. Halsey (2004: 176), citations showed that *Divisions of Labour* was among the ten most influential books in UK sociology in the 1980s. Halsey had already lauded Pahl (and J. Gershuny) as among the small group of researchers in the sociology of work who, standing on the shoulders of the preceding generation, could see 'further into the nature of urban labour markets and work organization, clarified theoretical puzzles, adopted new refined techniques of quantitative analysis, and established new connections between the sociology of production and the sociology of the family, household and community' (Halsey 1989: 369). Google Scholar gives a figure (December 2016) of 1,460 citations for the book. This figure is impressive in its own right and broadly on a par with other classic works of British sociology.

It is also noteworthy because of the range of disciplines that the citations of *Divisions of Labour* show the book reaching, the range of languages in which the citations occur and the duration of this influence. On the first of these additional points, we can note that the ideas contained in *Divisions of Labour* have been engaged with by scholars not only in sociology but in anthropology, development studies, economics, geography, political science, psychology, social history, social policy and beyond. This extraordinary ability to speak across disciplinary boundaries prompted the application to Pahl of the term 'interdisciplinary sociologist' (Crow and Takeda 2011); the term 'boundary spanner' also captures his role in promoting dialogue across disciplinary borders that are restrictive when over-zealously guarded. On the second point, it is readily apparent from the Google Scholar data that the book's influence has extended far beyond the English-speaking world, aided in part by its translation into Spanish. When Anthony Giddens listed seven British sociologists who had a worldwide reputation (1996: 6), Pahl was among them. Third, it is instructive that the book has been cited at a remarkably steady rate; it has achieved at least 200 citations in each five-year period since 1984, and its citation figures actually rose after the turn of the century. Figures have not tailed off markedly in the 2010s but merely returned to the levels of the 1980s. It can also be argued that these are not superficial 'ritual' references made for form's sake but rather have been prompted by active engagement with the book's ideas.

The things that lead to a book becoming widely known are of general interest. John Madge's work *The Origins of Scientific Sociology* looked at an earlier generation of 'seminal books' (Madge 1970: 524) that have played key roles in the development of the discipline. Madge highlighted three aspects of successful books relating to methods, theories and relevance to social problems. He looked for methodological rigour and empirical applicability but he also sought 'explanations rather than enumerations' (1970: 524), and as a result excluded studies that were reluctant to venture beyond description. Conversely, the studies included stand out for the rich 'heritage of concepts' (1970: 542) they bequeathed to subsequent generations of researchers. Madge also draws on Robert Merton's concept of 'practical curiosity' (1970: 514–5) to argue that the studies included in his volume produced knowledge that was of value not only for its own sake but also for the policy implications that might be drawn from that knowledge. For Madge, sociology's potential lies crucially in the power of its ideas, and the history of the discipline can be written through instances of the most far-reaching ideas that practitioners of the subject have generated.

Efforts to identify outstanding books to come out of British sociology in more recent periods include Gordon Marshall's *In Praise of Sociology* (1990) and Fiona Devine and Sue Heath's *Sociological Research Methods in Context* (1999). These authors follow Madge in selecting books that report on research projects that are theoretically and methodologically sophisticated with a distinctive purpose in commenting on the social world in ways that have some practical significance, and written in such a way that readers are made aware of how the research was actually undertaken. Although *Divisions of Labour* did not feature in these collections, there is no reason in principle why it could not have done.

W. G. (Garry) Runciman's reflections on the variety of things done by sociologists also support the case for treating Pahl as the author of a modern sociological classic, because of the range of its ambition. Runciman summarised the most usual and most important aims of sociologists to be 'reportage, explanation, description and evaluation' (Runciman 1989: 9), all of which can be considered to be present in *Divisions of Labour*. Runciman later went on to produce a fuller description of the sociological agenda that includes 'refining statistical methods, categorizing social relationships, ruminating about the human condition, championing the oppressed, rewriting the history of sociology, undermining the reputations of rival sociologists, [and] prophesying the future of the world' (1997: xiv). This extensive list was drawn from sociologists in general, but there is a sense in which each of these elements of sociological practice plays a part in Pahl's *Divisions of Labour* (which is, incidentally, included in the bibliography of Runciman's book). Pahl's ambition in the Sheppey study can be gauged by considering each of these items on Runciman's list in turn.

The development of statistical methods can be found in Pahl's efforts (with the assistance of Spyros Missiakoulis, acknowledged as joint author of chapter 10) to capture the complexities of the domestic division of labour. Pahl's interest in work in all its forms led him to present a rudimentary model of the different combinations of types of work that households can include in their work strategies, but even with simplifying assumptions that Pahl recognised to be unrealistic, the model still produced some forty-nine options (Pahl 1984: 149). The analysis of the survey results undertaken by Pahl's team required sophisticated statistical analysis including devising a new index of the domestic division of labour, called 'the DOMDIV index' (1984: 257). Without this, the results derived from the survey data on the gendered patterns of who does what in households would not have been presentable in the way that they were.

The development of the DOMDIV index in turn relied upon Pahl's **categorisation** of types of work, his efforts to develop 'new ways of looking at work' (1984: 139). Morgan's review of the book noted that: 'The familiar categories of work, class, family and household are broken up and reassembled in new and informative ways' (Morgan 1985: 615). The purpose of this endeavour was to look beyond paid employment in the formal economy to paid and unpaid work in the informal economy, and unpaid work in households using the term 'self-provisioning' as a more extensive category than 'housework'. At the outset of the Sheppey projects that culminated in *Divisions of Labour* there were the early indications of what would be known as the breakdown of the post-war settlement that had been built around nuclear families, the full employment of the male 'heads' of those households, and a redistributive welfare state. Pahl's research agenda was fleshed out incrementally, but was already germinating in the sense that he 'had in the early 1970s that the pattern was starting to shift and that a world [he] had got used to for twenty-five years would never be the same again' (1984: 2). The dismantling of the corporatist settlement and the movement into reverse (beginning in 1976) of the long-term trend towards the reduction of income inequality in the UK, the insistence of the women's movement that housework and care work should not be excluded from counts of work simply because they were unpaid, and the onward march of technology that was opening up opportunities for people to do more things for themselves all pointed to the need to fundamentally re-think 'work' and its associated social relationships.

Work in all its forms is a vital element in the human condition, and Pahl's style in *Divisions of Labour* and elsewhere included **rumination** about this. His later edited volume *On Work* (1988) included contributions from philosophy, as well as his own challenge to readers to consider why unenjoyable work is not better rewarded than enjoyable work. Starting out the main Sheppey project with the broad questions: 'how do all forms of work get done?', 'whose work?', 'and how is it changing?' (1984: 13) inevitably created scope for philosophical reflection, such as the observation Pahl made that: 'People have to grapple with the material circumstances of their existence' (1984: 155). Philosophical musing occurs throughout the book, as in the suggestion that conventional forms of social solidarity are in decline as 'the citizens of the middle mass are asserting themselves in their private lives' (1984: 326), the imaginative identification of similarities between the people of Sheppey and the inhabitants of the (then) Soviet Union in terms of patterns of self-provisioning (1984: 330), and the prediction made on the final page of the book's concluding chapter that: 'If there were a national minimum wage instead of the present system of benefits and allowances, the total amount of work done would almost certainly increase' (1984: 336). How much subsequent developments in UK labour market policy could be attributed to this latter sentence having 'impact' would be hard to determine, but it does illustrate the point that impact may be a very long-term phenomenon, and also one to which many incremental contributions may be made. (It was not until 1998 that modern minimum wage legislation came into effect in the UK.)

Championing the oppressed follows on directly from some of Pahl's ruminations about the perversities of the welfare benefits system as it operated on individuals whose acquaintance he made in the course of the research. This is most readily apparent in the story of Linda and Jim, which was used to portray the side of social polarisation that propels people downwards towards the disadvantaged positon of 'a deprived underclass of between 20 and 25 per cent in poverty' (1984: 320), in contrast to the processes that take Beryl and George to the relative comfort and security of the middle mass (revisiting an unconventional distinction Pahl had developed in another context (1984: 6)). In what is arguably the most compelling part of the book, Pahl used Linda and Jim's story to convey the wastefulness and suffering that accompanies people who unquestionably possess the work ethic but whose efforts to secure work are frustrated at every turn. He also chronicled how he took on the role of championing their cause with the authorities: 'Casting aside the dispassionate observer role, I raised the matter at the highest level in the county' (1984: 302). Linda and Jim epitomised the plight of people who were losing out as deindustrialisation and welfare state reform made their existence ever more uncertain and precarious The next book publication with which Pahl was associated, *Faith in the City*, would develop this theme of social polarisation, and also adopt an explicit campaigning stance on behalf of the downtrodden and dispossessed.

The elements of *Divisions of Labour* devoted to **re-writing the history of sociology** are not systematic but take the form of asides about past and current shortcomings and missed opportunities. It can therefore be rolled up with Runciman's category of **undermining the reputations of rival sociologists**. The book's themes on these points are that the discipline in general, and research in the field of community in particular, have suffered from the preference for 'higher-level theorizing' (1984: 3) over the type of empirical research that gets close to ordinary people's experience. Sociology has also been held back by unwarranted attachment to what Ulrich Beck was later to call 'zombie categories', which had outlived their usefulness and stand as an obstacle to the creative process required to capture new social and economic forms as they emerge. For this to happen, Pahl suggested that sociologists should practise two of Charles Wright Mills's injunctions in *The Sociological Imagination*, namely to link personal and public levels of analysis, and to think comparatively. At one point in *Divisions of Labour* a footnote bemoans sociologists' unfortunate capacity to keep separate 'personal experience and anecdote and general formulations' (1984: 3, fn. 5), while the comparative perspective that historians and anthropologists have to offer is celebrated for its encouragement of 'escaping from established categories' (1984: 12). The whole of Part One of the book moves between past and present in the analysis of forms of work, while the latter parts of the book consider material relating to several countries (including Italy, Hungary and the Soviet Union) for comparative purposes. At the time that *Divisions of Labour* was written the framework that located countries in one of the western capitalist, state socialist or third (underdeveloped) worlds held sway, but Pahl was not confined by this. By drawing on material about the informal economy from eastern Europe and the concept of strategies being developed by social anthropologists working in the global South, Pahl anticipated the need to go 'beyond the three worlds' (Crow 1997) in our understanding of the contemporary era.

This leaves the remaining element of Runciman's list of sociologists' activities, **prophesying the future of the world**. Pahl in *Divisions of Labour* was happy to do this, notably in Part III in a concluding section entitled 'All Forms of Work towards the Year 2000' (Pahl 1984: 334). In this as in his other forays into futurology, his style was self-consciously polemical. He was determined not to concede anything to forms of argument that bemoaned the downward descent of social arrangements from supposedly golden ages in the past (Crow and Takeda 2011), and also not given to extrapolation of indications of change for the better, certainly not where claims were made that attributed such developments to the benevolent effects of social engineering. Instead of 'a benign or a malign historicism', he recommended 'the kaleidoscope theory of social life' (Pahl 1984: 2) in which the search for new ways of looking at things was constantly renewed. The things that Pahl's 'sociological nose', as it has been described, sniffed out in the look ahead with which the book finishes include comments on new forms of social stratification as work in all its forms and property ownership in housing continue to evolve. The potential for the emergence of 'a more humane society' (1984: 336) is recognised, but with no illusions about its inevitability.

Using Runciman's catalogue of what sociologists do as a benchmark helps to illuminate the ambitious, varied and occasionally idiosyncratic character of *Divisions of Labour* and the grounds for considering it a modern sociological classic – all the more so, perhaps, when it is remembered that Runciman was definitely not expecting any sociologist to attempt all of the activities in a single project. The standards for this accolade ought to be demanding, but not impossibly high. One criterion for consideration as a sociological classic is that a book's agenda 'transcends its context to address perennial concerns' (Runciman 2010: 127). To ask about the nature of work and who does it (including the further question of who is prevented from working) is as vital a question as the related one posed by Pahl's PhD co-supervisor John Westergaard, *Who Gets What?* (Westergaard 1995). In this tradition Pahl had already asked *Whose City?*, and within that collection of essays used the formulation 'how much of the cake and for whom?' (Pahl 1975: 8).

These are the types of awkward questions that form the bedrock of social science by setting research agendas and using the results to promote debate. Pahl's sense of history and of the impermanence of apparently settled social and economic arrangements led him to topics that need to be posed anew with each generation, such as a society's work and inequality profiles. In the final quarter of the twentieth century it was apparent that certain categories of people were becoming systematically disadvantaged in their search for access to secure, rewarding and meaningful work, among them the young people whose marginal position in the labour market was focused on by Claire Wallace (1987) in her study *For Richer, For Poorer* which followed *Divisions of Labour* as a further major report on the body of Sheppey research undertaken by Pahl and his team. Three decades on, the wide interest generated by Guy Standing's (2014) work on the 'precariat', a social class among whom young people are disproportionately located, suggests that Pahl and Wallace's agenda was as prescient in this as it was in several other respects.

Classic status may also be judged by the way in which other researchers adopt and seek to address and develop the same agendas. This is the criterion of academic impact on thinking and research practice. Several examples of researchers seeking to make use of the research instruments of the Sheppey project could be cited. These include Marilyn Porter (1993) replicating the self-provisioning survey in her investigation of women's lives in eastern Canada, for which she offered the rationale that she 'wanted to examine Pahl's Sheppey findings in a different context' (Pahl 1993: 154). This she did, and although this presented challenges over what to do with activities like woodcutting that were somewhat removed from practices found on Sheppey, the comparisons were nevertheless instructive.

In north-west England, Alan Warde and colleagues treated *Divisions of Labour* as marking the start of a new phase of research into the division of labour within households, and first repeated and then duplicated and extended Pahl's approach in their own fieldwork (Warde and Hetherington 1993: 29). In the case of Dawn Lyon and her colleagues, the imagined futures essays written by school leavers on Sheppey in 1978 were not only re-examined as archive material three decades on from their collection; they were also complemented in a repeat study on Sheppey (Lyon *et al.* 2012). The high profile immediately achieved by *Divisions of Labour* is indicated by John Scott attributing his revised focus in his research on elite networks to Pahl's book's exposition of the case for a focus on households (Scott 1985: 256); Chris Harris's acknowledgement of the Sheppey project's influence on the central research questions of his study of redundancy in South Wales (Harris 1987); John Westergaard and his colleagues' engagement with the 'black economy' perspective which Pahl's work had shown to be 'shaky' (Westergaard *et al.* 1989: 15); and Jan Pahl's (1989) exploration of financial arrangements within households. The career of the concept of 'household work strategies' could also be mentioned here as an idea given significant impetus by Pahl's book. Even if it originated earlier and in different hands – Pahl's acknowledgements in *Divisions of Labour* to Sandra Wallman and Gershuny are relevant here – it remains true that his application of the idea prompted researchers to be more mindful of the merits of focusing on individuals as members of households, in which context the rationality of their actions may become more apparent (Crow 1989; Wallace 1993, 2002).

Impact beyond academia is harder to gauge, but not impossible. The fact that passages of the report of the Archbishop of Canterbury's Commission on inner cities, *Faith In The City*, are direct echoes of what *Divisions of Labour* has to say about social polarisation is one example of such impact, facilitated by Pahl's membership of that Commission. If others examples of impact beyond academia are less well known, it was not for want of trying on Pahl's part as he sought to influence policy-makers in areas such as apprenticeships, using arguments grounded in the analysis presented in his book. Apprenticeships had been the cornerstone of the occupational community that had grown up around Sheppey's Admiralty dockyard, and the effects of the closure of the dockyard in 1960 were still being keenly felt two decades on when Pahl and his team's fieldwork was being undertaken. Pahl can be credited with being ahead of his time in terms of pursuing the impact agenda through seeking to influence the attitudes of local employers and educationalists towards young people's acquisition of workplace skills. His efforts as a pioneer in archiving the data from the Sheppey project should also be noted, because this was far from standard in the 1980s, but has subsequently become a norm, providing significant resources for the growing community of users of social science archive material (Corti *et al.* 2014: chapter 10).

In proposing *Divisions of Labour* as a modern sociological classic we are not pretending that it is perfect. Its coverage of relevant literature was far from exhaustive, which was bound to be the case given the breadth of the project's agenda. Nevertheless, Sheppey's association with the early nineteenth-century pioneers of the co-operative movement (Brown: no date) is one curious omission. The choice of Sheppey as a fieldwork site was in some ways a constraint on the pursuit of developments in all forms of work. David Byrne rightly noted that the book reports on an interesting study of 'a rather unusual place' (Byrne 1989: 24), as Pahl himself seems to suggest in saying that 'in some respects the Isle of Sheppey can be seen to have some of the characteristic problems of a de-industrializing Britain in a particularly extreme form' (1984: 195). The pursuit of 'typical' fieldwork sites is, of course, problematic (Savage 2010: chapter 6), and the case for the *Affluent Worker* study's location in Luton because of that population's 'prototypicality' (its indicativeness of coming patterns) rather than its typicality is well known (Goldthorpe *et al.* 1968b: 10; Devine 1992).

Developments on Sheppey may have heralded the future in several respects, but the population's atypicality in terms of socio-economic profile meant that it was never going to throw up phenomena such as the work of au pairs, which have become a prominent feature of households in more affluent areas (Búriková and Miller 2010), nor be an ideal location for the re-emerging demand among the middle classes for nannies and cleaners (although Pahl's work is cited as helping to understand the expanding supply of such workers (Gregson and Lowe 1994: 130–2)). Furthermore, the account of the Island and its people was not consistently sympathetic; the description of the 'small elite of red-faced men with large stomachs, large Fords and tinselly wives with long fingernails patronize the Playa Club on Minster Cliffs and drink many gins before their steak or scampi and chips' (Pahl 1984: 154) is particularly unflattering and revealing of researcher bias (and indiscretion). The book may also have been unfair to other authors in attributing arguments to them that they did not necessarily recognise as their position, or in not making attributions for ideas as meticulously as people working in the same field might have considered appropriate. That said, the book still meets Michelle Lamont's standards of work characterised by clarity, originality, methodological rigour and innovation, significance, and general 'quality' (2009: 167) by which judgements are made about what constitutes the best social science.

The structure of *Revisiting Divisions of Labour*

Our intentions in putting together this book have been to bring together commentaries on various aspects of *Divisions of Labour* and the legacies of its analyses, and to place these alongside extracts from the original publication in order that readers may gain a flavour of Pahl's writing at first hand. We have placed these extracts after this Introduction and interspersed among the new contributions that discuss the case for revisiting *Divisions of Labour*, and readers are encouraged to move between the two. Readers do not have to go through the contributions in the order in which we have presented them, though there is a logic to that order. It begins with Tim Strangleman's account of how Pahl's characterisation of Sheppey as an 'industrial island' (1984: chapter 6, and reproduced here in the excerpts) can be read as an early analysis of 'deindustrialisation'. Pahl did not coin this term, but he was among the first to pick up on the significance of the phenomenon and one of the pioneers of its usage. Strangleman shows how *Divisions of Labour* involved not simply using but developing this concept. Deindustrialisation has several facets, and Strangleman shows how these are brought out in the local context at the same time as global connections are highlighted. The Japanese cars imported into the UK through the port at Sheerness that had once been an Admiralty dockyard provided a stark reminder of how the old order was changing, and Pahl's treatment of this phenomenon helped to pave the way for many subsequent studies of deindustrialisation that have mapped the evolution of the process around the world. The excerpts from chapters 6 and 7 of *Divisions of Labour* have particular relevance for Strangleman's contribution, as well as for the contribution from Dawn Lyon that comes later.

Chapter 2 by Jonathan Gershuny begins by rehearsing the discussion about the early speculations out of which *Divisions of Labour* arose. Gershuny's collaboration with Pahl grew out of their shared interest in the very broad question of what would come after the pattern of industrial society that was showing signs of unsustainability in its then current form. The chapter here conveys something of what it was like working with a colleague who was by turns engaging, enthusiastic, questioning, respectful, unconstrained by the niceties of academic convention, and always on the move in search of answers to an ever-shifting agenda. Gershuny's chapter then goes on to describe how that initial dialogue continued down the years, and has its latest instalment here as connections continue to be made and the effort to put records straight goes on. Nor has this dialogue been purely academic, because among its legacies can be included influences on the development of some key parts of the social science infrastructure. Gershuny's chapter considers the excerpts that precede it which are included to convey the mechanics and the fruits of Pahl's survey of 730 Sheppey households and the extensive quantitative data on work practices and strategies that this generated.

The chapter by Claire Wallace also involves tracing back an ongoing dialogue that began in the early days of the Sheppey 'laboratory'. Her conversations with Pahl and also with Gershuny have continued and expanded well beyond their initial reference points on Sheppey. Thus the discussion of work strategies has relevance to the understanding of how households endeavour to 'get by' in a range of contexts across the world, in many diverse contexts, including societies that have never had the norm of formal, waged labour and societies forced to go through rapid, radical reorganisation, such as in the former communist countries (Pahl and Thompson 1994). One of the enduring lessons of the study of strategies is that strategic action does not guarantee success. Wallace's Sheppey-based book *For Richer, For Poorer* differentiates between those young people who are 'swimmers' and those who are 'sinkers' (Wallace 1987: 140), reflecting the fact that the process of social polarisation which featured so prominently in *Divisions of Labour* did not hold off until adulthood to make its presence felt. The gendered nature of the uneven distribution of benefits and costs is also something that has been just as apparent around the world as it was on Sheppey. Richard Sennett's statement that: 'In the last quarter of the twentieth century, modern capitalism changed' (2000: 119) is presented as a global statement, but it is studies like Pahl's and Wallace's that confirm its veracity at a local level. The excerpt that precedes Wallace's contribution conveys the value of Pahl's reflection on his reading widely around the literature on gender and work, and his awareness as a result that scholars were failing to appreciate the significance of the widely noted phenomenon of the growth of women's employment during the long boom.

Dawn Lyon's contribution reflects on the potential of re-studies to inform the understanding of contemporary society. In an age now routinely referred to being characterised by globalisation, it is instructive to go back to the Sheppey study to gain a sense of how things have changed in the interim. In fact, despite Pahl's description of his fieldwork site as 'isolated' (1980: 2), this did not mean that its inhabitants were unaware of the wider world. The 'imagined future' essays that Pahl collected in 1978 included 10 per cent of the 141 envisaging living abroad, and many more going beyond the UK's shores for work purposes (notably through recruitment to the armed services), or for holidays. Put another way, 'globalisation' was understood in lay terms before the concept became an everyday term. Lyon shows how it was revealing to collect further material on Sheppey and compare that with the original Sheppey project materials that are archived. Given the scale of the original Sheppey project and the sheer amount of the data generated and archived, the work that she and her colleagues undertook could only ever have been a partial re-study, but the passage of a quarter of a century since the original fieldwork provided a rationale to return to Sheppey (Crow et *al*. 2009), even if the team were able to engage with only a fraction of the material available.

Working with archived material is also the subject of Chapter 5, where Jane Elliott and Jon Lawrence discuss the pivotal role played by one household in the Sheppey study, that of Linda and Jim. Readers of *Divisions of Labour* are not introduced to these individuals until the penultimate chapter of Pahl's book, but this merely serves to heighten the impact of the discussion of how they epitomise the downward social mobility that comes with the polarisation of workers' fortunes. Some working-class households did more than simply 'get by' in the challenging circumstances of the period, moving up into what Pahl called the 'middle mass' of households characterised by comfortable material circumstances that contrasted sharply with those of 'a deprived underclass of between 20 and 25 per cent in poverty beneath them' (1984: 320). In Pahl's analysis the upward movement into the middle mass is represented by Beryl and George, but it is Linda and Jim who have more of his attention. The analysis of Pahl's developing relationship with Linda and Jim was foreshadowed in a passage written well before the Sheppey project in which he noted the tendency of researchers to be 'on the side of the lower participants who may have suffered at the hands of insensitive local officials. It is understandably very easy for the researcher to view the situation through the eyes of disadvantaged local populations' (1975: 267). This is difficult ground for both researchers and researched, and tracing what happened to Linda and Jim in the period following the publication of Pahl's book, undertaken by Elliott and Lawrence, serves to underscore the bleak message of the book about life at the bottom of the socio-economic order. The excerpt from chapter 11 reveals Pahl's sympathetic engagement with what Karl Marx called 'the dull compulsion of economic relations' (Marx 1954: 689) as it plays out at the level of individual households.

The contribution from John Holmwood (Chapter 6) moves from the micro level of the implications of changes at the level of individual households like

Linda and Jim's to the macro level, and to Pahl's conception of sociology's role in engaging with issues of social stratification. Pahl was familiar with the concept of polarisation from his first publications onwards (Crow and Takeda 2011: 3.4), and well used to making the case that theories should serve the purpose of illuminating and de-mythologising the realities of the social and economic world that forces like social polarisation produced. Holmwood shows how *Divisions of Labour* was a continuation of Pahl's concerns to make sense of evolving patterns of stratification, and that this ongoing debate continued long after the book's publication, with Pahl an active participant in the process. In this respect, *Divisions of Labour* was not Pahl's final word, but rather an interim statement of ideas that he had by no means worked through fully. Sociologists at the time of the Sheppey project were deeply engaged in soul searching about the nature and purpose of their discipline (Abrams *et al.* 1981), and Pahl's contributions to these discussions regarding what Holmwood (following Andrew Abbott) calls sociology's 'jurisdiction' were if anything emboldened by his Sheppey experiences, as the short excerpt from Pahl's book's conclusion that precedes Holmwood's chapter conveys.

Our book concludes with an Afterword by Mike Savage in which he reflects on re-reading *Divisions of Labour* three decades on from having first done so. In the interim he has engaged with much of Pahl's other work, which makes him uniquely placed to reflect on the questions that have driven the other contributors to *Revisiting Divisions of Labour*, notably the issue of what makes the original book stand out. Part of his answer points to the importance of Ray Pahl the person for the way that the book turned out. Pahl was deliberately 'polemical' (1989: 710) not only in his Sheppey project but his subsequent engagement with class analysis which continued to think through the implications of the Sheppey project. In a 1988 paper in the *International Journal of Urban and Regional Research* he had returned to the themes raised in his speculative article that had been published in that journal at the start of the decade and before most of the Sheppey research had happened. He conceded that the empirical evidence required him to undertake 'a radical shift from the stance I adopted in my earlier paper' (1988b: 264). The indications of a shift in the pattern of stratification to one in which 'the middle of the onion is getting fatter but the top and the bottom may be visualized as being sliced off and are moving up and down respectively from the middle' (1988b: 258) had wider implications than simply for Pahl's understanding of social class; it also mattered to the consideration of policy options. His conclusion that revising his position in the light of new evidence and argument was preferable to maintaining an initial position with 'an unswerving commitment to consistency' (1993: 256) provides an insight into his approach to research that it is useful to bear in mind when reading the excerpts from *Divisions of Labour* reproduced in this book. They have been selected to convey something of the original work's breadth, ambition and style. Pahl did not want his readers to accept his arguments uncritically, but to engage with them, and to approach them with scepticism, which he called 'the sociologist's greatest strength' (1977: 147). To persuade a sceptic who has an argument placed in front of them to re-think their views is an ambitious aim, but that was what he set out to do. He was well placed to do this having lived and breathed Sheppey for the best part of a decade. It is also why we are encouraging readers to revisit and engage with this modern sociological classic and its provocative, at times infuriating, but always stimulating author.

Timeline of Ray Pahl's career

17 July 1935	Born in London National Service with Royal Air Force
1956–59	Undergraduate student in Geography at St Catharine's College, University of Cambridge
1959–64	PhD student London School of Economics and tutor for the Board of Extra-mural studies, University of Cambridge
1965	Publication of PhD thesis as *Urbs in Rure*; appointed lecturer in Sociology, University of Kent
1970s	Active in the International Sociological Association, helping to set up research network on urban and regional development; advisory and assessor roles for government and development plan for Greater London
1970	Publication of *Whose City?*
1971	Publication with Jan Pahl of *Managers and their Wives*
1972	Promotion to Professor of Sociology at Kent
1978	Fieldwork on the Isle of Sheppey commences; imagined futures essays collected from 141 sixteen-year-old school leavers; first of nine recorded interviews with Linda and Jim
1979–81	Joint publications with Jay Gershuny on the informal economy
1980s	Advisor to University Grants Committee
1984	Publication of *Divisions of Labour*
1985	Publication of *Faith in the City*
1988	Publication of *On Work*
late 1980s–1990s	Helped to establish the Institute for Social and Economic Research, University of Essex and the Central European University in Prague; research materials from Sheppey project and other projects archived with the forerunner of the UK Data Service at the University of Essex
1992	Final recorded interview with Linda and Jim
1995	Publication of *After Success*
1996	Retired from post at University of Kent

1998	Interviewed as a pioneer of social research (further interview 2009)
1999	Made Visiting Professor at ISER, University of Essex
2004	Elected to the Academy of Social Sciences
2006	Publication with Liz Spencer of *Rethinking Friendship*
2008	Elected to the British Academy
2011	Received lifetime achievement award from the British Sociological Association
3 June 2011	died in Churchstoke, near Montgomery, Powys

Excerpts from *Divisions of Labour*, chapters 6 and 7

Chapter 6, 'Portrait of an Industrial Island' (excerpts from pp. 152–84)

Introduction

The next six chapters are based on material gathered in the Isle of Sheppey in Kent. Inevitably, readers will want to have some idea of what the Island is like; however, as is shown below, to provide such an account is not entirely a straightforward exercise.[1] To understand the present situation it is necessary to know something of how that situation has developed, yet all historical accounts have to be partial and selective. The position adopted here is to acknowledge that the basic problems of getting by, of forming households and of caring for the young and the old have remained remarkably similar for centuries. Most people experience life as a struggle: they compare their own life with that of their mothers or fathers and perhaps gain some comfort that their life is better, but they might equally feel that things are getting worse. In the case of the Isle of Sheppey, those with long memories will almost certainly perceive the present as a sad and ugly decline from a better-ordered and more attractive past. Some attempt must be made to match 'scholarly' history with 'folk' history, recognizing that the latter may have more salience for contemporary attitudes and behaviour than the former.

Visually the Island has undoubtedly declined. When William Hogarth visited Sheppey in 1732, he and his friends walked through pleasant countryside to Minster, a little village on the highest part of the Island on which Minster Abbey stands, said to be founded in the seventh century by the wife of Ercombert, King of Kent. Old prints and drawings and even postcards dating from as recently as the early years of this century show a wooded countryside more reminiscent of villages in the more fashionable parts of the county today. Queenborough was a flourishing little borough in the seventeenth century, and Sheerness developed in the nineteenth century as garrison, Admiralty dockyard and seaside resort. So much was built between 1850 and 1900 that people's memories of a much cleaner town are likely to be substantially true.

1 A map of the Island may be found on p. 342. (The map is reproduced on p. 153 in this volume)

It is understandable that many islanders cannot see the present except in terms of its decline from the past.

Certainly, a contemporary visitor to the Isle of Sheppey is likely to be dismayed by its lack of visual character.[2] The road to the Island may well be clogged with huge lorries weighted down with containers, Japanese cars or steel rods from the mill. On one side, acres of marshland appear to be sinking under the weight of thousands of Toyotas and Mazdas; ahead, there is a pall of black smoke over the Sheerness Steel Mill with the Isle of Grain oil refinery towering in the background and appearing to be on the Island itself. On the other side, treeless marshes and sheep pasture stretch away for ten miles or so. The village of Minster in the middle of the Island is now overwhelmed by private housing development, put up in a seemingly chaotic way in the 1960s and 1970s. Much of the earlier development along unmade roads makes one forget that any Town and Country Planning Acts have been passed. Queenborough High Street has many of its period houses boarded up in bad repair, and turning off down Rushenden Road, past the industrial estate, the impression is of a northern industrial town. Heavy traffic has pitted the roads; factories making fertilizer, lavatory pans or glass bottles make little attempt to look presentable to visitors. Railway tracks cross the road; huge metal objects lie outside the rolling mill and iron foundry, and the horizon is again dominated by the endless sea of Japanese cars. Eventually, at the very end of the marshes where the Swale does a loop back before entering the Medway, there is the Rushenden Road Estate, an all too obvious machine for workers to reproduce themselves in. Remote from shops, privately built housing and such amenities as the cinema and swimming pool at Sheerness, visiting state officials or university researchers are viewed here with suspicion. Some of the houses look smart, with new front doors and obvious double glazing, indicating clearly that they have been bought from the council; others have the characteristic scuffed door and concrete path, with a scattering of broken toys and odd bits of wood that may or may not be rubbish in what was once a front garden.

The High Street of Sheerness, the town that houses about a third of the Island's population of 33,000, is the standard mixture of discount carpet stores, Tesco's, Boots and tawdry boutiques, interspersed with

2 In 1983 Swale District Council launched an 'Economic Programme', much of which was concerned with 'environmental improvements' on the Island. A new concern with the image of the area was based on the assumption that new investment would be clean and that industrialists would be attracted by physical appearances.

pubs and indeterminate shops selling sweets, greetings cards, cigarettes and newspapers. It could be transferred to New Cross, Kilburn or Wood Green in London and no one would notice the difference. Behind the shops, in the areas known as Marine Town and Mile Town, another pattern of owner-occupied working class housing can be seen. Here, terraces built in the mid-nineteenth century front straight on to the street. Corner shops and pubs punctuate the scene and little alleyways criss-cross the areas, full of running children at 3.30 as they come home from school. Mothers and married daughters go shopping together. In summer elderly women put wooden chairs on the pavement to sit and chat and a group of lads strip a motorbike on the pavement. 'For Sale' signs appear permanently in all the streets and every front door is painted a different colour. One little terrace house with green interlocking tiles, pink pebbledash and a frosted glass front door adjoins another looking much as it did a hundred years ago. The roads are lined with elderly Fords and chromey Datsuns. Women cross the street in carpet slippers. A large Ford van with a 'J' registration, painted entirely black, has the words 'Funeral Service' on the side, but further information has been covered in with more black paint.[3]

Following the coast road from Marine Town to Minster, views of the sea are hidden by the huge new concrete sea wall, recently built to avoid flooding. The road has to turn inland at Minster Cliffs, which are gradually sliding into the sea, although a contractor is struggling hard to shore it all up. The clifftop land from Minster to Warden is a jumble of unmade roads, riding stables, little smallholdings and caravan sites. A determined driver with little regard for his car can zigzag his way over potholes, past home-made bungalows with goats grazing in the front garden and the odd run-down farmhouse.[4] One can emerge at Warden Bay into a new estate of houses, being a mixture of neo-Georgian and south-coast Spanish. Then more holiday camps, overblown pubs offering live entertainment (male strippers on hens' evenings), before one reaches Leysdown-on-Sea. Bingo halls, a disco, amusement arcades and gift shops are the focus for acres of holiday chalets, caravan sites and holiday camps. In winter it is hard to find anywhere to get a cup of tea; in summer the place is awash with the highest priced beer in Kent. Returning by the main road along the spine of the Island, one

3 See plate 8. This is perhaps truly the black economy on wheels. I am grateful to Jim Styles of the University of Kent Photographic Unit for the sympathetic way he helped in providing this and other vivid documentation.

4 On one safari trip with Colin Ward, I slipped a disc heaving my car out of the mud. Anthropologists in far-away places are not the only ones with hazards to face.

passes through the agricultural village of Eastchurch with nothing but Eastchurch Open Prison and a few farms on the pastures sloping away to the Swale. At Minster there is a hospital and the comprehensive school. Some larger houses in the best positions on the high land have paddocks for ponies, power boats on trailers and two or more cars in the drive. A small elite of red-faced men with large stomachs, large Fords and tinselly wives with long fingernails patronize the Playa Club on Minster Cliffs and drink many gins before their steak or scampi and chips.

A perceptive observer visiting the Island would see and understand much by travelling about – the pub where the managers who live off the Island congregate for lunch, another pub (not always the same one) the centre for drugs and prostitutes, the fisherboats on Queenborough Creek, the light aircraft bringing in one of the farm owners from over the estuary in Essex, the Regency terraces, once the homes of officers in the dockyard and much the same as they were when first built, the apparently uncountable chapels and working men's clubs, the fish and chip shops, the markets on Tuesdays and Sundays, the truant teenagers in the coffee bars. Having spent six years visiting and doing fieldwork on the Island and spending time in particular factories, streets and communities, I feel daunted at times by the overwhelming wealth of information.

Nevertheless, it is important to try to make sense of the context: people's real or imagined knowledge of the past colours, to a degree, their present attitudes and pattern of behaviour. Newcomers to the Island have different traditions, to be sure, but Sheppey is a distinct milieu with its own distinctive traditions, experiences, possibilities and constraints. People have to grapple with the material circumstances of their existence, and because the Island is so relatively small and insular, in more than one sense, people can readily have a consciousness of its distinctiveness. Working-class culture is not an ahistorical response to existential circumstances – rather, it is an intensely conservative and traditional set of household practices for grappling with difficult material circumstances. In order to understand more of the complexity of the material context, it seemed necessary to gather a substantial amount of data on the historical development of the dockyard, the pattern of employment from 1960 to 1980 and a detailed analysis of housing development in the twentieth century.[5]

5 Each of these themes provided the basis for separate reports, only the main points of which are referred to here. See N. Buck, *An Admiralty Dockyard in the Mid-Nineteenth Century: Aspects of the Social and Economic History of Sheerness*, Final Report to the SSRC on a research project funded by grant no. HR6939/1, 1981;

The Decline and Closure of the dockyard

Some general conclusions can be drawn about the impact of the dockyard on Sheerness. Perhaps the best starting point is to consider the needs of the Admiralty. There was a need for a reliable and highly skilled workforce, since the quality of the product was of considerable importance. The Admiralty had to produce ships at a price competitive with private shipbuilders, who formed a powerful lobby against the dockyards in Parliament. Second, they needed to be able to maintain their workforce cheaply at times of slack demand, and expand it rapidly when the need arose. These needs were met by two strategies. First, the workforce was isolated from the rest of the labour market to reduce competition from other employers paying higher wages. In Sheerness there was virtually no other source of employment, apart from services, until the 1960s. This had very serious implications for women's employment possibilities. Furthermore, by keeping the shipwrights as the general constructors of the ships – a group with no parallel in private industry – they helped to reduce the potential for unionization and militancy. The second main strategy was to offer the dockyard workers considerable non-monetary compensations for wages which were low by comparison with the private sector – pensions, security, prospects of promotion, perhaps a higher level of control over the immediate production process than private workers, a slower pace. The Admiralty also offered the prospect of regular work for established men, and created a division between this group, which was the permanent workforce, and the hired men, whose employment depended on the amount of work – though even this group was in general more regularly employed than private sector workers.

These points may be illustrated by interviews with retired dockers whose memories cover the period from the First World War to the closure of the dockyard in 1960.[6] They emphasize the leisurely pace of work, the indulgency patterns whereby the dockyard authorities kept only modest control over the traditional occupational easement of making 'rabbits' – private jobs done with dockyard tools and materials – and the overwhelmingly Conservative political ideology. Talking to the

R. E. Pahl with J. H. Dennett, *Industry and Employment on the Isle of* Sheppey, University of Kent at Canterbury, part of the Final Report to the SSRC of project no. G00230036, 1981; and C. Wallace with R. E. Pahl and J. H. Dennett, *Housing and Residential Areas on the Isle of Sheppey,* University of Kent at Canterbury, part of the Final Report to the SSRC of project no. G00230036, 1981.

6 The argument is also very thorough documented for Chatham (Waters, 'Social history of the Chatham dockyard').

shop steward who had developed the Sheerness Labour Party in the 1920s, it was clear that the dockyard had little latent radicalism:

> You see, the working men's club in the dockyard, it was then, every man practically. Perhaps and in the Conservative Club too. ... The dockyard came first. Well you see the feelings in the dockyard are this – that the Tories are the people for war, they support that kind of thing and they were the people for a big navy, big army, you see, so you'd have a job to get the people in the dockyard to vote Labour, because they'd close the dockyard.[7]

In the event, of course, it was, ironically, the Conservatives who closed the Sheerness dockyard in 1960 and then twenty years later made the same decision for Chatham. Throughout the 1920s and 1930s, workers had no way of resisting cutbacks in employment and there were regular discharges. 'You stood there and you listened and you waited and you heard. It was last in and first out.'[8] Because the dockyard was the dominant source of income and the dominant employer in the town since its establishment as a community in the early nineteenth century, it dominated many other aspects of life. It promoted attitudes that stressed individual mobility and instrumental collectivism, which may not seem to some to be the basis for the ideal-typical traditional working-class community.

The Rise and Fall of casual work

Parallel with this formal, hierarchical, relatively well-documented world of the dockyard, there was another, rougher and less well-documented working-class culture more typical of Samuel's quarry roughs or White's Campbell Bunk. Even the pious and deferential Augustus Daly, who generally paints Sheppey in a very rosy hue, acknowledged that in the early nineteenth century 'the morals of the Sheppey islanders of this period were apparently, somewhat lax, for smuggling was not only exceedingly rife but was accounted an honourable vocation to pursue. The whole populace, it was said, were more or less addicted to this profitable pursuit.'[9] In common with other parts of East Kent, smugglers saw themselves as 'free traders'. This swashbuckling free-trader spirit flourished again in the 1970s, when large quantities of the goods imported into the docks found their way all round the Island. The peak of this activity was in the mid-1970s, before fieldwork on the Island began and

7 From an interview I conducted as part of the pilot work for the main project.
8 *Ibid.*
9 Daly, *History of the Isle of Sheppey*, p. 264.

a fierce crackdown by the police led, so it is consistently claimed, to piles of transistors appearing at the bottom of Minster Cliffs.[10]

Obviously, many Islanders go fishing and shoot and trap duck and rabbits on the marshes. Much of the Island gives a remote and desolate impression and, until recently, wildlife was abundant. For nearly a century, holiday-makers have doubled the population of the Island in the summer, bringing money and the opportunity for quick-witted entrepreneurs to make small fortunes out of food, drink and 'amusements'. Leysdown-on-Sea attracted hustlers and cowboys and provided apprenticeships in mild crookery for generations of school leavers who, in the 1950s, 1960s and early 1970s, went 'down Leysdown' to work as cheap labour, cleaning the chalets in the holiday camps, serving in cafes and bars and minding stalls and (later) machines in the fairgrounds and amusement arcades. The holiday trade provided a myriad opportunities for small business enterprises to start with little capital, and the regular flow of new clientele prevented the build-up of bad reputations: fiddles could be perpetrated all summer; prices could be exorbitant; and high labour turnover prevented possible protest but spread bad practices. Some parents refused to let their sons and daughters go off in the summer to pick up bad ways. However, such seasonal employment also had the useful function of providing independence, some pocket money and the experience of a number of bosses, without any opprobrium resulting from having 'changed jobs too frequently'! Being unemployed for a spell in the winter, 'helping your dad' or 'looking after your sister's baby' is perhaps more acceptable when there is a very strong likelihood of finding temporary employment at the beginning of May.

Unfortunately, by the late 1970s there had been a drastic reduction in the number of summer visitors. Debate raged on the Island about whether it was the lack of facilities or cheaper package holidays abroad.

For many years, Sheppey has been the haven for the poorer section of the south-east London communities. They have relied on the Island to provide them with holidays. Many have bought caravans, some older and more rundown than others, or chalets, on the many sites in and around the Leysdown area. The huge number of vans, chalets and villas

10 On my very first visit to the Island in the winter of 1977–78 one of my early informants was recovering in a pub after claiming much of a jettisoned cargo of timber, which had been washed up on the beach in the heavy seas. Getting it on to an inadequate truck in the dark was not easy work. On another occasion, during the same winter, driving down a remote track in the marshes opposite the Island late one very dark, wet night, I came across two heavy lorries loading by an isolated cottage. The tone with which I was told I had taken the wrong road convinced me that some fieldwork situations are best left unexplored.

has meant a constant flow of people to that end of the island and a constant flow of income to the arcade, shops, stall and entertainment owners.

Thus, an editorial in the local newspaper justified the development of underdevelopment and attacked a report of the South East England Tourist Board and the Department of Environment regulations that demanded hard standings, electricity and main drainage.[11] Few facilities and little surveillance were seen as positive attractions. More organization would reduce the desirability of Leysdown to 'the less affluent holiday maker from this side of London'. In the heyday of Leysdown's prosperity in the 1950s, there was a regular bus service from there to Leytonstone in East London.[12] While to officials in Maidstone and Sittingbourne, Leysdown was seen as 'a real planning disaster based on too-local decision-making',[13] it at least had the merit of attracting regular spare money which could circulate in the local economy.

The holiday trade was blamed by the school for generating an ideology of dishonesty and rule-bending, and in 1978 the truancy rate for the fifth year at the comprehensive school was said to be 20 per cent. Bobby Wilson, the Rolls-Royce-driving owner of the amusement arcade at Leysdown, was a regular recruiter of school leavers.[14] However, the possibility of leaving school early to get regular money was rapidly declining in the late 1970s.

Employment on Sheppey 1960–1980

There is no question that the closure of the Admiralty dockyard in 1960 was, in the words of the Chief Planning Officer for the District, 'a hammer blow to the economy of the Island' (even though, a few weeks later, the *Sheerness Times-Guardian* was describing 'Sheppey's most important occasion of the century ... when momentous history was made' when the new Kingsferry Bridge was opened by the Duchess of Kent). More than 700 dockyard workers were put out of work. Although many left the Island, and the Admiralty paid the fares for some to work in the Chatham yard for a short period, in 1960–61 local unemployment reached 11 per cent when the national rate was just over

11 *Sheerness Times-Guardian*, 24 April 1981.

12 This service ceased in the early 1970s.

13 It would be indelicate to reveal the precise source of this remark.

14 Bobby Wilson was killed in a car accident in October 1983. His death provoked many warm tributes and it was reported that 600 people came to his funeral at Minster Abbey. Wilson came to Sheppey in 1961 and was often referred to as 'Mr Leysdown' since at one time he owned most of the place. It is interesting that this rather swashbuckling entrepreneur should appeal so strongly to the Islanders.

2 per cent. The dockyard was bought by Building Developments Ltd for £750,000 as an industrial site. The industrial structure of Sheerness has developed entirely since 1960. The Navy playing fields provided the location for one industrial estate, and the Army playing fields provided the site for the steel mill in the early 1970s.

The development of Sheerness docks happened almost casually. In the early 1960s the odd vessel was being unloaded there and while other ports were moving into new technology, containerization and so forth, Sheerness was not in a position to do so. At a time, therefore, when few ports wanted conventional ships and the London docks were clogged up, Sheerness could unload faster and could get fruit and vegetables up to Covent Garden in two hours. A Stevedores Union was formed in the early 1960s and a distinctive element in the local labour market soon became firmly established. There was no tradition of labour militancy, and since dockers soon became among the highest paid workers on the Island, there was little reason for the situation to change. Furthermore, the dockers could easily get home for lunch: if there was no work they could simply go home and, in the words of the chief executive, 'upset the local decorating market'. In the late 1970s it might cost the owners of a ship £2,500 a day to keep a ship in the docks: in the desire to get ships away owners would pay almost anything, and therefore, in practice, the extra costs of overtime were paid without question and fiddles to extend the amount of permissible overtime were accepted with little argument. From the early 1960s to the late 1970s, registered dockworkers in Sheerness increased to between 360 and 380. The 'official' reason why Sheerness developed rapidly and effectively as a port was its 'good labour relations'.

However, there is another, darker side to the post-1960 development. Most workers on the Island in the early 1960s were largely unskilled and had no tradition of collective organization, shift work or hard industrial discipline. Somewhat unkindly, one official claimed that the workers in the dockyard had been provided with a legalized form of national assistance. More radically, another official claimed that the workers had been dispossessed from their own labour market as new, skilled workers had to be imported from outside to work in the new factories. There was no established union pressure to ensure that incoming employers hired local labour.[15] In the case of the steel mill, 90 per cent of the most skilled

15 The General and Municipal Workers' Union (now the General, Municipal and Boilermakers' Union) is the largest union on the Island, being at least twice the size of its nearest rival. Office holders change only on the death of incumbents and hence there have been only three branch secretaries at Queenborough since the Union was founded in the 1920s. The GMWU offers a whole range of facilities to its members and was at one time jokingly referred to as 'the funeral union' because of

workers came from outside the area. However, some of the new firms that were attracted to the Island recognized that its isolation and tradition of low wages were substantial resources. Factories in the clothing industry in particular were attracted by the availability of women workers, whom they could train and expect to keep. Some firms exploited the local labour force by paying low wages, while others paid more, knowing that the differential would ensure that their workers would not leave. The steel mill, which was established in 1972, employed more than 800 workers eight years later. Young, tough, stable, married men were needed who could stand hard, hot work, including shift work, and recruitment never posed a problem.

A detailed study of the industrial structure of the Island was undertaken in 1981,[16] demonstrating how top-heavy it was: of the 39 manufacturing enterprises, 15 employ more than 50 workers, a further 10 employ between 21 and 50 workers and a mere 14 firms employ up to 20 workers. Even if these 14 each had 10 workers, which it is known they do not, that would mean only between 100 and 200 jobs in the small-firm sector on the Island. Inevitably, this makes the Island extremely vulnerable, should the giants of the labour market get into difficulty. Typically, in a healthy labour market, a seedbed of infant industries produces growth, providing, as it were, an inflatable cushion should the main employers be obliged to shed labour. Also, the service sector is very poorly developed. There is a striking lack of any office employment of any scale whatsoever: the largest employers are simply the local branches of banks or building societies.

This dramatic skew in the structure of employment on the Island implies that the twenty-seven employers with more than fifty workers are more important than might be the case elsewhere. For good or ill, the future of the Island's employment is overwhelmingly dependent on them. This small group of the largest employers had about half of the workforce between them, and a representative of each of the main employers was interviewed at length between February and June 1981. As Table 6.3

the generous funeral benefits it offered. Most of its members treat it as a convenient private club. Union officials have a secure, highly respected lifetime job, which can be combined with chairmanship of the local Conservative Party with no sense of incongruity. Members regard the Union as a source of service provision and social security more than as a political and campaigning organization. As one union official remarked, 'In Queenborough you feel a sort of loyalty to the firm anyway because it's only a small firm. It's not so much a factory as a way of life after twenty years. The hours suit me and the money is good. It's a way of life, a local job and a very secure job.' Since he said that, the firm has twice been taken over by international corporations.

16 Pahl with Dennett, *Industry and Employment*.

Table 6.3 Isle of Sheppey firms, by size of workforce and proportion of women workers

No. of workers in firm*	No. of firms	Average no. of workers per firm	% of women in workforce
Over 750	3	800	11
300–749	3	325 }225	17 }23
100–299	2	150	43
Under 100	17	56	39
Total	25	185	20

* Total number of workers = 4,635

shows, women comprise 20 per cent of the workforce of the twenty-five largest companies, and their relative proportion of the workforce of individual firms is, by and large, inversely related to their size. Most of these firms have come to the Island since 1960 and half of them are ultimately owned by organizations based outside the United Kingdom. Four of the six largest employers are owned by multi-national firms. At the time of the survey, it was estimated that these twenty-five companies generated an annual turnover of about £100 million and those with the highest turnover are foreign-owned. The rolling mill at Queenborough and the steel mill at Sheerness were partly encouraged to come to Sheppey by the established shipbreaking yards on the Island. The post-war government granted a licence not only to break up ships but also to smelt them into raw material for the UK steel industry. The scrap from a de-industrializing Britain has helped to bring some new investment to Sheppey. The Queenborough rolling mill has moved from ships to old track and wagons from British Rail. It owns the old line which ran to Queenborough jetty in the days when it was a packet post. Owned and managed by an Italian, using an Italian rolling process and employing between twenty and fifty skilled Italian workers at different times, the mill employed about ninety workers in 1981. The rapid expansion was possible through finance from Swiss banks and the chance to buy 6 acres of industrial land adjoining the railway line for a mere £25,000.

Many employers mentioned the advantage of Sheppey's 'green labour' – people who could be trained and also had the 'right attitudes'. Wages were not high, and many managers who took part in the survey recognized that it would be very hard to bring up a family on £100 a week in 1981. They would prefer to employ fewer, more highly paid and more skilled workers.

Perhaps the most striking finding from an analysis of the wage rates of Sheppey workers was the glaring discrepancy between what women were paid for semi-skilled work and what men earn for the same category of work. In one company, the lowest paid semi-skilled worker was the maintenance fitter's mate: he earned £2.25 an hour in 1981, which is £90 for a 40-hour week. If this was his minimum wage, it was substantially above the rate that most women on the Island were paid. Women's rates varied from around £1.50 to £1.89 an hour and they generally worked a 37-hour week. In one firm no overtime was possible, so almost the complete female workforce earned a maximum of £55.50 a week. In other firms there was a range from £55 to £75 or £80. When asked about the rates for semi-skilled men and women in the same firm, the discrepancy would be explained by the fact that all the women were on piecework but that such work was not available to men. The fastest women on piecework in a number of factories could earn up to £80 or £90, and in two, exceptional, cases, women were earning over £100 for piecework. In one case that involved very long hours (54) and in the other, where women could rise above the basic rate of £80 to over £100 'easily' on piecework, 70 per cent of them were in their appropriate union.

Ten companies employed at least thirty women as semi-skilled workers, but the opportunities for women to become trained further so as to earn skilled workers' wages seemed very small. One employer claimed that, while there were opportunities for women to become skilled workers, they did not choose to do so. Another said that one woman was following the formal training procedures to become a skilled worker, but because of age considerations she was unlikely ever to become skilled.

Despite their low rewards, the women workers of Sheppey were highly valued and in many ways appeared to be better workers, from the employers' point of view, than the men. Many of the companies who employ a high proportion of women came to the Island specifically because unemployment was high and the women, perhaps more than the men, were trapped on the Island. Those who employed both men and women and who were prepared to make disparaging remarks about the men (about which more later) frequently made it clear that they exempted the women from these remarks. Typically, women workers are loyal, reliable and do not make trouble. Those employers who were seen to be fair and reasonable (and that does not seem to involve paying high wages) got a very loyal response. In one case, a rush of work led management to ask for extra work in the evenings and weekends, and half the staff volunteered to do this. In another instance, a firm found itself short of work and the managing director explained that if the workers insisted on keeping their existing hours of work, he would have to make some redundant. However, he was prepared to devise a work-sharing scheme to keep everyone on, but with reduced hours and earnings. This was accepted, even though this meant a low ceiling for the highest earners and a mere £40 a week for the lowest earners, with two-thirds of the workforce getting less than £50 per week. It seemed clear that the extra effort and complications that these arrangements created could not be justified on strict profit and loss criteria. 'It's a case of making a profit or coming out of it maintaining your staff. I always think that we must look forward to the time when we can employ all the staff full-time.' The idea was to keep the business going as a collective enterprise, partly because that was a decent thing to do. 'If I was ruled by a board of directors, I couldn't do it.'

The Island being a small community and with relatively few alternative wage-earning possibilities for women, some employers saw their future involving a few men to keep the machinery going, with women to do the packaging and boxing. Such work is always classified as semi-skilled, but, of course, it does not have to be done by females. Nevertheless, the wage rates ensure that it is. Employers have been flexible by, for example, allowing women to leave early on Friday to do the shopping and, in general, have been willing to take a woman back after she has left to have a family. As one manager remarked, 'often the wildest ones when they're young become the most reliable ones when they come back'. Since many of the factories are close to the council housing areas of Sheerness and Queenborough, women can even get home at lunch-time if they want to. This must be relatively unusual.

According to one employer, women have become relatively stoical about their marginal position in the labour market and see themselves as something of a reserve army of labour to be taken on in good times and the first to be discarded when times get difficult.

It certainly suits employers to imagine that redundancy causes less distress to women. As one manager remarked, 'we have got people here who are the breadwinners, who are single-parent families who'd obviously take any smashing of their income very hard. But the one who's been working in a family, even though their husband has been unemployed, doesn't regard herself as the breadwinner. You know, it's sort of "oh well, it was fun while it lasted".'

It would be extremely surprising if these two conflicting views of Sheppey women workers were equally true. Some employers see them as *more* loyal and committed than the men, whereas others see them as *less* committed. Some who take the former view are prepared to reciprocate with a similar commitment to their workforce. But one company, which employs 600 workers to assemble parts in their own homes, has been criticized for the low wages paid to these outworkers; according to the rate set by a time and motion study, the homeworkers might be expected to earn 60p an hour, although, of course, many manage to earn much more. This particular company can readily silence its critics by pointing out that it has a turnover of one in six of its outworkers a year and never has a problem of recruitment. The waiting list of those wanting to become homeworkers is as long as those actually on it. This must be clear evidence of the demand of the women of Sheppey to earn money. When wage rates are low, the need for a second wage earner may become a necessity.

All employers were asked how long it would take to replace a skilled manual worker (implying, of course, a man), assuming that they had to do so. The answer was always measured in days or, at most, a few weeks. Thus, in one small manufacturing company which employed no tradesmen, 'two weeks on the job' was said to be adequate to get enough skill to do the work. In another larger company, it was claimed that many of the workers could be trained in a day, although, exceptionally, some workers doing a particularly skilled operation would need three months' training. More typical, perhaps, was the reply that the time for training for both skilled and semi-skilled workers was 'about a fortnight for anything'.

Given these modest demands on male workers' capacities, it was difficult to know precisely what a good worker was. Most employers very generously spent time showing me round their works, and my subjective impression was that those exercising the most complex manual skills were more likely to be women. Indeed, women doing what is defined as semi-skilled work, say as machinists, would require up to six months' training – which is substantially more than the men doing what is called skilled work. Thus, despite the protestations of employers, it does seem that men do not necessarily have great demands put upon them. It is, of course, paradoxical that women who are expected to do relatively demanding and meticulous work are paid by piecework and get lower wages than the men.

When employers are talking about good workers, they do not really mean good workers: they mean good *employees*. That is to say, they want disciplined and reliable workers who accept their pay and conditions without protest or who respond in a very direct way to the stimulus of more income. There is an interesting contrast here in the way employers approach women: generally there is a strict limit on the amount of money they are prepared to pay, but there is more emphasis on their being decent, understanding and reasonable in order to bind the women with ties of loyalty. For the men, the pecuniary nexus was frequently held to be sufficient.

When managers were asked about the distinctiveness of the Sheppey workforce, they mentioned the isolation and 'rural' nature of the

Island, the ready availability of seasonal or casual employment until very recently, the family nature of social relationships on the Island, and a value system that expects bosses to be bosses and is suspicious of attempts to share responsibility. It is evident that these factors are interrelated, and it is also clear that previous experiences help to colour contemporary consciousness and understanding. The best bosses are not necessarily those that pay most or believe in power-sharing – rather, the best bosses are those who provide certainty, security and stability, are not too demanding, allow a degree of absenteeism and do not expect the work to be an all-enveloping life interest for the worker.

One manager, in attempting to put his finger on what was most distinctive, thought that the dockyard had created a particular style of worker: 'it gave employment with dignity'. The new employment that came onto the Island in the 1960s and 1970s demanded different qualities from the Sheppey workers. It demanded regular hours; it introduced all kinds of controls and disciplines. There was little concern for the workers' dignity, and, very frequently, firms closed or workers were made redundant as a result of takeovers, mergers or the rationalizations of larger companies which decided that they could dispense with their Sheppey plant. No longer was there a clear and obvious boss – whether of the dockyard, the bottle works, the potteries or the glass factory. As the manager of one of the older companies, which has a long association with the Island, commented: 'they're good workers but suspicious – and rightly so when they've been taken over three times in ten years.' Now, he admits, despite attempts to explain to the shopfloor about the takeovers, there is still confusion: 'they don't even know who owns them!'

There was nothing, it seemed, that many workers could do to avoid being made redundant from some of the companies that came and went in the 1960s. It was not lack of workers' efforts that led to closures and redundancies in the late 1960s; it was under-capitalization, changing markets or some other factor over which they had no control whatsoever. Given this utter powerlessness in the face of forces based largely outside the Island, it is perhaps not surprising that their time-scale should be foreshortened and their attitude to work should be ambivalent. Without exception, employers agreed that on occasions workers would rally round and give of their best when there was a clearly perceived need to do so. They *could* work hard, but did not always *want* to. An unusual comment, made by one of the most thoughtful managers on the Island, was that Sheppey had a 'very middle-class workforce'. By this he meant that there was a distinctive kind of individualism on the Island. Unlike the workers in the North of England from where he came, Sheppey workers show 'a variety of different forms of individualism' and he referred to their opinions, their leisure, pursuits and so on. Certainly, there is an unusually high proportion of home owners on the Island: overall, 69 per cent of the Islanders own their own homes and 61 per cent of manual workers do so. This compares with 45 per cent of manual workers in Britain as a whole who own their own homes.[17]

It seems likely that some of the larger and firmly established employers on the Island have managed to build up a committed workforce. By paying higher wages, they have encouraged their employees to raise their style of consumption so that they become more dependent on higher wages. In time, it is possible to buy in labour as long as working conditions are not too bad. One of the largest employers on the Island was able to claim that there is 'no such thing as bad troops, only bad management': few others were able or could afford to agree with such a sentiment. Most managers felt slightly baffled and beaten by 'the Island's mentality', the Island pace of work and the problem of motivating men to do noisy, repetitive, dirty and sometimes dangerous work for a wage that, as some managers admitted, was little better than the dole for many married men. I suspect that most managers would prefer not to have to employ people at all under these conditions, and many had plans to introduce more machines and to get rid of the worst jobs. A future pattern of factories in which machines are maintained by a few men and most other tasks are done by women seems likely in Sheppey.

A casualized secondary labour market could also be readily observed on the Island: youngsters in the amusement arcades, women behind the bars and pensioners filling in for everything from cleaning to skilled craft work, provide a very varied and fluctuating workforce. Wages for by-employment are always low: either the supply is short or the demand is great or both. By-employment can be hard, exhausting and demoralizing, especially perhaps for those with skills and experience. To see this kind of shadow wage labour as some kind of solution to the problems of a de-industrializing society is dangerous romanticism.

Before leaving this discussion of employment, two examples of other styles of waged work may be mentioned, which illustrate aspects of employment not obtainable from the formal survey. One 'employer' did not appear in the survey because he 'did not employ anyone'. However, he manufactures a product that requires substantial labour, and he has a milkman and several pensioners working for him. The milkman comes to the factory for three hours, four times a week for which he gets 80p an hour, paid monthly. He uses this as a compulsory form of savings to pay his electricity bill. In the afternoon he does voluntary work, caring

17 *Social Trends*, HMSO, London, 1981.

for the lawn of a bowling green. Another worker is a pensioner whose first job of the day is to open a newspaper shop and mark the papers. After he has been home for breakfast and walked the dog, he does three hours at the factory for £1.50 a day. Then, after a nap in the afternoon, our pensioner does his third job between 5 p.m. and 7 p.m. as a sort of night watchman at £3 a day. His total weekly income in 1979, on top of his pension, was about another £50. According to the owner of this factory, there was a network of spry old age pensioners ready to do these regular, relatively undemanding jobs at low salaries. For them it provides a distraction and a little extra money. Younger people, he claimed, would not accept the low rewards and the discipline of keeping regular hours. Somewhat fancifully, perhaps, I was told that these pensioners living centrally in Sheerness all had telephones and could be called up as an instant reserve army to deal with rush orders, a job of cleaning on the boats or whatever. With their pensions as a long-stop, a tradition of self-help and early rising, they were following the pattern of by-employment that has been described in previous chapters as part of the traditional pattern of getting the work done.

In April 1978 I talked to women on the Warden Bay estate at the east end of the Island, where the time and cost of commuting and the heavy burden of a mortgage put severe strains on married life. In one small close, five husbands out of thirty were unemployed. Opportunities for casual work were limited and competition was intense. Women who had skilled jobs before marriage, working for computer companies and the like, were obliged to accept 50p an hour serving in greengrocers or in the pubs. One woman, in desperation, worked at a day job seven days a week for which she got £21 and then served behind a bar from 7 p.m. till midnight. She worked days and nights for two months, earning less than £40 a week. She had two children aged 5 and 6 and simply never saw them. Some women will have a third weekend job but still not earn much more money. Buses to Sheerness run once every two hours in winter and in 1978 it cost £1 return. Prescriptions of Valium to the wives on the estate doubled during the year before fieldwork began.

Housing on Sheppey, 1960–1980

Four main developments in the housing of the Islanders have taken place: the expansion of Sheerness for the dockyard workers a similar development at Queenborough for the early industrial development there, often built by the factory owners themselves; the plotlands of Minster; and the chalet development at Leysdown. All these types of development offer considerable scope for individual domestic refurbishing and improvement, positively encouraged by the council. In the mid-1970s for example, the council focused on a cluster of streets in Marine Town, Sheerness, build between 1857 and 1865 – Alma Street, James Street, Richmond Street, Clyde Street and Unity Street. This small area, typical of working class Sheerness, had within it two general stores, a newsagent, a fish and chip shop, two hairdressers and a second-hand furniture shop. There were also three pubs. Most of the 296 dwellings (77 per cent) were owner-occupied, but 12 per cent were unfurnished, privately rented.

Overall, the council found considerable poverty, environmental dereliction and a striking lack of amenities in the houses examined. In just over half the houses, of which many were occupied by elderly people often living alone, the head of the household had no earned income. It was decided to designate the area as a Housing Action Area in January 1977. This allowed substantial funds to be made available, which had the inevitable effect of encouraging the younger occupants to benefit from the grants, often by doing much of the work for themselves. At the time of the council survey in 1976, it was found that the average length of occupation of houses in this area was seventeen years, and thirty two houses had had the same occupiers for more than forty years. Clearly an area such as this can change very quickly in its social composition as a high proportion of the population die or move to residential homes in the space of a few years.

Such an intensive survey of a few streets was not attempted in the programme of research reported here. As is shown in chapters 8 and 9, the sample survey provided a detailed snapshop of the whole Island in 1981 but could not pick up the contours of small, relatively self-contained social worlds. Nevertheless, it is most important to emphasize that these distinctive residential areas very often have different cultural styles and traditions which affect fundamentally the level of informal communal work that can be supported.

In 1981 there were 13,250 dwellings on the Island, of which 2,870 or 22 per cent had been built by the local authority. These are mainly in the Rushenden Road area of Queenborough and on the West Minster side of Sheerness. Smaller clusters of local authority housing are at Minster and Halfway. These two main clusters adjoin the two main industrial areas of the Island, providing the opportunity for women living there to get to and from work easily and for all workers to get home for a midday meal if necessary. But this is offset by the disadvantages of pollution and a bad environment. Thus, in July 1981 the dust and fumes from Sheppey Fertilizers were stripping paint from cars and causing sore throats, coughs and watery eyes. Residents claimed then that the dust had been falling on and off for three years but that the last few months had been particularly bad. Complaints led to more thorough tests and the plant was shut for a time. Although the firm was registered with the alkali inspectorate, this occasion was said to be the first they had heard of a problem.[18] Later in the month the firm pleaded guilty to using a wrong chemical mix and was fined £75 in the Magistrates' court. Similar complaints were regularly made against the steel works and a chemical plant in Sheerness, which is now closed. Certainly, it was the common experience of the researchers coming from the clean air of Canterbury that collars and cars soon got very dirty in the industrial areas. More washing and cleaning would be necessary in working-class Sheppey. The compensation of being able to walk to shops and most facilities relatively easily, which may encourage neighbourly meetings, applies more in Sheerness than Rushenden, but, as will be shown later, these two areas do typify in many respects urban working-class industrial communities. Most local authority housing was built before 1968 with only 14 per cent of the stock built since that date. Perhaps the most striking element in the housing development on the Island in the 1970s was the new private development at Minster and Warden Bay. Between 1965 and 1976 some 2,000 private houses were built there. Such properties are between 20 and 40 per cent cheaper than on the mainland.[19]

However, it would be wrong to assume that newcomers in privately built houses contrast with established Islanders in the local authority estates. It is a common aspiration on the Island for a self-improving family with upwardly mobile aspirations to move to Minster, or at the very least to Halfway, when money for the down payment and mortgage charges has been saved. Just over half the survey respondents had lived in three or more houses on the Island and 15 per cent had lived in five or more houses.

18 Reported in *Sheerness Times-Guardian*, 17 July, 1981

19 This figure was derived from comparing prices of equivalent housing in Faversham and Sheppey advertised by the same estate agent on the same day (18 July 1981) in a local newspaper. The cheapest home in the paper for Sheerness was £9,500 for three-bedroomed terrace in the town centre in need of 'modernization'. In Faversham, the cheapest was £16,500 for a two-bedroomed equivalent house, some distance outside the town. Similar houses with full modernization and central heating cost £15,500 in Queenborough and depending on facilities and construction, whereas in Faversham the lowest price was £26,000, and the highest £65,000. The prices for virgin land are just as disparate, since in Minster it costs just £9,000–£10,000 for a plot on an unmade road with a 40 ft frontage, whereas in Sittingbourne, and equivalent plot costs £20,000–£25,000. Faversham is about fifteen miles from Sheerness, and Sittingbourne about eight miles from Sheerness, and they fall under the same local authority area.

This high level of intra-Island dwelling mobility reflects a particular kind of household work strategy, which depends on home renovation and improvement as a means of raiding the values of the property, selling with a capital gain and gradually moving up the housing market and acquiring capital at the same time. The very varied housing stock, the peculiar structure of the land market at Minster and the policy of Swale District Council to sell local authority houses provides a diverse opportunity structure. Older, three-storey houses in Sheerness, once the basis of the boarding house trade, can be converted into flats; the smaller terrace houses can have bathrooms added at the back and the two downstairs rooms made into one with a reinforced steel joist; and the early plotland bungalows can be extended over the years from very modest dwellings to substantial detached houses if adjoining plots are later acquired. At the bottom end of the market there are some 4,900 caravans and 2,000 chalets, which can always serve as temporary accommodation if there is no relative willing to put up a family moving between a house already sold and another in the process of conversion.

Housing is, therefore, a crucial element in the Island's political economy. While the unemployed man in a council house who owned his 'second home' round the corner which he was refurbishing with the income from his wife's employment and his own labour was exceptional, he illustrated nicely a household work strategy involving both housing and employment.

The different areas of the Island are to a degree polarized politically, with Conservative members of the local council more likely to represent Minster and Warden Bay, and Labour councillors representing Queenborough and Sheerness. Before the local Island council was formed in 1968 there were three separate councils, each with its distinctive political style. Local action groups are typically community-based rather than focused on wider issues. The separate identities of the different areas of the Island have deep roots. The trade unions are also locality- rather than industry-based, even though members could be working in any part of the Island or even on the mainland.

Chapter 7, 'Myth and Reality in Sheppey in the 1980s' (excerpts from pp. 185–97)

When I started research on the Isle of Sheppey I spent many evenings simply talking generally to people about the Island, as I met them in their homes or in the cafes or pubs.

Theories from Below: Islanders' Ways of Making Sense of their World

In the early days, when I was getting the feel of the place, I was presented with three contrasting theories by ordinary people I chatted to as I spent time exploring, in a relatively unfocused way, the Island's character. Since I cannot now recall whether it was Dave, Colin, Steve, Helen or anyone else who most clearly first articulated these theories to me, I will assign my own labels to them.

The Durkheimian Theory

The problem with the Island, according to those who propounded this theory, was that it never recovered from the sudden closure of the dockyard in April 1960. A strong sense of social cohesion existed, built up over the centuries, based on the pride of craftsmanship, the patriotism associated with working for the Army and navy, and the solidarity based on working men's clubs and the co-operative movement. In the old world, so tradition had it, there was meaning in people's lives provided by the ritualized Admiralty hierarchy and reflected in a status hierarchy outside the dockyard, with the skilled men living in more respectable areas, supporting church and chapel and having total occupational security.

The shock of suddenly finding the *raison d'être* of a way of life taken away so quickly knocked the self-esteem of the community with a force it could not handle. The decay and dereliction that set in as soon as the announcement was made in 1958 blighted the Island and undermined its *conscience collectif*. Without a clear focus for the community's identity, it fell apart. Youngsters no longer went to the technical school or competed for the much-prized dockyard apprenticeships. (This was the beginning of the end of apprenticeships generally. A hundred years ago there were well over 100 craft apprenticeships on the Island; now there are less than ten.) The Island lost its tradition of skill: new factories were less demanding; an anomic and privatized war of all-against-all in the labour market developed. Unemployment rates began to rise: the Island would never be the same again.

The Marxist Theory

According to this theory, the Islanders have always been an isolated, trapped labour force valued for its docility. Different waves of capital have washed across the Island at different periods, exploiting, extracting and polluting. In the late 1950s and early 1960s the Island had Development Area status, and firms were attracted to it with local and central government assistance, turning underdevelopment into a resource. This wave of investment was largely dissipated in a decade as many of the firms collapsed or were taken over in the merger boom of the late 1960s and early 1970s and then closed by the new parent companies. Islanders were rudely ejected from employment with little redress. Then, in the early 1970s, international capital invested heavily. In particular, a large, new, Canadian-based steel plant was erected, but by the early 1980s it, too, started to shed labour.[1] By then, competition from the cheaper labour in the Third World countries made it impossible for some companies to hold their markets. Finally, the penetration of foreign products, consequent upon and encouraging the de-industrialization of Britain, led to acres of land changing from sheep pasture to enormous car parks for foreign-made (mostly Japanese) cars. It was estimated that, of the total of 800,000 cars imported into Britain in the early 1980s, 100,000 came through Sheerness, encouraging the local MP to say that this was putting Sheerness 'at the centre of world trade'.[2]

Proponents of this theory see a captive reserve army, deskilled and demoralized, buffeted and bruised by world processes of capital accumulation eddying round a backwater.

The Weberian Theory

Those who adopt this stance point to the continued rationalization and bureaucratization of all aspects of the Island's life. In 1968 the three Island local authorities were merged and the system of education became comprehensive, despite much local opposition.[3] The technical

1 A total of 172 men were made redundant on 2 June 1982.

2 *Sheerness Times-Guardian*, 23 September 1983.

3 A research project to monitor this change was funded by the Kent County Council Education Committee at the University of Kent at Canterbury. This was

school was closed and one large comprehensive school was built in the middle of the Island for just under 2,000 pupils. Then, in 1974, local government was reorganized once again; the District Offices were established on the mainland at Sittingbourne and councillors were more likely to be mainland farmers and businessmen.[4] The growth of the welfare state organized everyday life, generating a resentment against pervasive surveillance and control. People came on to the Island during the day to check, to organize and to inquire. Planners, school attendance officers and careers advisers sorted, sifted, chased and advised.

A resentment against the apparently ever-expanding state was a common topic of pub conversation in working-class areas, fuelling those who supported this theory. The development of new, modern estates and the sale of council houses developed or encouraged sharp status distinctions among manual workers, based less on mutual respect and understanding and more on the outward signs of a given style of life. Family members drew apart from each other as the ambitious, hard-working and overtime-seeking moved out to owner-occupied houses in Minster and emphasized their distinctive patterns of consumption. It was the new value system, developed by an aspiring consumer-oriented stratum, that divided and weakened the established community.

These three theories, sketched out by ordinary people trying to make sense of the context in which they live, are all founded to some degree on fact. The dockyard did indeed close, abruptly changing the nature of the town of Sheerness. But Sheerness housed only a third of the Island's population, and it is unlikely that that one event could have had such an effect, although the *Sheerness Times-Guardian*, widely read on the Island, did (and still does) much to spread the myth. Features on various aspects of local history appear frequently in its pages and those with personal memories of the 'good old days' are given generous space in the correspondence columns. Elderly people living in other parts of Britain or in other countries – particularly Canada or New Zealand – write regularly with anecdotes. The Island in the past is frequently equated with the Admiralty dockyard.

directed by Professor Paul Stirling and carried out by Cyril Rodd. Substantial disagreement about the 'usefulness' of this work led the Education Committee to abandon the project. An interim report, reflecting the bitter resentment of local teachers, was deposited at the Library of the University.

4 A suggestion put forward by the Boundary Commission in 1983 to put Sheppey into *West* Kent for the purposes of the next election to the European Parliament in June 1984 led the *Sheerness Times-Guardian* to complain, with some justification, 'If you confuse people often enough, as the Boundary Commission seems intent on doing, they will become apathetic and that is bad for democracy' (29 July 1983).

The theory about the effect of the ruthlessness of capitalist exploitation is also based on some facts, but the imputed consequences are questionable: in terms of the effects on people's consciousness, employers are more likely to be perceived as benefactors – providing employment is seen to be the most useful way to help the Island. Agencies of the state, on the other hand, are viewed with greater resentment and hostility.

Finally, the organization and management of the Island has, indeed, become more remote. Companies are controlled by distant corporations based overseas and the local government is based on the mainland at Sittingbourne. However, in practice, multi-national corporations are more likely to provide *better* conditions of service for their employees, and the new Swale District Council claims that it is providing proportionately more resources for the Island to make up for its previous neglect. A new swimming pool costing £1 million opened during the period of our research, and a further £1 million was spent on a covered sports centre that was completed in 1984. It is likely that the Council's claim is valid.

These three theories are therefore inadequate in different ways, and it would be hard to say more than that there is something in all of them. And that, of course, is where the discussion in the pub generally ends. Social scientific rigour should do better than that.

There is, however, a fourth, which might be called the psychogenetic, theory often held by those living off the Island and visiting it as an employer or member of a local government or welfare state organization. It was claimed that Sheppey was distinct because its population was stable and self-contained (even in-bred), and had been so for generations. Accounts of the origins of the population varied: some claimed that many were escaped convicts from the prison hulks that were moored on the Medway in the eighteenth century; others suggested that there was substantial inbreeding among a small number of landless quasi-gypsy families or that more recently cockneys had migrated to the Island early in the twentieth century and had created a distinctive cultural style. The IQ of Sheppey schoolchildren was said to be lower than the county average, there was a greater problem in dealing with ESN pupils, and there was a higher proportion of mentally handicapped people on the Island. All this was due to the isolation and the peculiar genetic make-up of the Islanders.

Needless to say, this pernicious myth is completely false, but islanders are aware of it and adopt a mocking, self-deprecating tone often hiding a fierce pride. I was shown on a number of occasions how a crude drawing of East Anglia and the Thames Estuary could demonstrate that 'Sheppey was a piece of shit in the arse 'ole of England.' But then the conversation would quickly shift and many would emphasize that it was curious how often people came back to the Island after leaving it for a time. It was frequently said that the rest of the world was unfriendly: people felt at home on Sheppey. As one woman unselfconsciously remarked, 'I like it here because it's so central: you've got London and city life in one direction and Canterbury and rural life in the other.'

This is the complex material context in which households struggle to get by. In 1984, as in 1784 or 1284, ordinary people know (in T. S. Eliot's words)

> Birth, and copulation, and death.
> That's all the facts when it comes to brass tacks:
> Birth, and copulation, and death. (*Sweeney Agonistes*)

The way in which households form and organize their work practices is a complex process: following through the domestic cycle and getting by is constrained fundamentally by material circumstances. The historical development of the material circumstances that make the Isle of Sheppey today is not simply an account of the growth of capitalism. Throughout the nineteenth century, capitalist enterprise hardly penetrated the Island. Such capitalist activity as did exist up to the 1890s was small-scale petit-bourgeois trade and service activity. While Queenborough was industrialized with relatively heavy industry in the early twentieth century, the Island as a whole escaped until the 1960s and 1970s. Hence, since having a number of employers is a relatively new phenomenon on the Island, this may be a reason for them to be viewed as supporters of the Island rather than class enemies. Over and over again during the six years of fieldwork, employers in general were described in favourable terms, despite the very low wages many paid and the dangerous, dirty and boring work many of them required.

Towards the Year 2000 with a Labour Market in Decline

During the period 1978–83, when the Island was the focus for the research reported here, unemployment was rising steadily. In some desperation the Medway Ports Authority made an unsuccessful application for Free Port status to be granted to the reclaimed Lappel Bank and the Neats Courts Area. In many respects the Island is well-placed for an experiment in removing state controls: as has been shown, aspects of its local government history have provided it with substantial experience in the consequences of neglect by public authorities. Perhaps institutionalized neglect would provide some economic impetus.

De-industrialization and jobless growth are not ideas that have to be introduced to the Islanders. The development of Sheerness as a port for importing Japanese cars makes the contrast transparently clear. On the same site where Pilkingtons once employed over 400 people, there are probably three times that number of Toyota cars driven there by a handful of workers. Certainly, the car-importing firms are expanding and firms may take on a few extra workers, but this is rarely likely to reach double figures in a year. As the managing director of one successful firm explained, 'We don't just take people on and lay them off. I would rather work my existing staff a little harder than take on more people to let them go after a few weeks.'[5]

Even if Free Port status had been granted, or if controls such as the quota restrictions on imported cars were relaxed substantially, it is unlikely that very many new jobs will be created. The investment of £1.4 million in the new Klippon factory to create twelve new jobs was widely noticed and discussed. Indeed, so sceptical are the Islanders that some resistance to the designation of more land for industrial development at Queenborough was reported. A local councillor argued at a public meeting that, since new industrial development would be unlikely to provide a significant number of jobs for local people, it would be better if it did not come. One speaker at the meeting was reported as saying, 'The council continues to push industry down on us but the time has got to come when we say enough is enough. It's about time other areas had their fair share.'[6] This response from an area with one of the very highest levels of unemployment in southern England may appear surprising. However, it may be a sign that, if there are few realistic hopes for new, decent jobs, people at least want to live in a pleasant environment. This certainly may account for the correspondence addressed to the local (Conservative) MP deploring his willingness to support the expansion of Japanese car imports for the sake of a handful of jobs.

There are certainly very clear signs that Kent County Council believes that it has to make efforts 'to create more wealth' on its own account, without relying on much central government support; and, in common with other local authorities, it is energetically pursuing contacts overseas. A delegation went to Japan in the autumn of 1983 in order to attract Japanese manufacturing industry or assembly plants to Kent. With increasing protectionism in the European Economic Community, the county can claim to be well-placed to distribute products owing to its geographical advantages. Perhaps more significantly, Kent is attempting

5 Quoted in the *Sheerness Times-Guardian*, 22 July 1983.
6 *Sheerness Times-Guardian*, 22 July 1983.

to sell a particular kind of labour to international capital. The leader of the county council reported that when in Japan Kent's 'stable workforce' was one of the advantages that was particularly stessed.[7] The county has also established its own Kent Economic Development Board, chaired by a former director general of the National Economic Development Council, Sir Ronald McIntosh. He, too, emphasized the 'good industrial relations record' of Kent workers as one of the county's main assets in an attempt to attract overseas investors to Kent.[8]

It was clearly accepted without question by the management that 'wealth-creating' investment in the county would be universally welcomed by the workers. But in Sheppey, one of the main sites for such investment, attitudes are likely to be ambivalent. Public subsidies for private profits are seen by some as a sensible way of getting more wealth, which can then be redistributed through the taxation and social security systems. But if relatively few new jobs are to be created and the unemployed are still unemployed, it is understandable that Sheppey people should feel it adds insult to injury if the new investment simply spoils their view. It may be that in the later 1980s the county management will be hurt by what they perceive as the mulish and ungrateful opposition of the apparently deprived to the introduction of foreign investment.

As an alternative pattern of development, women may more readily accept employment at relatively modest rates and, more likely, on a part-time basis. The most docile of all labour, and with, as has been shown, a developing tradition on the Isle of Sheppey, it seems likely that women's position in the labour market may be moderately good, at least until the end of the century. The implications of this pattern of employment which may produce part, but not all, of a household's income will be considered in the final chapter. Here it is simply worth noting that in some respects the Isle of Sheppey can be seen to have some of the characteristic problems of a de-industrializing Britain in a particularly extreme form. People, goods and capital are likely to flow through the Island, adding little to the quality of life of those living there. The people come straight off the ferry and do not wish to stay overnight; the goods, mainly imported cars, cover much of the Island in an unsightly way or are moved out in heavy container lorries jamming the Island's roads; and the capital, from plants employing few, but relatively highly rewarded workers, goes to Chicago, Osaka or Rotterdam. Various clever financial arrangements ensure that little of the value added by the people and locality accrues to the National Accounts. The county gets some benefit

7 *Sheerness Times-Guardian*, 11 November 1983.
8 Reported in the *Sheerness Times-Guardian*, 4 November 1983.

from initial investment and the increase in rateable value, but the level of unemployment remains high. International corporations are not noted for employing school leavers.

Such seems to be the most plausible scenario for the formal economic development of the Isle of Sheppey towards the year 2000. One of the Island's well-known 'characters', long-serving councillor Charles Nevill, wrote an ironic letter to the *Sheerness Times-Guardian* which was published on 7 October 1983. It expresses many of the views and resentments that regularly appear in the correspondence pages, and since the Island appears to be at another turning point as it suffers the impact of de-industrialization, the letter is quoted in full:

> **Queue here for Falklands tickets ...**
>
> Sir,
>
> Applications are being accepted for emigration to the Falklands Islands. It is advised that those interested should not delay in applying as a large response is expected.
>
> It is felt that Sheppey's residents are well suited for such emigration as they have experience of an isolated life-style. But, of course, there is a vast difference between the Falklands Islands and the Isle of Sheppey.
>
> For example, on Sheppey the cost of a child's bus fare to attend school is either unobtainable or under review; the cost of £1.50 per year per pupil for sports-clothes cleaning equipment cannot be afforded; the repair of roads and pavements is almost a thing of the past; and employment [*sic*] is maintained to equal the blackspots of the United Kingdom unemployment figures.
>
> Although equal in rate contribution to those on the mainland, it is a fact that they fail to receive the equal proportion in return, whereas, on the Falkland Islands, each resident is maintained at well over a million pounds a year.
>
> In order to encourage visitors, a contract has just been given to a British firm (an umpteen million-pound contract!) for a floating pontoon accommodation for visitors.
>
> Of course, there are disadvantages; there are no cinemas, dance halls or amenities, but, as stated previously, this is why Sheppey residents are considered to be ideal immigrants.
>
> They should take full advantage of the current situation. If the money does not come to them, then it would be best if they go to where the money is.
>
> Apply now! Don't wait until Sheppey is threatened by foreign invaders before money is ploughed back in.
>
> All applications are expected to be processed in time to fly direct and land on the new Falklands Islands airstrip in the course of construction.
>
> Go Falklands! Be a millionaire; and you will not be as lonely as there are even some of our sheep there to make you feel at home.

> And remember, there you have the Government's ear far more than you have where you live now. Enrol today!
>
> – Regional Enrolment Officer for the Falklands, c/o Charles Neville.

This and the previous chapter have provided some account of the arena in which the people of our case study live out their lives. Not every local context will have such a sharp contrast between myth and reality, for, as I have suggested, being an island probably helps. However, it is important to recognize that most people read their local newspapers with greater care than the national ones. There is a sharp disjunction between the national and the local that strongly persists and will no doubt continue to do so. Those who have commented on the changes in British society from 1959 to 1984 have tended to aggregate the local into a national – or perhaps metropolitan – perspective. Thus, for example, discussions about de-industrialization, the decline in manufacturing and shifts in employment have been largely national in orientation. Yet it is clear that these larger processes of change have very distinctive local impacts.

It is possible that variations in life chances between different localities will become much more marked in the next quarter of a century. Some areas will develop rapidly with new jobs and capital investment; other areas will continue to decline. Patterns of geographical polarization, already in evidence, may well become more acute. In the same way that households may retreat within themselves as a way of coping with a turbulent and apparently uncontrollable environment, so too may localities come to look more within themselves. It is not unlikely that there will be greater vigour and determination to cope with social and economic problems at a local level than at the national level.

And it is at the more local level that all forms of work outside employment have their greatest salience. Local initiatives to organize various forms of informal and communal work are developing very vigorously.[9] It is not, perhaps, too fanciful to expect the rediscovery of local products, local crafts and ways of marketing local identity and historical associations. The stubborn concern of many people on Sheppey not to forget what they see as their 'past' should, perhaps, be considered seriously. The interest in old photographs, old postcards and old people's memories seems to be growing. A local publishing company has been established to supply this new market. Meresborough Books, in Rainham, Kent has published over forty books about places in Kent

9 See the Report *Whose Business is Business?* Community Business Ventures Unit, London, 1982 and other studies sponsored by the Calouste Gulbenkian Foundation.

and other county-related topics, and has published a monthly journal, *Bygone Kent*, since 1979.

This nascent localism is a form of social consciousness that cannot be ignored. If, as I argue, the nature and meaning of work can be understood only in a specific social context, then perhaps the general understanding of the way all work is done in our society will inevitably have to be rooted in a deeper understanding of local contexts, such as the Isle of Sheppey.

1 Portrait of a deindustrialising island

Tim Strangleman

Introduction

Ray Pahl's *Divisions of Labour* represents an influential, if somewhat neglected classic text for sociologists of work. Combining formal and informal work patterns alongside discussions of both public and private realms, it was part of an upswing against a more traditional industrial sociology which privileged traditional, often male-dominated forms of employment (see Salaman 1986; Gallie 1988; Strangleman 2005). What Pahl realised in his writing was the need for a broader sociology of work which could encompass a wider set of pressures, influences, links and networks that shaped work, and were in turn shaped by work. As a piece of historically and sociologically aware writing about economic life it was in many ways prescient.

In this chapter I want to explore another way in which *Divisions of Labour* is a neglected classic, and this is in terms of its attention to the issue of deindustrialisation. Pahl was writing at a time when the label 'deindustrialisation' was increasingly applied to the contemporary experience of industrial change. The word crops up six times in the book's index, both as a general phenomenon, as well as specifically about Sheppey as a site of industrial loss. I want to argue that *Divisions of Labour* was a ground-breaking book in a number of ways precisely because of the way it understood the topic of deindustrialisation. Pahl realised that a tight focus on a confined geographical space could reveal a more general set of trends, and therefore understandings, about change.

Pahl's Sheppey was in many ways an exemplar of deindustrialisation in the UK as it contained within its boundaries many of the complex elements of deindustrialisation, indeed he did describe Sheppey as a 'post-industrial laboratory'. Rather than seeing the problem as 'simply' about job loss and industrial closure *Divisions of Labour* identifies and unpacks a whole series of often contradictory processes involved in deindustrialisation, processes which often occlude rather than reveal the reality at work. By developing his unusual temporal device of projecting forward, thinking through what developments might yield in the future, Pahl was, by accident or design, anticipating many of the ways in which deindustrialisation has been conceived of subsequently. Pahl was up close to the developments he discussed, but he was able to put his contemporary observations in historical context and, crucially, able to think about how this process of industrial change might unfold into the future. What makes Pahl's book so important is that he senses deep-seated change in the economy but avoids what he described as 'exagger-books' which argued that society was undergoing complete change. In what follows I look first, briefly, at the scholarship around deindustrialisation, both contemporaneously to Pahl's work and in later writing. This sets the scene for a discussion of the theme of deindustrialisation within *Divisions of Labour* and how we can identify a number of distinct ways in which Pahl was thinking in very original ways about the process. Finally, using these ideas I want to explore how *Divisions of Labour* can in turn throw new light on to debates about both deindustrialisation and the sociology of work in our own time.

Deindustrialisation

Pahl's *Divisions of Labour* of 1984, and his research for it dating back to the 1970s, was right at the cusp of a profound change in western economies. While the term deindustrialisation had been around for some time it really became an issue in the early 1980s and, in academic and policy circles in particular, with the publication of Bluestone and Harrison's *The Deindustrialisation of America* (1982). The novelty of Bluestone and Harrison's approach lay in the way they studied the economic, political and social effects of industrial decline, seeking to understand economic decisions as hedged around by a complex web of factors, both domestic and international. They identified important trends in North American disinvestment domestically, and the parallel investment in developing nations as at the heart of deindustrialisation. They called for moral and ethical questions to be answered by US corporations over these actions. Understandably, much of the attention paid to industrial decline centred on what was rapidly becoming known as the 'Rust Belt', a corridor of disinvestment from the North-east states – New York, New Jersey and Pennsylvania through to the Mid-West – Ohio, Indiana, Illinois and Michigan.

During the 1980s and 1990s interest in the process of industrial loss grew among academics, journalists and policy-makers. Many of the early studies sought to understand the immediate effects of closure on local communities struggling with industrial loss. Often these accounts emphasised the vulnerability of mono-industrial towns or regions and the attempts to fight closure or reopen plant (Lynd 1982; Bensman and Lynch 1987). As time passed, greater emphasis was placed on linking the plight of individual places with broader issues associated with plant closure. These included a focus on internal migration, of white flight and racial ghettoisation. Later still, attention was paid to the ongoing and long-term effects of change within and across generations. Deindustrialisation attracted the attention not only of sociologists like Pahl but also geographers, economists, anthropologists as well as humanities scholars interested in how reaction to this deindustrialising process was increasingly being manifested in cultural creation such as creative writing, poetry and visual media (see Strangleman 2013; Strangleman and Rhodes 2014; Strangleman *et al.* 2013).

Later there developed a trend towards making broader sense of deindustrialisation, to attempt to synthesise the more local, small-scale accounts of change to try and capture the great meaning and significance. In a special issue of *Urban Anthropology and Studies of Cultural Systems and World Economic Development*, published in 1985, editor Katherine Newman envisaged the contribution that the field of urban anthropology could make to the study of deindustrialisation. Recognising what she saw as the transformative powers of deindustrialisation, as well as its social and economic costs, Newman saw it as a pertinent area of inquiry, owing to the way in which, 'it offers a means of integrating the study of urban subcultures into the larger economic landscapes which surround them' (Newman 1985: 14). She argued that the, 'deindustrialisation paradigm',

> takes us beyond purely economic issues. Deindustrialization ultimately affects family life, the ways in which people age, the extent to which their communities remain intact or fall victim to outmigration, and the very nature of the urban dweller's worldview. In the most general sense, the research on deindustrialization turns the urban anthropologist toward the social problems side of our informants' lives, since many of the pathologies of city life can be traced to the effects of economic dislocation. (1985: 15)

This was echoed by Stefan Goch, who observes in relation to the study of deindustrialisation in the German Ruhr:

> Whereas the economic dimensions of structural change were constantly discussed, certain other dimensions only became evident with time, needed more time to be even recognized … These were the social and cultural, particularly political-cultural dimensions that arose with de-industrialization, the change and diversification of the economic structure, the emergence of service industries, the production of knowledge, and the accompanying pluralisation of the working world and life in general. (Goch 2002: 88)

In 2003 Jefferson Cowie and Joseph Heathcott published *Beyond the Ruins*, an edited collection bringing together authors from a range of disciplines and perspectives studying the phenomenon of deindustrialisation across the USA. Cowie and Heathcott used their introduction to 'move the terms of the discussion "beyond the ruins"' (2003: 1). While the editors made clear they were not dismissing the important testimonies from workers caught in the midst of plant shutdowns, they instead argued that:

> the time is right to widen the scope of the discussion beyond prototypical plant shutdowns, the immediate politics of employment policy, the tales of victimization, or the swell of industrial nostalgia. Rather, our goal is to rethink the chronology, memory, spatial relations, culture and politics of what we have come to call 'deindustrialization'. (2003: 1–2)

They argued for a more considered view as to what this all meant: what were the longer-term patterns and issues and what was at stake? This emphasis on the long-term consequences of industrial change coupled with a desire to reach back historically to ground an understanding of industrial culture gives a particular richness to debates and commentary within the USA, arguably one that is lacking in the UK. More recently still literature scholar Sherry Linkon has developed the phrase the 'half-life of deindustrialisation', in order to grasp the medium and long-term impact of social, cultural and economic change. As she explains:

> Deindustrialization has a half-life, and like radioactive waste, its effects remain long after abandoned factory buildings have been torn down and workers have found new jobs. … We see the half-life of deindustrialization not only in brownfields too polluted for new construction but also in long-term economic struggles, the slow, continuing decline of working-class communities, and internalized uncertainties as individuals try to adapt to economic and social changes. It is not yet clear how long it will take for the influence of deindustrialization to dissipate, but the half-life of deindustrialization clearly extends well into the twenty-first century. (Linkon 2014: 2)

As we will see Ray Pahl was alive to many of these issues and ways of exploring industrial change in the context of Sheppey.

Deindustrialisation and *Divisions of Labour*

The first mention Pahl makes of deindustrialisation is towards the end of his introduction to Part II, where he notes his three primary reasons for selecting Sheppey for his study. After its sociological distinctiveness, and its reputation for informal economy, he notes:

> The third main factor that drew me to the Island was its pattern of unemployment. As an Admiralty dockyard from the late seventeenth century and also a military garrison, Sheerness had almost three hundred years of industrial history which might have produced a mature working-class culture. The dockyard had closed twenty years before the fieldwork began, but it was in the front of the minds of all those who had been living on the Island at the time. There were other traditional industries, such as glass and pottery manufacture, and more modern plants making pharmaceuticals and electrical components. A very wide range of manufacturing industry made the Island a more attractive area in which to explore the implications of de-industrialization[1] than any other alternative town within a reasonable radius of my home university. Furthermore, its level of unemployment was between 10 and 14 per cent in the early stages of the project, rising above 20 per cent in the autumn of 1983. In so far as other forms of work could serve as a compensation for the decline in employment, Sheppey seemed an appropriate choice to explore such a pattern. (Pahl 1984: 145)

1 I have kept Pahl's original spelling and configuration of de-industrialization for consistency.

There are a number of points to pull out of this extensive justification for choosing Sheppey. Most important for this chapter is that Pahl makes the distinction between unemployment and deindustrialisation, a more obvious point now, but not quite so clear cut in the early 1980s. Interesting too in his portrait of an industrial island is how he pays attention to an industry which had disappeared physically from the Island some two decades before, but which at the same time continued to exercise a ghostly presence on its latter-day inhabitants. While that initial mention of deindustrialisation was essentially backward looking, in the final section of his introduction he projects forward from the period of the mid-1980s to the turn of the millennium, and from the local context of Sheppey to the rest of the UK:

> although the account of the process of de-industrialization on the Isle of Sheppey will surely prompt the reader to consider whether what the smaller Island faces in the 1980s its larger neighbour will face, in increasingly acute form, towards the year 2000. (Pahl 1984: 151)

In both Pahl's historical sense of the process of deindustrialisation, and in his anticipatory projection forward over a quarter of a century into the future, he was at the forefront of discussions of the phenomena. A careful study of the bibliography of *Divisions of Labour* reveals little contemporary writing he could draw on to discuss the topic. The big exception was the collection *De-Industrialisation*, edited by Frank Blackaby (1979) which explored the issue through a variety of policy and disciplinary perspectives and Jonathan Gershuny's (1978) *After Industrial Society?*, which uses the term 'post-industrial', rather than 'deindustrial'. Interestingly, he did not reference Daniel Bell's 1973 book *The Coming of Post-Industrial Society* in the 1984 book although he had in previous publications (e.g. Pahl 1980). Understandably, given the timing of his writing, Pahl seems to have been unware of Bluestone and Harrison's (1982) *The Deindustrialisation of America* mentioned earlier.

Industrial decline was though a hot topic during this period as an ideological war was being fought out over the economy and how it might be reformed. Much was made of the nineteenth-century antecedents of the 1980s recession, most notably seen in the publication of Martin Wiener's 1981 book *English Culture and the Decline of the Industrial Spirit 1850–1980* and his assertion of the notion that the roots of Britain's industrial decline date from the 1880s and in particular the gentlemanly capitalism that failed to grasp fully the need to invest in new technology and efficiency. In sociological accounts of the economy contemporary researchers were more likely to discuss the issue of unemployment, usually in policy terms, rather than as sociologists of work (see Marsden 1982; Massey and Meegan 1982; Fineman 1987; Westergaard *et al.* 1989). Other sociologists of work and economic life were later to use the term deindustrialisation as the economic programme of the Thatcher administrations gradually became clearer (see for example MacInnes 1987; Eldridge *et al.* 1991). By contrast Pahl was not only using the term deindustrialisation, but was also differentiating between its various forms.

Three concepts of deindustrialisation

The most straightforward account of deindustrialisation in Pahl's book is in his discussion of industrial closure. His chapter entitled 'Portrait of an Industrial Island' gives a flavour of Sheppey's industrial past and present:

> Queenborough High Street has many of its period houses boarded up in bad repair, and in turning off down Rushenden Road, past the industrial estate, the impression is of a northern industrial town. Heavy traffic has pitted the roads; factories making fertilizer, lavatory pans or glass bottles make little attempt to look presentable to visitors. Railway tracks cross the road; huge metal objects lie outside the rolling mill and iron foundry. (Pahl 1984: 153)

He goes on to describe the Rushenden Road Estate in the language of the Marxist analysis of the time as 'an all too obvious machine for workers to reproduce themselves in' (1984: 153). If this is an industrial scene it is clearly one Pahl reads as being in decline, just like scores of similar industrial communities of 'the north'. It is the process of industrial loss that attracts Pahl to the story of the dockyard and the way its fortunes wax and wane before the eventual terminal closure of 1960.

Importantly, Pahl draws attention to the peculiarities of naval dockyard employment wherein a particular form of secure vulnerability was engendered, a feature common to all the historic naval dockyards in the UK (see Lunn and Day 1999). These were workplaces that featured high levels of job security, relatively low wages, provision of pensions and relative autonomy over work patterns. These then were secure 'good jobs', but vulnerable in the sense of being subject to government strategic review. Seven hundred dockyard jobs were lost in 1960 although some workers transferred to the Chatham yard, which itself was to close two decades later as part of a more established wave of deindustrialisation. Pahl was clear that in order to grasp contemporary patterns of work on the Island he had to understand the legacy of the type of work culture that had been engendered by the naval dockyard. This was something that had grown up not over decades but rather centuries. In the interviews with employers he picked up the sense of legacy:

> One manager, in attempting to put his finger on what was most distinctive, thought that the dockyard had created a particular style of worker: 'it gave employment with dignity.' The new employment that came on to the Island in the 1960s and 1970s demanded different qualities from the Sheppey workers. It demanded regular hours; it introduced all kinds of controls and disciplines. There was little concern for the workers' dignity, and, very frequently, firms closed or workers

> were made redundant as a result of takeovers, mergers or the rationalizations of larger companies which decided that they could dispense with their Sheppey plant. No longer was there a clear and obvious boss – whether of the dockyard, the bottle works, the potteries or the glass factory. As the manager of one of the older companies, which has a long association with the Island, commented: 'they're good workers but suspicious – and rightly so when they've been taken over three times in ten years.' Now, he admits, despite attempts to explain to the shopfloor about the takeovers, there is still confusion: 'they don't even know who owns them! (Pahl 1984: 175; the excerpts from 'Portraits of an industrial island' provide a fuller context for this quote.)

There was then a sense of earlier deindustrialisation and closure as making contemporary Sheppey vulnerable to new waves of closure; the original dockyard closure creating a pool of labour more at risk of insecure employment even in an era of virtually full employment. While *Divisions of Labour* more obviously focuses on the decline of industrial work Pahl also mentions the decline in non-industrial forms such as informal work on the land or in the tourism sector, all in serious decline by the time Pahl began his project.

Pahl's second conceptualisation was less straightforward than simple loss of industrial work. Scattered throughout the book are mentions of the new 'industry' whereby Sheppey was being developed as a place to off-load, store and prepare new Japanese cars before they hit the forecourts of Britain. Here the story was of Sheppey's role in undermining the domestic automotive industry. It clearly made a big impression on Pahl, in his description of the industrial nature of the landscape he notes in his portrait 'and the horizon is again dominated by the endless sea of Japanese cars' (Pahl 1984: 153). The presence of this particular trade flow was noted on the map of the island that Pahl included in the book (1984: 342) as 'parking areas for Japanese cars' (indicated by shading); the map is reproduced in Dawn Lyon's chapter in this book (p. 153). Car importation was even captured in one of the images used to illustrate the book, with a picture of empty rail car transporter wagons returning to the Island to collect another load of imported cars. Pahl was explicit in his analysis of this trade that it was fundamentally linked to the wider process of UK deindustrialisation, as he argues later in the book:

> Finally, the penetration of foreign products, consequent upon and encouraging the de-industrialization of Britain, led to acres of land changing from sheep pasture to enormous car parks for foreign-made (mostly Japanese) cars. It was estimated that, of the total of 800,000 cars a year imported into Britain in the early 1980s, 100,000 came through Sheerness, encouraging the local MP to say that this was putting Sheerness 'at the centre of world trade' (Pahl 1984: 187)

Later still he again draws on this servicing industry to illustrate a wider point about economic change on the Island:

> De-industrialization and jobless growth are not ideas that have to be introduced to the Islanders. The development of Sheerness as a port for importing Japanese cars makes the contrast transparently clear. On the same site where Pilkingtons once employed over 400 people, there are probably three times that number of Toyota cars driven there by a handful of workers. Certainly, the car-importing firms are expanding and firms may take on a few extra workers, but this is rarely likely to reach double figures in a year. (Pahl 1984: 194)

By making these connections so early in the process of deindustrialisation Pahl was uncovering the complexity of what was happening to the wider economy in the UK through the lens of the process on Sheppey. As he notes:

> Here it is simply worth noting that is some respects the Isle of Sheppey can be seen to have some of the characteristic problems of a de-industrializing Britain in a particularly extreme form. People, goods and capital are likely to flow through the Island, adding little to the quality of life of those living there. The people come straight off the ferry and do not wish to stay overnight; the goods, mainly imported cars, cover much of the Island in an unsightly way or are moved out in heavy container lorries jamming the Island's roads; and the capital, from the plants employing the few, but relatively highly rewarded workers, goes to Chicago, Osaka or Rotterdam. (Pahl 1984: 195)

Pahl understood that this form of development added little value to the local or national economy, and tied in with his recognition of the significance of the fact that 'In 1983, for the first time in 200 years, Britain recorded a deficit in trade with the rest of the world in manufactured goods' (1984: 335). This was typically service sector work for low-skilled and low-paid workers. Flows of investment made by multinational companies also made Sheppey and places like it vulnerable to changing business decisions made far away. *Divisions of Labour* then makes the link between industrial decline and 'precarious' work nearly three decades before Guy Standing (2014) promoted the term in his writing.

The third main type of deindustrialisation identified in Pahl's book was a form of what could be called, following Schumpeter, 'creative destruction'. This was the way in which industry on the Island was stimulated as part of the very process of wider domestic deindustrialisation.

> The rolling mill at Queenborough and the steel mill at Sheerness were partly encouraged to come to Sheppey by the establishment of shipbreaking yards on the Island. The post-war government granted a licence not only to break up ships but also to smelt them into raw material for the UK steel industry. The scrap from a de-industrializing Britain has helped to bring some new investment to Sheppey. The Queenborough rolling mill has moved from ships to old track and wagons from British Rail. (Pahl 1984: 171)

Pahl does not mention that Dr Beeching, the architect of dramatic cuts to the UK's railway network in the 1960s, had been born on Sheppey, but the irony would not have been lost on him. Some of the expansion of the new activity was, Pahl notes, due to the cheap abandoned industrial land on the Island – brownfield sites before that term became popular. What is striking about Pahl's insights some three decades ago was how *Divisions of Labour* rehearsed many of the ways in which deindustrialisation is now discussed and understood. This example of industrial development stimulated by deindustrialisation – industrial development as both symptom and cause – is a common one in contemporary coverage of the topic, notably in the USA (see Walley 2013).

One of the best examples of this contemporary writing can be found in Paul Clemens's *Punching Out: One Year in a Closing Auto Plant* (2011), in which the author spends twelve months working with a gang of skilled workers who strip out the capital equipment from a redundant factory. Clemens's account is a careful exploration of this process and is a sympathetic portrayal of the men who, having once been skilled fitters in plants like Budd (the automotive plant on which his study is based), now find employment using that skill and knowledge carefully dismantling the still operational machinery ready for shipping to Mexico or elsewhere in Latin America. Clemens is keen to make the distinction between the highly-skilled gang he observes and the scrappers – both legal and illegal – who now populate Detroit's abandoned industrial landscape. *Punching Out* places this trade in redundant machinery in its wider US context. He shows how a whole industry has been created to systematically strip out plant from the US economy ranging from those who actually dismantle machines and transport them through to the intelligence produced on where closures have occurred. Clemens talks at length about *Plant Closing News*, a twice monthly listing of industrial distress. At one point the paper was reporting on an average of 100 plant closures a month, but the figure is often reported as being much higher. In both the case of the skilled dismantlers Clemens reports on, and lower-level scrappers, the impression is of an economy consuming itself; hastening its own decline, feeding off its own body fat built up over a century. Clemens is aware too of the irony of the workers he becomes close to as working themselves out of jobs as they finish dismantling Budd.

> I felt as if I'd witnessed an execution. I watched the process of dismantling a press many times, and never found the sight any less awesome, or any less saddening. At Budd, all of the skill of the Arkansas Boys – and of Jeff, Matt, Guy, and Nedaz [those he worked with] – was in the service not of making things but of taking apart the things that had made things. It seemed a waste of such talents, a wound somehow self-inflicted – an act of violence against the prospects of blue-collar Americans by blue-collar Americans, who had no other choice. (Clemens 2011: 253–4)

Pahl then understood what was happening on Sheppey in terms of the scrap management as a very real and poignant form of economic cannibalism in much the same way as Clemens would, nearly three decades later and over three thousand miles from Sheppey.

Reassessing deindustrialisation in *Divisions of Labour*

As we have seen, Pahl identified three distinct but interlinked forms of deindustrialisation underway in Sheppey in the late 1970s and early 1980s. In its most basic form this was the simple loss of industry, the closure of plant which is what most of us, certainly at the time Pahl was writing, would have associated with the word. Second, he was identifying the way industrial depression was sucking in newer forms of investment attracted by cheap labour and plentiful land. Crucially, Pahl recognised that this was not employment or economic activity that was likely to add much value, being neither highly-skilled nor well-paid. It was also, and perhaps most importantly, not sustainable in the longer term. Indeed, this type of economic activity might even prevent the development of other forms of investment and job creation. Finally, *Divisions of Labour* saw the industrial activity in the scrap metal sector on the Island as a symptom of an industrial cannibalism, a country systematically stripping out its productive manufacturing capacity. What was and still is impressive about this dissection is how it can simultaneously hold these developments apart but see them as interlinked and intertwined. They are all part and parcel of the same process of a wider deindustrialisation.

But what more can *Divisions of Labour* tell us about the process of deindustrialisation, and how it might throw new light on contemporary industrial decline? As the excerpts from chapters 6 and 7 illustrate perhaps the most important aspect of what Ray Pahl was doing in his book and wider research was placing economic activity into a geographic context as well as a historical perspective. As a geographer by training he was sensitive to an understanding of the relationship between place and human development. Space and place were not containers in which activity took place but rather each shaped the other over time. This temporal sensitivity was and is important, and is one of the reasons why *Divisions of Labour* has stood up so well as a study to return to. In examining economic activity occurring in the 1980s Pahl understood the deep roots of industrial culture, the multiplicity of sedimented customs and practice and how these were accreted over time. Though he did not use the phrase one could almost sum this up as a recognition of an industrial structure of feeling.

Dave Byrne has used this phrase to explore the legacy of industrial work in the North-east of England after deindustrialisation (Byrne 2002; Byrne and Doyle 2004). Using Raymond Williams's work, Byrne charts the persistent traces of a culture shaped by specific types of work in a region – most notably in his research on the coal industry. In many ways Pahl was thinking in very similar ways about the development and decline of industry on Sheppey. Thus in talking about economic life in the 1980s, Pahl felt the need to revisit the creation of industry in the seventeenth century and thereafter trace the way that industry (especially the naval dockyard) grew, matured, declined and then finally closed. Crucially, though, he understood that the closure of the 1960s was not the terminal point of that particular story. As a good historical sociologist Pahl knew that two decades after that closure it still influenced economic, cultural and social life and would continue to do so. It still could be found in traces among those who had directly experienced closure as well as in subsequent generations shaped by their parents or grandparents. As Pahl notes in his introduction:

> Furthermore, the past may provide clues for the future: if de-industrialization is, in some sense, the reverse of the process of industrialization, then by, as it were, running the film of history backwards, we may discover a guide to the future. There may be possible parallels between what happens in the 1980s and 1990s and what happened two hundred years earlier. (Pahl 1984: 2)

Here again Pahl's work has powerful resonances with the way many scholars of deindustrialisation are thinking about their subject (Strangleman 2016). There is a general recognition that the study of industrial change has to, in the words of US historians Jefferson Cowie and Jonathan Heathcott, move 'beyond the ruins' or the 'body count' approach to talking about deindustrialisation. As we have seen, authors such as Cowie and Heathcott wanted to move away from the immediacy of plant closure and the struggles to save them, important as they undoubtedly were or are.

By examining deindustrialisation that had occurred in 1960 Pahl was making some important points about its study. Again, though he does not use the phrase, effectively he was talking about what US literature scholar Sherry Linkon describes as the 'half-life of deindustrialisation', the ongoing intergenerational legacy of industrial work. As Linkon puts it:

> People and communities are shaped by their histories – by experience, by memory, and by the way the economic and social practices of the past frame the structures, ideas, and values that influence our lives long after those practices have ceased to be productive. (Linkon 2014: 1)

The past, she contends, remains both as a source of pride and pain and it is the tension between these that leads to a selective reworking of the past in the present. As she continues:

> Thus, even as the active memory of industrial labor may fade, the landscape, social networks, local institutions, as well as attitudes and cultural practices bear the stamp of history. (*Ibid.*)

Pahl's writing is suggestive of just such a half-life existing on Sheppey when he explains his need to trace the history of the Sheerness naval dockyard:

> Nevertheless, it is important to try and make sense of the context: people's real or imagined knowledge of the past colours, to a degree, their present attitudes and pattern of behaviour. Newcomers to the Island have different traditions, to be sure,

> but Sheppey is a distinct milieu with its own distinct traditions, experiences, possibilities and constraints. People have to grapple with the material circumstances of their existence, and because the Island is so relatively small and insular, in more than one sense, people can readily have a consciousness of its distinctiveness. Working-class culture is not an ahistorical response to existential circumstances – rather, it is an intensely conservative and traditional set of household practices for grappling with material circumstances. In order to understand more of the complexity of the material context, it seemed necessary to gather a substantial amount of data on the historical development of the dockyard, the pattern of employment from 1960s to 1980 and a detailed analysis of housing development in the twentieth century. (Pahl 1984: 155)

In *Divisions of Labour* Pahl was sensitive both to the history and chronology of deindustrialisation. He was very unusual for his time, and arguably still is unusual in actually talking about industrial change of the 1960s as deindustrialisation. Even in the 1980s the term was a controversial one with some seeing such change as creative destruction, or a process of maturation, rather than something to be particularly concerned about. In a slightly different register Pahl's labelling chimes with the more contemporary trend towards tracing deindustrialisation's antecedents further back than the 1970s, to the early post-war period, the inter-war era or even earlier. Recent scholarship in the field such as David Koistinen's *Confronting Decline* (2013) for example is a historical account of deindustrialisation in the New England textile industry. He argues powerfully that the process of industrial retrenchment began during the 1920s as mills in the north-east states came under intense competition from newly industrialising southern US states. This competition in part was a function of newer technology, but was mainly due to lower wages commanded in the South as a result of a general lack of unionisation. Thus the relatively high wages of the North were progressively undermined through the 1920s and the Depression era of the 1930s. Indeed, Koistinen suggests that the first signs of the structural weakness of the textile sector in New England were detected in the 1890s, which brought the response of investment in textile schools to train workers and especially managers in improved industrial techniques. Even earlier evidence and use of the term deindustrialisation can be found in Christopher Johnson's *The Life and Death of Industrial Languedoc 1700–1920* (1995) suggesting decline in the 1820s.

In sum then, Pahl recognised relatively early on that we need to study the historic roots of industrial decline – both local and national. Like contemporary writers his stress was on process rather than deindustrialisation as a discrete event (see Mah 2012). He was aware of the way the industrial past continued to bubble up, to haunt the present. He even hinted at what would later be termed a form of 'smokestack nostalgia', where Island residents looked fondly back on more benign economic times, as he notes:

> Queenborough was a flourishing little borough in the seventeenth century, and Sheerness developed in the nineteenth century as a garrison, Admiralty dockyard

and seaside resort. So much was built between 1850 and 1900 that people's memories of a much cleaner town are likely to be substantially true. It is understandable that many islanders cannot see the present except in terms of its decline from the past. (Pahl 1984: 152–3)

Conclusion

In this chapter I have made a sustained attempt to argue that Ray Pahl's *Divisions of Labour* represents an important contribution not only on how work is understood in all its forms, but that he was also a pioneer in his focus on deindustrialisation. It was by no means common to discuss economic change in the early 1980s using this term. Many of those talking about industrial decline during the late 1970s and early 1980s were in many ways too close to events to really be able to apprehend what was happening in all its complexity. Pahl's analysis stands out, even today, not only because of how he used the term but also the subtlety and complexity with which he engaged with the issues that confronted Sheppey and wider Britain. He recognised the complexity of the changes being wrought on Sheppey and that these were part of a long-term evolving process with its roots in the Island's initial industrialisation. He saw that the trajectory on which Sheppey found itself in the mid-1980s had been shaped by events in the 1960s which continued to unfold into the future. He was also ground-breaking in terms of his ability to differentiate between various elements of deindustrialisation. In doing so he went beyond a straightforward account of industrial closure and loss. He also paid close attention to what often must have appeared as contradictory developments, such as the stimulation of new industrial processes and services by deindustrialisation on and off the Island itself.

When people think about *Divisions of Labour* they often remember the way it calls for a sociology of economic life which takes seriously both paid *and* unpaid work. What Pahl and others called for as part of a move away from the strictures of industrial sociology's focus on paid, manual, often male, work undertaken in factory settings, was a broader understanding of the role and context of household survival strategies. This was an acknowledgement that the division of labour in the private sphere was as important as that which went on in public, in the formal employment relationship. In just the same way his discussion of deindustrialisation was rooted in place, context and community. He understood work culture, and its decline, as shaped by local and national events historically. As he noted:

> Those who have commentated on the changes in British society from 1959–1984 have tended to aggregate the local into a national – or perhaps metropolitan – perspective. Thus, for example, discussions of de-industrialization, the decline of manufacturing and shifts in employment have been largely national in orientation. Yet it is clear that these larger processes of change have very distinctive local impacts. (Pahl 1984: 197)

He went on to project, with great prescience, what might unfold in the future:

> It is possible that variation in life chances between different localities will become much more marked in the next quarter of a century. Some areas will develop rapidly with new jobs and capital investment. Some areas will continue to decline. Patterns of geographical polarization, already in evidence, may well become more acute. (*Ibid.*)

Pahl's genius in writing about deindustrialisation in the pages of *Divisions of Labour* was to recognise the complexity of the story that confronted him. In his later edited collection *On Work* (1988) Pahl indulges himself with a rant on what he describes as '"The future-of-Work Industry": a Polemic on Polemics'. Here he rails against the likes of André Gorz and Charles Handy and what he considered their naivety and superficiality, in discussing the nature of work. As he acknowledges:

> I agree completely with those in the future-of-work industry who urge us to look with fresh eyes at all forms of work. My fear is that too many will turn their eyes but not much will come into focus. Understanding the new strategies of employers and households and how they interact from the local to the global level is obviously a demanding and wide-ranging project. (Pahl 1988: 751–2)

One could make an argument that the relative neglect of *Divisions of Labour* has a great deal to do with Pahl's mission to not engage in what he describes as the 'future-of-work industry', or what I have described elsewhere as the end of work debate (Strangleman 2007). It was perhaps Pahl's insistence on focusing on change in an isolated Kent coastal community that made his insights seemingly less important than those that indulged in more Jerimiah-like predictions as to the future nature of work. For this writer it is precisely Pahl's ability to resist melodramatic conclusions that makes his work as relevant to contemporary readers as when it was written over three decades ago.

Excerpts from *Divisions of Labour*, chapters 8 and 9

Chapter 8, 'Class, the Domestic Cycle and Sources of Labour' (excerpts from pp. 198–231)

I was able to commission a large-scale survey to take place in the spring of 1981.[1] I required information on both the *forms* of labour in which household members were engaged and the *sources* of labour that the household drew on to get certain tasks done.

Gathering information on forms of labour is fairly straightforward. Questions on the nature of the present occupation of respondent and partner elicited data that could be readily collapsed into class categories. Information was also gathered about other earners in the household and about household income. All these data enabled households to be precisely categorized in relation to their involvement in formal labour. Other questions were designed to draw on all the other work respondents did for employers or for any other person or institution outside the household, whether or not they were paid. Inevitably, such questions had to be phrased more and more generally in order to encompass all the possible tasks and activities that respondents could do.

A further set of questions explored the sources of labour that households used to get forty-one distinctive tasks done. These tasks were chosen in the light of the knowledge derived from my earlier work in Sheppey. Broadly, sources of labour were provided either formally, through the market (for example, garages), state services (for example, the home help service) or members of the household themselves, or through informal sources (friends, neighbours, relatives or others 'working off the books'), which might have been paid or unpaid. There

1 This survey was undertaken in the exemplary manner by Social and Community Planning Research of London (SCPR) under the direction of Gill Courtenay. The construction of the interview schedule and the analysis of the pilot survey was a joint effort by Gill Courtenay, Claire Wallace and myself. SCPR organized the fieldwork of the main survey and coded the data. The team at the University of Kent were provided with straight hole counts of the data in the autumn of 1981 together with the tapes. The problems of transferring these data to the University of London computer so that it could be analysed using SPSS (Statistical Package for the Social Sciences) took longer than expected owing to a number of minor misunderstandings and difficulties. I am very grateful to Spyros Missiakoulis and Joan Dobby for helping with these problems.

was substantial variation among households in the divisions of labour between different sources, and this chapter explores the connections between *forms* of labour (focusing specifically on class and income as indicators of a household's position in relation to employment) and the balance of *sources* of labour for the Island's households as a whole.

Put more precisely, what I wanted to know was: 'How do household work practices and divisions of labour relate to the sources of labour used for the provision of services?'

In 1980 I thought that the central objective was to explore the trade-off between time and money. I was over-influenced by the frequently heard statement that 'it paid me to take a week off work to paint the house', so that in earlier publications I had assumed that informal work, whether for oneself or for others, was in some sense an *alternative* to full-time employment. The notion that levels of productivity were higher in the so-called domestic economy had persuaded Scott Burns, Gershuny and, indeed, myself that, in some senses, people had a choice to be better off working for themselves than by engaging in formal employment.[2] I embarked on this research project to see whether, indeed, those that did more 'work for themselves' had a different rationality, a modification of the work ethic that, as it were, distracted them from a complete commitment to formal employment. The practical and political implications of such considerations seemed to be of outstanding importance and significance. If the way people do their work is changing in some fundamental way – a kind of re-negotiation of the social division of labour, as some have described it – then detailed documentation of this would clearly be an essential research task. If people were valuing *time* more than *money*, and if, indeed, higher levels of productivity could be achieved with one's own tools in one's own time, then fears about the consequences of high levels of unemployment might be unfounded.

Furthermore, important differences in attitudes to employment and work might exist between men and women, and these distinctive rationalities should also be explored. A quiet revolution in everyday life might be undermining the central importance of employment as a means of livelihood, a form of social control and a fundamental support for personal identity. It cannot be denied that these are important questions and that too much debate has been conducted on hearsay, anecdote and

2 R. E. Pahl, 'Employment, work and the domestic division of labour', *International Journal of Urban and Regional Research*, 4; 1, 1980, pp. 1–20; J. I. Gershuny and R. E. Pahl, 'Work outside employment: some preliminary speculations', *New Universities Quarterly*, 34: 1, 1979, pp. 120–35; J. I. Gershuny and R. E. Pahl, 'Britain in the decade of the three economies', *New Society*, 3, January 1980, pp. 7–9.

unacceptably feeble empirical data bases. This was the context and challenge for the Sheppey survey, and these considerations very considerably determined the way in which we designed the research instrument.

It is quite clear that we initially underestimated the importance of household composition and the domestic cycle. Evidently, the household is a constantly changing social unit as members age and other members come and go. Hence, the connection between the work that is provided and the work that is supplied is mediated by the intervening variable of the stage in the domestic cycle of the household. This I now see is a crucial issue, which I must address in as much detail as the expected connection between employment and other forms and sources of labour.

The overwhelming problem in the Sheppey study was that, with very strict resource limitations, we required both a large enough sample to allow the numbers in the cells to be adequate for analysing distinctive household work practices and divisions, and information on all household members. In practice, that generally meant both partners in households based on couples.

An unclustered random sample was selected from the electoral register for each of the eighteen polling districts on the Island. A special effort was made to interview alternately the head of household or the housewife in all households where that was appropriate. These terms were not gender-linked: the 'head of the household' was the person who owned or rented the property and the 'housewife' was the person – usually though not necessarily a woman – who was mainly responsible for the catering and domestic arrangements of the household.

An inevitable consequence of having a completely random sample was that a high proportion – 28 per cent – were single-person households, most of whom were retired. However, since many of the questions related to how a range of tasks was done, these households provided an important demonstration of the sources of labour of households who were unable to do much work for themselves and therefore needed other households to help them.

The Formal Labour Provided by Households

The main source of income for most people is their formal occupation, and on the basis of this all respondents and their spouses were collapsed into three classes with a further, fourth, category for full-time housewives and occupations inadequately described. Broadly speaking, Class 1 is composed of professional and managerial workers, Class 3 is composed of manual workers and Class 2 are those in between.

Knowledge of the Sheppey local labour market helped in the allocation of marginal or ambiguous categories. Thus, personal service workers were put in Class 3 and foremen in Class 2, reflecting the way these categories were perceived on the Island. Perhaps more debatably, intermediate non-manual workers were left in Class 2, even though this category might be more appropriately classified as Class 1.

Using these categories, and focusing in this case only on the male's occupation in couple households, Sheppey has a similar class structure to the country as a whole. Given the particular characteristics of the Sheppey sample, a distinction is made here, which will be used throughout the analysis that follows, between the 204 households with only one, generally elderly, person and the 526 households in which there is a couple of a male and female partner. Evidently, only those households with more than one person can have a domestic division of labour.

If therefore, for present purposes, we disregard the single-person households (many of whom are lower-status people who have moved into cheaper housing on the Island on retirement), and focus attention on the 526 households in which both partners were classified by socio-economic status, some important intra-class variations can be highlighted. To anticipate later analysis, I may emphasize now that the pattern of household sources of labour is related closely to total household income and also to household tenure. The first substantially influences whether work is done by household members or whether other labour is engaged to do it, and the second influences the kind of work that is necessary to be done.

Tables 8.2(a) and (b) bring together information on households' class, income and tenure, and hence provide a composite guide to their material circumstances. Fully 69 per cent of Class 3 households based on a man and woman couple own their own homes, which is, of course, a reflection of the very high levels of home ownership on the Island as a whole; the proportion of Sheppey working-class 'couple-based' home owners is some 15 percentage points above the average for all households in Britain. Households are classified in this table not simply by the male's occupation but by the occupation of both partners to produce a household class with the male's class given first so that, for example, a Class 2 male married to a Class 3 female would produce a household class of 2.3. By having the class of both partners, it is possible to show the wide variation within categories defined by the occupation of the male chief earner alone. Thus, home-owning couples of Class 3 males married to Class 1 or Class 2 females have very much higher proportions earning 'high' incomes: the difference of 60 and 40 per cent for household classes 3.1 and 3.2 and 18 and 14 per cent for 3.3 and 3.4

Table 8.2(a) Social class of household by household income: home-owners (couples only)

Social class of male partner	Social class of female partner	Household income (%):* High	Medium	Low	Total sample N	%
1	1	50	50	0	4	1
	2	48	42	10	31	9
	3	29	41	29	17	5
	4	11	56	33	9	3
2	1	50	50	0	4	1
	2	43	42	15	74	21
	3	36	39	25	28	8
	4	26	63	11	19	5
3	1	60	20	20	5	1
	2	40	52	9	58	17
	3	18	63	19	62	18
	4	14	43	43	28	8
4	2	0	0	100	3	1
	3	33	33	33	3	1
	4	100	0	0	1	0
Total (N)		115	166	65	346	
Total (%)		33	48	19	100	

* In this and subsequent tables households were divided into three household income bands based on *net* income. The way this was done is set out as follows:

	Annual net income	Weekly net income	Proportion of households %	N
'Low' income	Less than £3,499	Less than £70	33.4	244
'Medium' income	£3,500–£7,499	£70–£149	36.5	267
'High' income	Over £7,500	£150 or more	18.9	138
Don't know, refused to answer, couldn't remember			11.1	81
			100.0	730

No information was provided by 17% of Class 1, 13% of Class 2, and 10% of Class 3

is very striking. It will be seen that the high-earning, working-class households in household classes 3.1 and 3.2 who own their own homes have a higher proportion earning 'high' household incomes than household classes that would appear conventionally higher in the household hierarchy; household classes 1.3 and 1.4 and 2.3 and 2.4 have lower proportions in the high household income category than 3.1 or 3.2.

Table 8.2(b) Social class of household by household income: non-home-owners (couples only)

Social class of male partner	Social class of female partner	Household income (%):*			Total sample	
		High	Medium	Low	N	%
1	1	0	0	0	0	0
	2	67	0	33	3	3
	3	33	67	0	3	3
	4	0	25	75	4	4
2	1	0	0	0	0	0
	2	29	43	29	14	13
	3	33	50	17	12	11
	4	20	60	20	5	4
3	1	0	100	0	3	3
	2	0	75	25	12	11
	3	19	53	28	43	38
	4	0	50	50	10	9
4	2	0	100	0	2	2
	3	0	100	0	1	1
	4	0	0	0	0	0
Total (N)		20	61	31	112	
Total (%)		18	54	28	100	

* See note to table 8.2(a)

Evidently, Class 1 males earn higher salaries, in general, than Class 3 males. However, the particular circumstances of the Sheppey labour market means that working-class women – or, more precisely, women who are prepared to do working-class jobs – are better placed. That is to say, it is easier for women to find 'working-class' employment than 'middle-class' employment. There is little doubt that Abbotts Research Laboratory would just as readily employ a female as a male research chemist with a doctorate; the difficulty is that the men who are in Class 1 on the Island are not married to women with PhDs in chemistry. The opportunities open to the women they are married to are more limited. As a result, the incomes of middle-class women in employment may not be much higher than those of working-class women. Furthermore, working-class women employed as routine factory workers may have greater security than their husbands. In addition, the expenditure patterns of working-class households may, for a variety of reasons, be less demanding than for middle-class households. For example, certain manual tasks connected with maintaining the house or car may be done by members of working-class households themselves whereas, as will be shown later, middle-class households may have to purchase such services formally. Thus, paradoxically, working-class households, given the possibility of multiple earners, may be in a better position to accumulate savings. The fact that they may use these savings to buy their own dwelling, perhaps from the local authority, is another matter. The point I want to make here is simply that working-class households may, in certain labour market contexts, be in a better position to raise their household income through having multiple earners.

Seven per cent of Class 1 males live with partners of the same occupational class as compared with 55 per cent of Class 2 and 49 per cent of Class 3. Also, of 203 women in employment whose partners are also in employment, 20 per cent are in Class 1, 34 per cent in Class 2 and 46 per cent in Class 3. Where both partners are employed there is a very strong likelihood that the couples will own their own homes: only 18 per cent of households where both partners were in employment did not own their own dwellings.

The Domestic Life Cycle of Households

Presenting information on the material circumstances of households by occupation, economic activity, number of earners and housing tenure is relatively straightforward. However, it is clear that economic circumstances vary between different stages in the domestic life cycle.

In the context of the present discussion, I am focusing primarily on the position of women in relation to their family-building cycle, as this is the main factor affecting their economic activity rates.[3] In some ways, stage in the life cycle is the greatest leveller here, although the dependence on one earner when children are young is inevitably a greater burden for those in households where the single earner has a lower income. Those 384 households in which the male partner was in full-time employment are selected in Table 8.7 in order to show the relationship between domestic cycle and female activity rates.

Women aged 35 or under without children are likely to be in full-time employment and those with children under 5 are likely to be full-time housewives. However, by the time the youngest child is aged 5, most women on Sheppey will be back in full or part-time employment. If

3 The point about the social acceptability of female entrepreneurship has been well made by R. Scase and R. Goffee, *The Entrepreneurial Middle Class*, Croom Helm, London, 1982.

Table 8.7 Life-cycle characteristics of female partners of males in full-time employment, by economic activity

Female partner	Full-time employed		Part-time employed		Housewife		Other		Total	
	N	%	N	%	N	%	N	%	N	%
Has youngest child under 5	4	5	9	10	73	83	2	3	88	23
Has youngest child aged 5–15	31	23	51	38	47	35	4	3	133	35
Has no children in household aged:										
35 or under	29	80	2	6	4	11	1	3	36	9
36 or over	37	29	37	29	43	34	10	8	127	33
Totals	101	26	99	26	167	43	17	4	384	100

those households where the youngest child is aged 5–15 are divided according to whether there is or is not another person aged 16 or over in the household, no difference appears in the overall proportion that are in paid employment. Where there is an older person over 16 in the household, however, 29 per cent of women are employed full-time and 32 per cent part-time, whereas without the additional older person only 20 per cent are employed full-time and 42 per cent part-time. It is significant that, for women without dependent children and aged 36 and over, the proportion employed full-time and the proportion employed part-time is the same – 29 per cent. This may reflect problems of re-entry into the labour market for older women, or perhaps women of that generation prefer part-time employment.[4]

The household's composition and stage in the domestic cycle is of crucial importance in influencing the involvement of household members in different forms of labour. Before turning to consider how households with these different characteristics relate to different sources of labour, it is important to examine a further intervening variable, namely the local area in the Island where the household lives.

Households' Sources of Labour

I found that it was extremely difficult to get systematic information over time about all the work that individuals do for others, whether they get paid or not. Diaries and time budget analysis are, of course, very valuable, and the work by Gershuny and his colleagues, based on Mass Observation data for Britain in the 1930s and BBC Audience

4 J. Chaney, *Social Networks and Job Information: The Situation of Women Who Return to Work*, Equal Opportunities Commission, SSRC/EOC, Manchester, 1981.

Research data at different periods in the post-war period, throws considerable light on general trends of certain broad categories of work.

However, these sources were not designed to deal with the complexities and subtleties of informal work. Formal work in employment can be measured fairly precisely, although difficulties arise with some occupations such as university teaching or with those doing creative work. Housework is hard to measure precisely: polishing a floor seems to be self-evidently housework, but if a neighbour comes in with his tool for sanding the floor, is he doing the 'housework'? Given that non-precise definitions such as 'housework is the work women do in the home' carry with them conventional assumptions and norms that may well be changing, and that, indeed, are part of the focus of this study, ideologically charged terms were consciously avoided.

The alternative approach is to focus on the labour that is done *for* households, including whether or not they do it themselves. The practical and pragmatic notion that work is any task that it is possible to pay someone else to do for one evidently embraces almost all activity. However, with the decline in servants, members of households have to do much of their everyday work for themselves. Friends, relatives, neighbours and the official home help service may do anything from making the bed to washing up for those who are elderly or incapacitated. Not all of these may define doing such a task as work: clearly the woman in the home help service will do so, but the dutiful son or daughter may be 'helping mum'. Certainly, it gets out of a lot of difficulties to focus, in a non-evaluative way, on the characteristics of those doing specific tasks – whether they are paid and whether they are a friend, relative or representatives of a formal firm or agency. This also enables analysis to be made on the basis of whether work is done by household members or non-household members and hence permits exploration of distinctive divisions of labour: divisions between household members, between some households and other households and between households and the money economy, including the distinction between whether the money is paid formally or informally.

Sheppey Survey Work Tasks

1. *House maintenance* (3)
   1 Indoor painting
   2 Plastering
   3 Mending a broken window
2. *Home improvement and decorating* (7)
   4 Double glazing

5 Putting in a bathroom
6 Building a garage
7 Building an extension
8 Converting an attic to living space
9 Putting in a reinforced steel joist (RSJ)
10 Putting in central heating

3. *Routine housework* (12)
11 Washing up
12 Tidying house or flat
13 Hoovering or brushing carpets
14 Cleaning outside windows
15 Cooking family meals
16 Making a packed lunch
17 Getting a take-away meal
18 Shopping
19 Washing clothes
20 Washing sheets
21 Ironing clothes
22 Ironing sheets

4. *Domestic production* (8)
23 Baking a cake
24 Making clothes
25 Knitting
26 Repairing clothes
27 Growing vegetables
28 Making jam
29 Making bread
30 Making beer or wine

5. *Car maintenance* (4)
31 Washing the car
32 Checking the oil
33 Tuning the engine
34 Repairing or checking the brakes

6. *Child care* (7)
35 Bathing child
36 Changing nappies
37 Looking after a sick child
38 Collecting child from school
39 Seeing schoolteacher about child
40 Taking child to doctor
41 Getting child's hair cut

With these considerations in mind, we selected a list of forty-one tasks to cover a wide range of activities. All respondents were asked if they had ever done each task on the list and then, in the case of house maintenance and similar tasks, they were asked, 'Who did all or most of the work?' In the case of more common domestic tasks, respondents were simply asked who usually does them. Respondents were also asked to name who actually did the task inside the household; outside the household they were asked to say whether it was done by a relative, friend or official firm and whether or not it was paid for. With the answers to these questions, it was possible to group those tasks that were done by distinctive sources of labour – household members, friends and relatives, paid or unpaid (informal sources), firms, garages, landlords or whatever (formal sources of labour).

The remarkable result to emerge from the analysis of these tasks was just *how much work* of various sorts was being done. Thus, of the full sample of 730 households, 80 per cent had done indoor painting themselves and a further 17 per cent had had it done for them at some time, 84 per cent had made a cake themselves, 25 per cent had mended the brakes on the car themselves, 32 per cent had made jam themselves and 8 per cent had put in a reinforced steel joist (RSJ) themselves (with a further 6 per cent getting the job done for them). Most of the labour involved in the work was unpaid: the overwhelming amount was being done *inside the household*. This is expressed diagrammatically in Figure 8.2: both sides of the diagram add up to the total proportion of the sample doing the task, with those not doing the task at all bringing the total up to 100 per cent. Thus, taking the example of tuning the car, half the sample got this task done and it was split remarkably evenly between unpaid and paid work.

Finally, and in striking confirmation of earlier remarks on the relative insignificance of the so-called 'informal economy', the main tasks on which informally paid labour was used were painting, plastering and domestic cleaning (mainly windows). People were more likely to be paid in cash for home decorating, cleaning the windows and general domestic cleaning.

Analysis at the level of the 730 households in the full sample gives some general understanding of broad divisions of labour. I now mention briefly a number of obvious points. Those who own their own homes, own cars and have children have a potential demand for more tasks than, say, couples without children living in a local authority rented dwelling. Yet again, older people may have a demand for fewer tasks and yet have to have more of them done for them. So income and life-cycle stage are self-evidently important, remembering that income needs

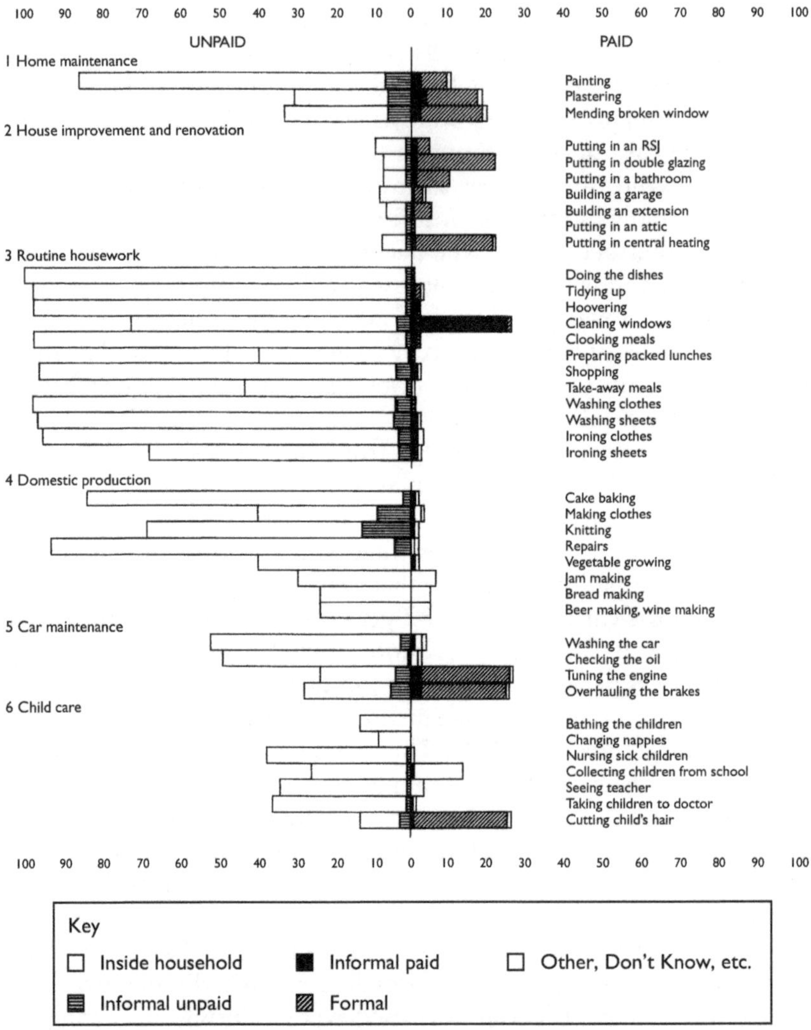

8.2 Sources of Labour for 41 work tasks

to be seen in its cultural context. That households spend their money in different ways is an obvious truism: an affluent manual worker may engage in more tasks when refurbishing his older house than a professional worker with a high mortgage on a new house. At this stage in the argument we are looking entirely at the demand side, at the differential use of services or demands for labour.

I should make it clear that, for present purposes, certain tasks are more significant than others. By and large, the tasks fall into the following general pattern:

(i) *tasks that are done by almost all households by household members:* these include the familiar cooking and cleaning, but also painting;
(ii) *tasks that are done by some households and generally done by household members:* these include child care, vegetable growing, car washing and beer or wine making;
(iii) tasks done by fewer households and generally paid for in the formal market sector*: these include most of the house improvement and extension tasks;*
(iv) *tasks that are done with a variety of forms of labour:* these are overwhelmingly painting, plastering, making cloths, knitting, tuning the car engine and fixing brakes.

Evidently, life-cycle and income effects are likely to operate in each category. Figure 8.3 shows the effect of household income on divisions of labour. Low-income and, as we shall see, elderly households are more likely to pay for home maintenance and routine housework; high-income households are also more likely to pay for home maintenance and car maintenance.

In Table 8.3 households' social class is related to the sources of labour for those doing two tasks – repairing a broken window and doing work on the brakes of a car. The tasks are much more likely to be done by households in Class 1 or with 'high' annual household incomes.

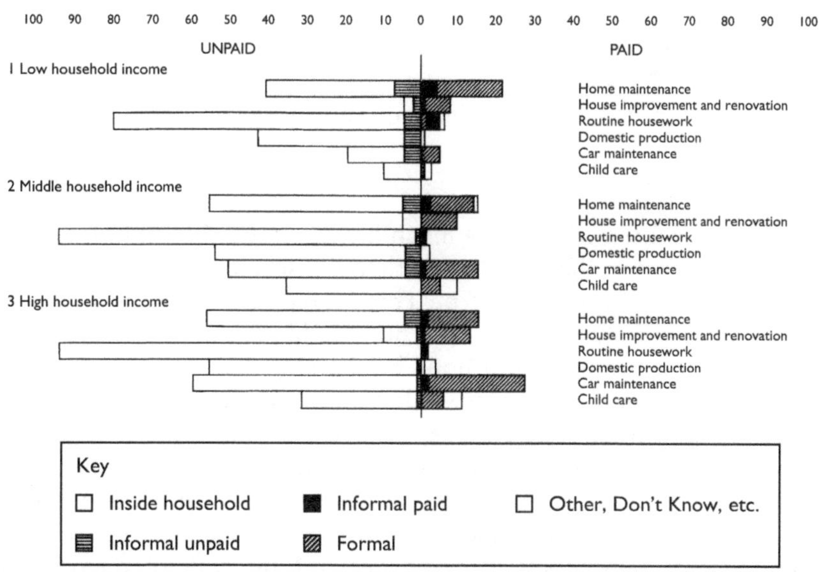

8.3 Sources of labour for 41 tasks by household income categories

Table 8.8 Getting two tasks done

(a) Class by source of labour

Class	Task	Those in class doing task %	N	Of those doing task: source of labour (%) Household	Informal Paid	Informal Unpaid	Formal
1	Repairing a broken window	62	61	46	13	5	34
	Doing work on the car's brakes	75	74	28	4	4	62
3	Repairing a broken window	51	174	58	8	1	32
	Doing work on the car's brakes	48	161	58	12	4	26

(b) Household income by source of labour

Income Range*	Tasks	Those in class doing task %	N	Of those doing task: source of labour (%) Household	Informal Paid	Informal Unpaid	Formal
'High' income	Repairing a broken window	62	85	63	4	–	33
	Doing work on the car's brakes	83	115	45	1	5	48
'Low' income	Repairing a broken window	46	112	36	13	7	43
	Doing work on the car's brakes	23	56	34	20	4	41

* 'High' income= £7,500 or more p.a. in 1981; 'low' income = £3,500 p.a. in 1981. See also note to Table 8.2.

However, it is interesting that a much higher proportion of Class 3 has the task of seeing to the car's brakes than households with low incomes – 48 per cent as against 23 per cent. This is a reflection of the high household incomes of some working-class households. Second, it is significant that the highest proportion of households using their own members as a source of labour to repair a window are those in the 'high'-income category – presumably also those most able to pay others to do the task for them. Low-income households, including many pensioners, are more likely than Class 3 to pay for the two tasks to be done informally, but it is also interesting that the same proportion of Class 1 households as low-income households (13 per cent) get the task of repairing a broken window done by paying someone informally. Not surprisingly, the lowest proportion of any of the four categories using a household member to work on the car's brakes is in Class 1 households; they would be most likely to take their car to a garage. However, 12 per cent of Class 3 car owners and 20 per cent of car owners in 'low'-income households would pay someone informally to do the work. These distinctions between class and household income are particularly important, showing how a household's capacity to gain income through multiple earners may offset its class position to some extent.

We are now in a position to consider how these activities are divided among different sources of labour. In each cluster of tasks, the high-income households did more activities apart from child care. For present purposes, the most interesting clusters of tasks are house maintenance and home improvement and renovation. In these two areas, the 'high'-income households are most likely to get the work done but *less* likely to use formal sources of labour.

Not only are richer households more likely to do more work, they are more likely to do tasks with their own labour. Thus, 74 per cent of the home maintenance and 39 per cent of the home improvement and renovation are done by members of 'high'-income households. The same category is also most likely to use household labour in domestic production and car maintenance. Those with cars, children, their own homes and high-household incomes appear to do a very great amount of work. There is little sign that households with higher incomes are that much more likely overall to use formal service provision – or, indeed, to use more informal sources of labour for which they have the means to pay. In every cluster, the higher-income households have the lowest percentage of informally paid sources of labour. By contrast, the poorest households use informal sources, most particularly *unpaid* informal sources of labour. It is important to bear in mind the degree of unreality produced by this aggregation of tasks, but it does provide some clarity at a high level of generality.

Age makes a difference to the amount of work that is needed, and people do less of all kinds of work as they grow older. However, the very busiest age category is aged between 31 and 50 – a time when, for all sources of labour, households in this category have the highest percentage doing various tasks, although child care is the first cluster of tasks to decline from the early forties. A similar pattern is found if one focuses on the forms of labour: the higher proportion of households using their own labour is always one of the two youngest categories.

Although age is important, it should perhaps be considered in the context of the household structure. More detailed analysis focusing on couples with and without children and on single-parent families produced clear and unequivocal results. Couples with children were busy in every sphere of activity, being more likely both to do the activities and also to use their own household as a source of labour to do them. Single-parent households, by contrast, were much more likely to get work done informally using unpaid sources of labour. For single parents, sources of labour follow a distinctive pattern showing that this category is obliged to adopt a distinctive household work strategy. The connection here is not simply that of low income and sources of labour, although that indeed is likely to be a crucial connection, but, particularly, a distinctive household structure. For much of the work that has to be done, partners of different genders provide a convenient work unit. I was initially surprised when I heard someone say that she was going round to a friend to 'borrow her husband for a while'. I later discovered that the phrase was not considered improper, although it was always said with a smile, if not with a wink: it was just a way of tapping a crucial and necessary source of labour.

Single-parent households are obliged to be more dependent on others; couples are more self-contained. The indications are, therefore, that households build up to a peak of activity as they build up their family, establish a comfortable and convenient home and acquire consumer goods such as the motor car, which needs to be repaired and serviced. This, then, raises a paradox. At the very time in the domestic cycle when so many tasks need to be done, the need for money is equally demanding: it is one thing to get the brakes on the car fixed; it is another matter to get the money to buy the car and then tax and insure it. How, then, does the general economic activity of household members relate to all the activities that are being discussed in this chapter? This question is getting close to the heart of the complex issue of household work strategies.

First, what difference does it make if women are employed full-time, part-time or not at all and if their partners are in employment? The results are set out in Tables 8.12a and 8.12b for two spheres of activity. These findings are remarkably consistent: whether or not the female partner is full-time employed, part-time employed or a full-time housewife, the *same amount of work* of the types presented (by and large) seemingly has to be done. One might have expected that in households where both adults are in full-time employment there would be less time for baking a cake or growing vegetables, but that does not seem to be the case. Sheppey full-time housewives do not seem to be living in households where the *overall* divisions of labour are that different from households in which the woman is in full-time employment. However, it is important to remember that nothing has been said so far about *who* does the work in the household: that is discussed in Chapter 10. Here it is simply noted that the employment characteristics of the female partner do not seem to affect the overall pattern of how

Table 8.12 Economic activity by sources of labour for two selected clusters of tasks, male partner in employment

	Household member (%)	Informal: Unpaid (%)	Informal: Paid (%)	Formal provision (%)	Not done (%)	Other (%)
Cluster (a): Sources of labour for aggregated home maintenance tasks						
Female partner						
Employed full-time	48	5	2	13	33	0
Employed part-time	55	3	3	14	26	1
Full-time housewife	56	3	2	11	27	1
Cluster (b): Sources of labour for aggregated domestic provisions tasks						
Female partner						
Employed full-time	50	1	0	0	46	2
Employed part-time	53	3	0	0	41	2
Full-time housewife	55	3	0	0	38	3

much work is done in the household. (Childcare is not appropriately considered here, since evidently it is largely an obligatory activity in households with children!)

However, if the economic activity of the female partner apparently makes little difference, the total number of adults employed in the household certainly does. Employment in the formal economy as a factor determining what other sources of labour are used may be more a matter of numbers than of gender: in almost every task the likelihood that it will be done (if it is done) in the household increases with the number of adults in employment. This applies particularly to tasks connected with home renovation or extension. The proportion of households in which painting is done at home, for example, increases from 78 per cent of households with no workers to 100 per cent with three. Couples with unmarried employed offspring living at home and with school-age children old enough not to inhibit the female partner from taking employment *need* more tasks done and are busiest doing them. The position of the household in the domestic cycle is one of the chief determinants of the sources of labour that are used. What needs doing differs throughout the life cycle, and the source of labour varies substantially between youth and old age and between households based on couples and those with only a single adult. The latter, typically, do not have the income to use formal provision of services (although, of course, local authority and welfare provision are important); hence, single-parent households and old people are obliged to use informal sources of labour.

It might, at this point, be useful to digress to consider the question of how frequently tasks are done. Since the intention in this chapter is to present only a very general account of sources of labour, the questions of the *cumulation* of different tasks in the same household or the *repetition* of a few tasks very frequently have so far been ignored.

Before concluding this chapter, I return to the discussion of class and the sources of labour. Do middle-class households have a markedly different pattern of access to sources of labour than working-class households? Do they consume more services and rely more on the formal economy to supply them? Do middle-class female partners do more or less domestic production than their working-class counterparts? Do Class 2 households – the respectable petit bourgeoisie – exhibit more home-centred values than the classes above and below them? Do Class 3 households use more informal sources of labour than Class 1? For the purpose of this analysis, households were allocated to each of the three classes by the occupation of the male partner in couple households and by the occupation of the respondent in single-person households. The results were remarkably consistent: the divisions of labour were almost exactly similar for each social class. The similarities were so great that there seems little value in any extended illustration. Thus, the proportion of each class engaging in domestic production of one sort or another was 54 per cent for Class 1, 54 per cent for Class 2 and 51 per cent for Class 3. There was some variation in house and car maintenance, since Class 3 households were less likely to own these. And there was some class variation in the sources of labour to do these sets of tasks. This table reflects the greatest difference that can be shown between classes at this aggregated level of analysis. Certainly, Class 1 households are less likely to do these tasks within the home and to buy in formal services from outside. When class is combined with economic activity, differences appear greater within the middle class (Class 1) than within the working class (Class 3). For example, when Class 1 couples are both employed, there is a much greater likelihood that they will pay for (house maintenance) tasks to be done.

Conclusions

Some important conclusions about sources of labour and divisions of labour have emerged in this chapter, but I have emphasized that the analysis has been at a highly aggregated level. Households in a given category – class, economic activity or income range – have been scrambled together and all the tasks of a given type analysed together. This provides a kind of understanding but, as with all abstraction, does some violence to reality. I have presented enough to show that, in terms of patterns of work and sources of labour, household structure, particularly as that reflects the number of earners and the domestic cycle, appears to be more significant than social class. It is one of the main themes of this book that this has always been so. One recognizes that sociologists will be accused of rediscovering the wheel once again – or at least recognizing the force of history. In the same way that late medieval households needed someone of the opposite sex in order to get by and to help to get the work done, so the exigencies of the domestic cycle and the demands of capitalist consumerism make couple households with multiple earners the best unit for getting by in the late twentieth century, albeit for different reasons.

But if class appears less important than the number and levels of economic activity of household members and the stage of the household in the domestic cycle, it would be rash to jump too readily to the conclusion that, if the domestic cycle is the great leveller, social harmony is attained by the hidden hand of 'birth, copulation, and death'.

Chapter 9, 'The Divisions of Labour of Households' (excerpts from pp. 232–53)

In the last chapter I was not concerned with the patterns of labour used in getting work done by individual households. Thus, all middle-class households, for example, were grouped together and analysis focused on the combined total of all their sources of labour. However, it is quite possible that, within such a category, some households do substantial work for themselves, whereas others rely entirely on formal or other sources of labour. The emphasis in Chapter 8 was on *clusters* of tasks and the balance between different sources of labour in getting these clusters of tasks done as a whole. Here I emphasize the sources of labour, and how far distinctive types of household use distinctive sources. To explore these divisions the focus of analysis shifts from the *nature of the task* to *the source of the labour*. Which households are more likely consistently to prefer one source of labour to another? What patterns emerge when the cumulative effects of using distinctive sources of labour are considered?

The last chapter showed that a remarkable amount of work is done by members of individual households for themselves.[1] Much of the data were presented in a highly aggregated form and the analysis was inevitably coarse-grained. Now I intend to aim at a finer grain of analysis and to ask whether those households who, say, do their own home decorating also, perhaps, fix their own cars, make jam and also grow their own vegetables. Is there a cumulation of what is termed 'self-provisioning', or do some households specialize in decorating for themselves whereas others specialize in other spheres and use the formal market provision of services for those spheres in which they do not have competence?

Similar questions can be asked in relation to the other sources of labour: do those who use formal services also do more work for themselves or do they get other tasks done informally? What, indeed, are the alternatives? How are the three sources of labour interrelated? Are

1 Thus, for example, of the 97 per cent of households who had had painting done, 83 per cent of those did it for themselves, and, of the 53 per cent of households who had had a broken window fixed, 53 per cent of those did the work themselves.

the formal and informal sources equivalent alternatives for different categories of households? Do all households use a little formal labour or do some use a great deal and others hardly any at all?

Scales of Measurement

These questions require precise answers and we devised three separate scales to indicate how households used the same source of labour over a range of different tasks.

The self-provisioning scale (self-prov) measures the spread of activity that given households do using the labour of members of the households themselves: that is, not simply the *number* of tasks, but rather the *range* of tasks that are done using the labour of household members. Each household gets a score from 0 to 6 depending on the use of its labour over a carefully selected range of possible tasks.

The scale does not show whether a household is able to do its own plastering *and* painting *and* glazing, but whether it has the capacity to do *one* of these activities *as well as* vegetable growing *and* a car maintenance task, and so on. The six-point scale was based on distinct spheres of household or domestic tasks that could be bought in the market. People can buy vegetables, cakes and jerseys; they do not have to dig, bake and knit. Indeed, jerseys bought in shops, in the market or at a bring and buy sale may well be substantially cheaper than those made at home. The tasks for the six-point self-prov scale were then arranged so that households could score one point if they did just one task within each cluster. Tasks of a fairly routine nature were included in the self-prov scale only if they were performed with some frequency, but the larger tasks were included if they were performed at any time at all. The clusters of tasks for the self-provisioning scale are, therefore, as follows:

SPS 1:
Vegetable growing at any time
SPS 2:
Either painting *or* plastering *or* mending a broken window in the last year
SPS 3:
Either checking the oil level *or* tuning the engine *or* doing the work on the brakes of a car at any time
SPS 4:
Either putting in an RSJ *or* double glazing *or* central heating *or* building a bathroom *or* an extension *or* converting an attic at any time

SPS 5:
Either making jam *or* beer *or* wine regularly
SPS 6:
Making *or* knitting clothes at any time

The informal labour scale (inf-lab) was constructed in a similar manner to the self-prov scale, but with the substitution of two other tasks for vegetable growing and the home production of certain items that were, in practice, limited to self-provisioning. Households could score from 0 to 6 on the scale, depending on the range of tasks or clusters of tasks for which they used informal sources of labour, namely friends, neighbours or relatives. Such informal labour might be paid or unpaid and no distinction is made on the scale. Although information was gathered about payment, in practice the distinction was very hard to draw and it seemed to make better sense to put all sources of informal labour in the same category. The tasks making up the scale are as follows:

ILS 1:
Either getting painting *or* plastering *or* a broken window mended in the last year
ILS 2:
Either getting the car oil level checked *or* the car engine tuned *or* work done on the brakes at any time
ILS 3:
Either getting an RSJ put in *or* double glazing *or* central heating *or* building a bathroom *or* an extension *or* converting an attic at any time
ILS 4:
Getting clothes repaired *or* knitted *or* a dress made
ILS 5:
Getting the outside windows cleaned
ILS 6:
Getting a child's hair cut

The formal provision of services scale (form-prov), like the inf-lab, is a six-point scale and was constructed using exactly the same clusters of tasks as the inf-lab. Here, however, the source of labour was a firm or business for domestic maintenance and improvement (form-prov 1 and 3), a garage or firm for work on the car (form-prov 2), a professional dressmaker or knitter for clothes (form-prov 4), a public agency for window cleaning (form-prov 5) and a barber or hairdresser for cutting a child's hair (form-prov 6).

Thus, these three scales measure the range of tasks using each of one distinctive source of labour. I discuss each scale in turn and then, finally, consider the way in which each is related to the others. Using these scales, a relatively precise measure is given of the degree to which specific households use different sources of labour.

The self-provisioning scale (self-prov)

Why do some households do more work for themselves than others? Do they choose to do it as a form of self-expression, or are they almost compelled to do it by the lack of other resources, because they have no money to buy services formally and no other resources to repay informal labour reciprocally? From what has gone before, we may expect that those households based on couples including a number of young children require more tasks to be done and, because of a reduction of income per head owing to the number of dependants in the household, are obliged to do more tasks for themselves. These arguments might apply *a fortiori* to households headed by a manual worker, who is likely to have a lower individual income than a middle-class earner but where both partners are, perhaps, more likely to have skills to do self-provisioning work than are middle-class couples, less well-trained in manual skills. In this way, perhaps, differences in levels of living between the two classes are reduced. Furthermore, it is likely that such high self-provisioners would own their own homes, be inward-looking, privatized and perhaps also more likely to vote Conservative. There might be a secondary peak of self-provisioning at a later stage of the life cycle, in the years before retirement after children have left home, when there is time and energy to devote to domestic tasks as a way of demonstrating a particular style of life.

Certainly, it is quite clear that couple households score more highly on the self-prov scale, as Table 9.1, relating to the sample as a whole, indicates. If the self-prov scale is dichotomized into 'low' (scores 2–4) and 'high' (scores 5–6), then over half the couples score in the 'high' category. This is a better basis for the assertion that substantial domestic work by households takes place, since it avoids the problems posed by certain tasks being appropriate only at certain stages of the life cycle. Particular individual circumstances are thus reduced by using the scale.

For ease of analysis, the dichotomized self-prov scale is used to illustrate some important differences. Selecting only those households where the male is in full-time employment, high self-prov scores are more likely the greater the involvement of his partner in formal employment. Thus, where both partners are in full-time employment, 65 per cent of

Table 9.1 Household type, by self-provisioning scale (percentages*)

Self-prov. scale	Couple households	Male-headed non-couple households	Female-headed non-couple households	All
1	–	–	–	–
2	3	13	31	10
3	13	37	31	19
4	28	30	28	28
5	40	17	9	32
6	16	3	1	11
Total (N)	526	40	164	730

*Throughout this chapter, percentages in tables do not always sum up to 100 because of rounding

households score 'high' on the self-prov scale, whereas when the female partner is retired the 'high' proportion falls to 50 per cent. Taking the 65 households with more than two earners, 69 per cent scored 'high' on the self-prov scale. Finally, selecting those households where both partners were in full-time employment but at least one of them was on shift work, the proportion scoring 'high' on the self-prov scale rose to as much as 74 per cent. Yet when male shift workers had as a partner a non-employed full-time housewife, the proportion scoring 'high' dropped to 43 per cent.

These findings are unequivocal: employment and self-provisioning go together, rather than one being a substitute for another. Furthermore, in line with the analysis in the previous chapter, class did not make a substantial difference: indeed, counter to the initial hypothesis, the proportion scoring 'high' on the self-prov scale ranged from 64 per cent in Class 1 through 59 per cent in Class 2 to 50 per cent for Class 3. Evidently, this result is partly the consequence of higher car and home ownership in the higher classes, but it still does not follow that households should, apparently, choose to do so many tasks with their own labour.

Some interesting intra-class variations appear when the combined household class classification is used. Thus, when Class 1 males are married to Class 3 females, the proportion scoring 'high' on self-prov scale rises to 70 per cent as against 64 per cent for Class 1 as a whole. Similarly, when Class 3 males are married to higher-status females, their scores are substantially above the rate for the class as a whole. This suggests, perhaps, that status inconsistency between partners is a source of tension or of complex feelings of guilt, which generates a distinct dynamic element into the household work strategy. Lower-status men and women may compensate to their partners by doing more conventionally gender-linked tasks. So lower-status men may do more decorating or car maintenance and lower-status women, more of the female-type tasks. Thus the internal dynamics of the couple modify what would otherwise seem to be a direct linear relationship between higher class and higher rating on the self-prov scale.

Child care work does not appear on the self-prov scale, yet couples with children were overall more likely to score higher than couples with no children (60 per cent compared with 47 per cent). However, the very highest score (79 per cent) is for couples having their youngest child aged between 5 and 15 with the wife or partner over 35 years of age; where there are also older children or other adults in the same household the proportion of 'high' scorers on the self-prov scale is 67 per cent. These latter may, therefore, be contributing not only extra money but also extra working capacity to the household. Analysis showed that level of income *on its own* was less important as a factor affecting levels of self-provisioning, which it must be remembered relate to a range of tasks done by different household members in and around the home. For this reason it is perhaps less surprising that the more adults in the household, the higher the score.

Households, then, do more activities with their own labour if they have a larger gender-divided pool of hands and access to land and capital. Growing their own vegetables requires access to land, whether a garden or an allotment, and owning a house or car requires capital. However, the land and capital by themselves do not necessarily encourage the use of the household's own labour. Ownership of property does not mechanistically determine behaviour: there is not a direct linear correlation between household work practices and household income.

Higher income is a necessary but not a sufficient condition for higher rating on the self-prov scale. A process of polarization has developed on the Island: this produces at one end busy households with many workers, some of whom are in employment, in which a wide range of domestic tasks get done by household members; at the other end are the households with only one or two earners, without a car and probably not owning their own homes or, if they do, having insufficient energy or strength and also insufficient resources to be able to maintain them adequately.

The informal labour scale (inf-lab)

We now move to a division of labour between the producer and the consumer of a service, where the source of labour is outside the household that consumes the service. Informal sources of labour, that is, friends, neighbours and relatives, can be paid or unpaid, and one might initially assume that informal labour is more a resource for the poor than for the rich, for the established than for the newly arrived and for older rather than younger people. One might expect Class 2 and particularly Class 3 to use more such informal sources than Class 1. While informal sources of labour count for quantitatively very little in the overall division of labour, such work can still be highly important for certain specified households. These expectations or hypotheses are now explored.

Informal sources of labour were not so sharply divided by income as we initially expected. The inf-lab scale was dichotomized into 'low' (0 or 1) and 'high' (2 or more). The proportions scoring 'high' on the scale in income categories 'low', 'medium' and 'high' were 17, 16 and 14 per cent respectively. Analysis by social class showed a similar pattern, with the comparable proportions being 17, 16 and 11 per cent, falling from Class 3 to Class 1. Evidently, these are not particularly significant distinctions. Turning then to the number of earners in the household, which were important in the case of the self-prov scale, in the case of the inf-lab scale no significant variation was found, the proportion of households with two or more earners scoring 'high' being much the same as in households with no earners.

Interesting variations did, however, appear when we considered household structure: while, for the sample as a whole, 16 per cent scored 'high' on the inf-lab scale, in the case of single-parent households the proportion rose to 37 per cent. Couples living on their own had only 10 per cent scoring 'high' (see Table 9.2).

A similar pattern is shown for tenure, with those in privately rented accommodation having a markedly greater likelihood of using informal labour. Proportions scoring 2 or more on the inf-lab scale were 15 per cent for owner occupiers, 16 per cent for those renting from the local authority but 26 per cent of the 47 households in the sample renting from a private landlord. Inevitably, in the case of single-parent families, household type and tenure go together. Households living in certain

Table 9.2 Informal labour scale rating by household type (percentages)

Inf-lab scale	Single person	Single person with child	Couple only	Couple with children	All others	All households
Low score						
0	43	22	56	46	60	48
1	40	41	34	37	30	36
High score						
2 or more	17	37	10	18	10	16
Total (N)	129	49	195	317	40	730

areas of the Island were also more likely to use informal labour, with the older established areas of Sheerness and Queenborough scoring higher on the scale than the more newly developed areas of Halfway and Warden Bay.

Table 9.3 shows that households in which women are in full-time employment use less informal labour those in which the woman is employed part-time or is a full-time housewife, suggesting that women may have a more significant role to play than men in reciprocating informal labour. This is an important aspect of informal work that is considered below. Where informal labour is unpaid it has to be repaid with reciprocal services. Those in employment may not have the time to provide such reciprocity and those too old or infirm cannot reciprocate. Hence, it may be that the households who use paid informal labour are those that cannot do the task themselves but, equally, cannot afford the formal market prices.

Perhaps some forms of informal labour, as is the case with formal labour, depend on the capacity to repay – but in a different currency. For the sample as a whole, younger respondents use more informal labour than older ones (Table 9.4), giving some support to the suggestion that they can repay more readily: 22 per cent of those households with respondents aged 30 or under score 'high' (2 or more) on the inf-lab scale as against 15 per cent of those households where the respondent is 65 and over.

Table 9.3 Inf-lab scale rating by the economic activity of selected households with male partner in full-time employment (percentages)

	Occupational status of female partner			
Inf-lab scale	F/T empl.	P/T empl.	F/T H'wife	All
0	58	49	46	192
1	31	32	41	140
2+	11	19	13	53
Total (N)	102	99	184	385

Table 9.4 Inf-lab scale rating by the age of respondent (percentages)

	Age of respondent				
Inf-lab Scale	30 or under	31–50	51–64	65 and over	All
0	38	51	51	46	48
1	39	35	33	39	36
2+	22	14	16	15	16
Total (N)	117	267	144	202	730

However, if we consider the age of respondents in single-person households only, it is clear that older people living on their own are obliged to rely on informal sources of labour, both because of their need for services and because of their lack of material resources.

For those single persons aged 65 and over, 18 per cent scored 2 or more on the inf-lab scale. If we compare the two tasks of painting and plastering, it is striking that among couples only seven out of nine households who pay informally for painting to be done are 65 and over and none are under 40, whereas for plastering, of the twenty-one households who paid for this task informally, thirteen are under 40 and none are 65 and over. This differentiation of task by age is an important distinction: younger people get plastering done for them informally; older people get painting done.

So far we have considered the economic variables of class, income and number of earners and some of the variables associated with household structure. The final factor to which I turn is the stage in the domestic cycle for couple households. The results are set out in Table 9.5.

The pattern is clear: women with young children at the early stages of the domestic cycle need more informal help and are in a position to repay it. By and large couples living alone, especially when they are older, use fewer informal sources of labour. However, households with a more complex structure, including more adults, use more informal labour: these households probably have dependent relatives and,

Table 9.5 Household structure and inf-lab scale ratings

	Inf-lab scale (%)			
Household characteristics	0	1	2+	Total (N)
Couple household with children under 16				
Youngest child under 5	32	49	19	94
Youngest child 5–15	46	38	16	98
Partners living alone with no children under 16				
Female partner aged 35 or younger	67	21	12	42
Female partner aged 36 and over	53	38	8	150
More complex households				
Couples with other people all over 16	54	25	20	83
Couples with other people over 16 and youngest child 5–15	70	23	7	43
				510
Other household types				16
All couple-based households				526
All households	51	35	14	

perhaps, are more dependent on informal and communal supports or, with more household members, are better placed to provide reciprocal services.

To conclude, I have shown that there are certain well-defined categories that are most likely to use informal sources of labour. These are:

1 single-parent families with no other adult in the household;
2 married couples with children under 15, particularly those with women under 30;
3 single persons 65 and over living on their own.

These findings run counter to much received opinion, and I discuss them again after the analysis of the informal labour that is done for other households. Finally, I should emphasize that, on the whole, households scored very modestly on this scale. While 55 per cent of households scored 5 or 6 on the self-prov scale, no household scored more than 4 on the inf-lab scale and only 14 per cent of households scored 2 or more. This is an emphatic refutation of the notion that the use of informal labour is very widespread.

The formal provision of services scale (form-prov)

This scale, on the face of it, would seem to be the simplest to analyse. Households will use formal sources of labour when they cannot do the work for themselves, owing to age or ill-health, or when they have enough money to be able to pay for services, thus freeing them for other activities which they prefer to do. The hypothesis is, therefore, that older, more established households with multiple earners would use this source of labour most. These expectations were borne out by the data. The higher the household income and the greater the number of earners in the household, the higher the score on the form-prov scale. Of households in the 'low'-income band, 16 per cent scored 2 or more points on the scale, whereas for those in the 'high'-income band, 46 per cent scored 2 or more. Those in the 'middle'-income category had a similarly intermediate position on the scale – 30 per cent scored 2 or more. The relationship between income and form-prov scale score was direct and unequivocal.

There was a similar direct relationship with number of earners: 14 per cent of households with no earners scored 2 or more against 45 per cent in those households with two or more earners. The correlation was, again, direct and positive, as it was also with the number of adults in the household. With only one adult, 9 per cent of such households scored 2 or more on the form-prov scale. This rose to 31 per cent for households with two adults, 41 per cent for households with three and

36 per cent with four or more. As one might expect, owner-occupiers relied on the formal provision of services more than did tenants, and council tenants more than private tenants. Most of this form of labour is in the new housing areas of Halfway and Warden Bay: precisely the opposite pattern found for the inf-lab scale. Consistent with the foregoing, there is a clear linear relationship between social class and form-prov scale: the higher the social class, the greater the use of formal sources of labour.

From this account there is little in the analysis that refutes expectations. Households in which both partners are in employment (whether or not the woman is full-time or part-time) will score higher than those in which the partners are retired or unemployed. Again, as one would expect, couples between the age of 31 and 50 were the most likely to use formal sources of labour, as Table 9.6 clearly shows. While 28 per cent of the sample as a whole scored 2 or more on the form-prov scale, households with respondents aged 31–50 had 43 per cent scoring at this level.

However, as with the inf-lab scale, the more detailed analysis of the domestic cycle of couple households is revealing (as Table 9.7). Households with children aged over 5 and with one or more other people aged over 16 (apart from the children's parents) in the household score the highest, and older couple without children score the lowest.

The conclusions relating to households' use of formal sources of labour are clear. Households which consume the most labour from formal sources are likely to have the female partner in employment, for her to be over 35 and for there to be other adults in the household adding to the household income. The youngest child is still likely to be under 15, which helps to increase the household's demand for services, but with multiple earners and higher household incomes these demands can be met. The higher the social class, the greater the level of economic activity, and where partners are aged between 35 and 50, the greater the propensity to employ formal labour. The pattern is neat and coherent:

Table 9.6 Formal provision of services scale rating by the age of respondent (percentages)

	Age of respondent				
Form prov scale	30 or younger	31–50	51–64	65 or over	All
0	30	20	31	53	33
1	45	36	44	36	39
2	21	30	23	11	22
3+	2	13	1	–	6
Total (N)	117	267	114	202	730

Table 9.7 Household structure and form-prov scale ratings

Household characteristics	Form-prov scale (%) 0	1	2+	Total (N)
Couple households with children under 16				
Youngest child under 5	21	36	42	94
Youngest child 5–15	14	43	43	98
Partners living alone with no children under 16				
Female partner aged 35 or younger	33	47	19	42
Female partner aged 36 or over	36	41	23	150
More complex households				
Couples with other people all over 16	22	51	29	83
Couples with other people over 16 and youngest child 5–15	21	21	58	43
				510
Other household types				16
All couple-based households				526
All households	25	40	34	

it shows by contrast the more complex pattern of the other two sources of labour scales.

Interrelationship of the Scales

It may now be helpful to draw together some of the findings related to these three scales and to explore their interconnections. First, I have shown that there is a direct linear relationship between both the self-prov and form-prov scales and household income and an inverse linear relationship between income and the inf-lab scale. Higher-income households either use their own labour or buy it in the formal sector: more typically they do both. Lower-income households do less informal work for themselves, with certain specific categories of low-income households depending disproportionately on informal labour from outside the household. All three scales are directly related to the number of earners in the household, but again the inf-lab scale runs in the reverse direction to the other two. The more adults in a household, particularly if they are earners, the more self-sufficient it is and the less it has to rely on community resources. The same pattern is reflected in housing tenure: owner-occupiers use more services than tenants but also, in general, have higher incomes. Local authority tenants appear to be more dependent on locality and kin support. We have seen that the scales vary according to area of the Island, but this is more because locality is an intervening variable than because it has a causal influence in its own right.

I have consistently stressed the importance of household structure: couples with children where the woman is over 35 are the most vigorous in consuming services, using their own labour and drawing on the formal provision of services. Where the woman is employed, particularly on a full-time basis, and where there are other earners in the household, the scores on the self-prov and form-prov scales will be greatest and the scores on the inf-lab scale the lowest. These relationships with household structure are stronger than with social class, although, again, the relationship of high self-prov and form-prov scale ratings with higher class and high inf-lab scale rating with lower class was in general found to be the case, but there were important differences *within* classes depending on the social class position of the woman. Table 9.8 illustrates those households scoring 'high' on each of the three scales by household class. In the self-prov scale there is a distinction among households with males in Class 3 and their wives in different categories, with 20 percentage points between those in 3.1 and 3.2 and those in 3.3 and 3.4. In the case of informal sources of labour, higher-status wives in households with males in Class 1 receive more services, whereas where the male is in Class 2 or 3 the position is reversed – except in the case of housewives: all households with full-time housewives receive more informal labour, and a high proportion of these are likely to be elderly. When the woman is in employment less labour is used from informal sources: the proportion of households using no sources of informal labour declines from 58 per cent, when both partners are employed full-time, to 46 per cent where the woman was a full-time housewife. The impact of female employment on the three scales is shown in Table 9.9.

Perhaps surprisingly, in Class 3 households having both partners in employment, more formal services are bought than in Class 1 households where the woman is employed part-time. It is also significant that the Class 1 households where both partners are in employment do more self-provisioning work than any other category, followed by Class 3 households with both partners employed. (I should mention that the highly paid stevedores and steel workers are classified as Class 3. Such men have both high income and more time, owing to shift work and the uneven flow of cargo through the docks, so that they are able to buy services and do more work for themselves.)

It is an important and significant conclusion of this study that household self-provisioning is not a substitute for formal services, as has sometimes been asserted. For example, Richard Rose has argued:

Table 9.8 Household class by proportion of households scoring 'high' on the three scales (percentages)

	Household class												
Male partner	1				2				3				
Score / Female Partner	1	2	3	4	1	2	3	4	1	2	3	4	All
'High' (5–6) on Self-prov scale	67	65	70	50	60	59	64	54	62	65	43	42	55
'High' (2+) on Inf-lab scale	–	19	8	4	–	14	17	7	–	15	17	9	14
'High' (2+) on Form-prov scale	50	56	47	57	20	38	41	32	13	33	24	25	35
Total number in each household class	6	43	23	14	5	100	47	28	8	75	120	43	512

*14 households for which there were inadequate data have been omitted from this table.

Table 9.9 Economic activity of both partners, by proportion of households scoring 'high' on the three scales* (percentages)

Household class	1			2			3			
Female partner's economic activity	F/T empl.	P/T empl.	F/T h'wife	F/T empl.	P/T empl.	F/T h'wife	F/T empl.	P/T empl.	F/T h'wife	All
'High' (5–6) on Self-prov scale	71	74	58	59	64	64	66	60	49	61
'High' (2+) on Inf-lab scale	15	16	16	12	9	16	10	27	13	15
'High' (2+) on Form-prov scale	57	47	63	25	51	46	46	32	21	39
Total (N)	21	19	19	32	33	34	41	47	63	309

*Households selected only where male partner is in full time employment. In this table the class categories are based solely on the male partner's employment.

> When demand for labour in the Official Economy slackens, individuals will spend less time in work, and marginal workers will be counted out of the labour force. But this gives more time and more incentive for individuals to produce goods and services in the Domestic Economy.... When the Official Economy is slack, individuals can use their domestic resources to maintain consumption.[2]

According to data gathered from the Sheppey survey, Professor Rose is mistaken and has been misled by unreliable sources.

Self-provisioning and the formal provisioning of services go together, with the same households scoring high on each. The informal labour scale is related strongly inversely to the formal provision of services and less strongly inversely to self-provisioning.

Correlation between	*Spearman's coefficient*
Self-prov and form-prov scales	+0.4061
Inf-lab and self-prov scales	–0.1072
Inf-lab and form-prov scales	–0.767

So much, then, for the way different sources of labour are interrelated in getting the work of the household done. However, I must finally consider the work that members of the household do for other households. The division of household labour is discussed in the next chapter, since this issue is an accepted focus of discussion in the literature. I have already considered the household's participation in the labour market, so that the only work that remains for me to discuss here is the unrecorded work that members of households do for others, whether or not they are paid.

Unrecorded Labour Performed by Household Members for Members of Other Households

In response to the question, 'Do you currently do any work on your own account to get extra money?', only 4 per cent of the sample replied in the affirmative; a further 1 per cent of respondents acknowledged that they did other work for an employer or firm for which they got

2 See Richard Rose, *Getting By in Three Economies: The Resources of the Official Unofficial and Domestic Economics,* Centre for the Study of Public Policy, University of Strathclyde, 1983, pp. 33–4. I regret that some of my earlier more polemical writing may have misled some commentators, but Professor Rose does not make much of that. Rather, he cites a variety of other sources, some of which have been discussed above in Chapter 4. All the evidence of the present study suggests that Professor Rose had been substantially confused.

paid (presumably in cash or some other informal way). This is what might be termed 'shadow wage labour': that is to say, payments may or may not be declared to the Inland Revenue. Given that the respondents were alternately male and female, the numbers of each sex who acknowledged that they got some extra money informally were very small. Of the 11 who were men, 10 were also in full-time employment and the other one was unemployed.[3] Of these 10 male full-time workers, 5 were in households in the 'high'-income category. By contrast, of the 16 women, half were full-time housewives and 10 were in households in the low-income category. The relationship between economic circumstances and paid informal work appears to be differentiated by gender, but even with a sample of 730, the numbers were too small for findings to appear very significant.

The main source of information on the labour of household members for other households was in response to a question that was posed as follows: 'We have talked about a number of tasks that are done in the household. Now I'd like to know if there are any jobs that you do *outside* your home, for other people?' One in four of respondents answered in the affirmative, and they were asked to name these tasks and were prompted to say if there were any others. These replies were separately coded from the verbatim answers into appropriate categories. It is these data that form the basis of the analysis that follows.

Which households were those most likely to provide informal labour for others? Were they the older established Islanders well committed to local social networks? Were they younger or older, with children or without? Do working-class households provide more informal labour than middle-class households? Does income make a difference? Are those in formal employment who are also busily engaged in self-provisioning too occupied to do more? What divisions are there between men and women in doing informal labour for others?

These were the questions that the analysis set out to answer: many of them could be answered briefly and precisely. If households are divided according to whether they arrived on the Island before 1970 or in 1970 and thereafter and whether the respondent was aged 40 and under or 41 and over, the proportions are exactly the same in both cases. Similarly, if weekly household income is cross-tabulated by the number of earners in the household, there is very little difference between households in the categories so devised, although there are interesting indications of

3 No doubt sections of the popular press would want to make much of this one 'honest scrounger' whom we found in our sample. Other labour-for-others by unemployed men will be discussed below.

Table 9.10 Number of respondent's relatives on Island by whether informal work is done (percentage)

Respondent's relatives on Island	Informal work is: Not done	Done	All
2 or less	60	48	57
3 or more	40	52	43
Total (N) = 100%	550	180	730

*The question on which this table is based is as follows: 'We have talked about a number of tasks that are done in the household. Now I'd like to know if there are any jobs that you do *outside* your home, for other people. [if yes] What are they? Are there any others? [list below]:'

variations between men and women. The numbers in the cells are rather small but there are very strong indications that women in the households with lowest incomes provide more informal labour and men in the more affluent households do more. This differentiation between men and women by income of household is one of the most interesting conclusions to come out of the analysis of this question. Analysis by class and by area of the Island showed no significant variations. Even the occupational status of the respondent made very little difference to the amount of labour provided by the household overall. Perhaps the most striking finding is the importance of having a number of relatives on the Island, as Table 9.10 shows.

The divisions between informal labour done for relatives and for non-relatives were also explored. Of a total of 269 separate tasks mentioned by respondents, 39 per cent were done for relatives and 61 per cent for non-relatives. Table 9.11 shows that for the sample as a whole approximately equal proportions of men and women do informal labour but they engage in different tasks. Men overwhelmingly do home improvement and women do routine domestic work, mainly shopping, for others. Women also do more voluntary work.

Both the main survey and the in-depth interviews, which were held with selected respondents a year later, suggested that people typically claimed that they did more informal work for others than they received themselves, indicating, perhaps, the general concern of people not to appear dependent on others. The most surprising conclusion, despite all our considerable efforts to document the so-called 'informal' or 'black' economy of popular misconception, was how little labour for other households was given in comparison with the efforts of self-provisioning within the household. By far the most common tasks done for other households with informal labour were simply extensions of work done

Table 9.11 Tasks performed informally for other households*

	For relatives (N)		For non-relatives (N)		Totals (N)	
Tasks	M	F	M	F	M	F
1. Shopping	5	6	4	25	9	31
2. Babysitting	3	12	–	8	3	20
3. Housework	2	10	–	2	2	12
4. Washing clothes	–	4	–	2	–	6
5. Visit, 'stay with', keep company	–	–	2	4	2	4
6. Hairdressing	1	4	–	1	1	5
7. Pet care	–	–	1	4	1	4
8. Gardening	7	4	13	2	20	6
9. Dressmaking	–	3	–	3	–	6
10. Decorating	9	1	7	2	16	2
11. Provision of transport	1	1	3	4	4	5
12. Repairs, carpentry, etc.	14	–	22	2	36	2
13. Help with local activities	1	1	6	7	7	8
14. Help with voluntary work	1	–	3	12	4	12
15. Other help	10	5	9	16	19	21
Totals	54	51	70	97	124	145

Summary

	Men		Women		Totals	
Type of work	N	%	N	%	N	%
Routine domestic work (1,3,4)	11	18	49	82	60	22
Social support (2,5,7)	6	18	28	82	34	13
Personal services (6,9)	1	8	11	92	12	4
Home improvement (8,10,12)	72	87	11	13	83	31
Formal community work (13,14)	11	35	20	65	31	12
Transport (11)	4	44	5	56	9	3
Other help (15)	19	48	21	53	40	15
Totals	124	46	145	54	269	100

*See notes from table 9.10

within the household – home improvement and maintenance and routine domestic assistance. There was little indication from the survey data that unemployed men did more or less informal labour than the average. This is a very important point. We analysed in some detail the use unemployed men made of informal *sources* of labour and discovered that unemployed people simply did not use such labour. This was partly because they could not afford to run a car and hence had no need of someone to fix it, or were not living in dwellings that they owned. The one task where unemployed men did use informal labour

Table 9.12 Household's self-prov rating by respondent's informal work for others*

Self-prov scale score	Informal work by respondents for other households			All (N)
	Not done (%)	Done (%)		
		M	F	
Low (2–4)	78	7	14	415
High (5–6)	71	17	12	315
Total	75	25		730

*Informal work is defined in the note to table 9.10

was in plastering, but even with this task those men in employment were more likely than unemployed men to use informal sources of labour.

In general, men are likely to do more informal work if they are in full-time employment, whereas women are more likely to do more if they are full-time housewives. This is because the informal labour that men do involves tools and materials and the informal labour that women do requires time (shopping for elderly neighbours and the like).

Finally, informal labour for other households is analysed in relation to the sources of labour scales that we discussed above. Those using formal sources of labour to do various tasks were also more likely to provide informal labour for others. Thus, only 19 per cent of those using no formal provision of services do informal labour for others against 32 per cent of those scoring 2 on the form-prov scale. The inf-lab scale shows no variation at all between different points on the scale. Relating work done inside the household with work done outside for others, there was a variation by gender, as Table 9.12 shows. More informal work is done for others in households that do more work for themselves.

Furthermore, it is likely that informal work for other households is given by men with skills who also do much self-provisioning work for themselves. As we have previously noted, the busy people do more: households scoring high on the self-prov scale do more for others, and there is a clear division by gender between high-scoring households and low-scoring households on this scale. This conclusion was borne out by more detailed analysis of a small category of manual workers individually earning high incomes[4] and most owning their own homes. These 'affluent' manual workers were also doing high levels of informal labour for others. The polarization of households in terms of all forms of work was strikingly confirmed.

4 More than £125 a week net in 1981.

Those who do informal work for others are, therefore, more likely to be choosing to do so. Doing informal work is not so much a coping strategy of the poor as a reflection of a particular kind of life style based on the skills and reciprocities of the work of everyday life. On the other hand, those who, as it were, consume informal labour are more likely to be the less well-off elderly people, single-parent families and households with children under 5.

An Excursus on Do-It-Yourself

In all the scales we have considered so far, the emphasis was entirely on *range* and not on *depth* of sources of labour for clusters of tasks. In order to compensate for this bias we devised a new DIY scale, where we put together all the ten domestic repair and maintenance tasks into one scale and households scored if they had done one or more of these tasks by using the labour of a member of the household:

1. Painting
2. Plastering
3. Mending a broken window
4. Putting in a reinforced steel joist
5. Putting in double glazing
6. Putting in a new bathroom
7. Building a garage
8. Building an extension to the home
9. Converting an attic
10. Putting in central heating.

We limited analysis to couple households. Table 9.13 shows the DIY scale by age of respondent. The dominance of those in middle life is clear: again, it is households in this age range with children that dominate. Among those who did not score, 69 per cent were couples without children as against 31 per cent with children. By point 4 on the scale these positions were reversed – 29 per cent of childless couples reached this score against 66 per cent of couples with children.

More DIY is done in working-class households with multiple earners. The relationship between the employment status of the couple and the DIY scale is set out in Table 9.14. The remarkable conclusion illustrated by this table is that the employment status of the female partner makes little difference to involvement in DIY activities: if anything, those couples where both partners are employed do *more* of such activity than other households! The DIY scale underlines in a most emphatic

Table 9.13 Age of respondents in couple households, by DIY scale

	Age of respondents				Total	
DIY scale	30 or under	31–50	51–64	65+	N	%
0	17	31	9	43	42	8
1	19	42	20	18	187	35
2	21	43	23	13	150	28
3	13	63	18	5	84	16
4	–	75	25	–	38	7
5	20	50	20	10	8	2
6	–	–	–	–	10	2
7	–	–	–	–	6	1
8	–	–	–	–	2	–
					527*	100

*The total is aberrant since one household could not be classified in all the other couple tables for lack of information but the age of the respondent is known.

Table 9.14 Economic activity of females in selected couple households where the male partner is in full-time employment, by DIY scale (percentages)

	Female partner is:		
DIY scale	F/T empl.	P/T empl.	F/T h'wife
0	9	6	2
1	33	30	23
2	30	28	14
3	17	17	11
4	6	9	5
5+	3	4	4
Total (N)	102	99	167

fashion the conclusions derived from analysis of the self-prov scale. Economic activity and high levels of the use of household labour for self-provisioning go together. Those most committed to the labour market are also the most committed to using their own labour in their own time for their own purposes. I return to discuss some of the wider social and political implications of this finding in the final chapter.

2 Informal, but *not* 'an economy'

Jonathan Gershuny

Errors, and first encounters

We sometimes learn important lessons by, first, getting things wrong. Ray Pahl was initially enthused by Sheppey as representing what he called 'a post-industrial laboratory', in which the household would provide a viable alternative locus of production to the capitalist market economy. His well-designed research programme very soon revealed exactly how wrong this was, and this discovery led not just to his own important contributions to the sociological understanding of work in households, but also to much wider and even more important developments in general British sociological activity. I have always felt that Ray rather unfairly blamed me for his initial error, misrepresenting his own over-enthusiastic adoption of 'the informal economy' as 'Gershuny's model'. In fact he himself had – rather like my old teacher Richard Rose – taken a rather exaggerated and over-determined version of my still somewhat underdeveloped understanding of the operation of modern economies. He subsequently distanced himself, cordially, respectfully, but firmly, from a theoretical position that had always actually been much more his own than mine.

I first met Ray sometime in 1977, introduced by Krishan Kumar (subsequently a lecturer in Ray's department at Kent, but at this time working as a radio talks producer in the BBC). Krishan somehow had a copy of the typescript of my first book *After Industrial Society?* (perhaps writing a publisher's review for Macmillan) which he passed to Ray. Ray invited me to give a seminar at Kent, starting a friendship, and an academic conversation, that continued until his death – indeed I'm continuing it here.

In the mid-1970s I too had got something seriously wrong. I thought Daniel Bell was correct when he told us (in his 1973 book *The Coming of Post-Industrial Society*) that the central feature of future developed economies would be individuals' and households' ever-increasing consumption of the product of the 'service sector' of developed economies. The empirical evidence Bell provided was, however, exclusively about growth, not of consumption, but of *employment* in service industries and occupations. My contribution was to be, I thought, providing the clinching evidence by looking at household expenditure (which is, as I amplify in what follows, not actually consumption at all), initially in the UK Family Expenditures Surveys from 1954 to 1974. But once I adjusted household incomes in this data series to constant prices, I discovered to my surprise, and initially intense disappointment, that rather than proportionally increasing this expenditure, British households, from the 1950s to the 1970s, had actually *reduced* their expenditure on final services. While the Engel's Law-type cross-sectional relationship remained, richer households consuming larger proportions of their incomes in the form of services than poorer households, nevertheless, regularly over successive decades, at each level of real income, proportional expenditure on services declined: the service-consumption-by-income curve shifted downwards.

I realised (after briefly thinking that I should move on quickly to some other field of enquiry entirely) that my negative result was in fact a significant discovery. I had uncovered a process of substitution in which households at each level of real income moved proportionately from buying services, to buying goods that related to similar sorts of final consumption: cars instead of bus or train trips, washing machines instead of laundry services, televisions instead of cinema visits, and so on. Before the mid-1950s televisions and other 'white goods' were found only in middle-class households; they were widely diffused across the whole social spectrum by the mid-1980s. Borrowing a term from transport economics, I called these shifts 'changes in modes of provision'.

This substitution was to be interpreted as implying a '*self*-service economy', the subtitle of my 1978 book: 'economy' in this context, of course not denoting any sort of independent sphere of economic action (though the Greek origin of the term meant literally 'household' in the grand sense of 'landed estate'). It was always clear to me that, in general, only those with secure paid employment would have the money to buy the domestic capital equipment and materials. This was simply a mechanism for acquiring some final services without the involvement of some specific sorts of paid final service labour: a contrast, in short, to the pre-war 'servant economy', and to Bell's original interpretation of the 'service economy'. It implied, among other things, that various sectors of employment and output that had previously been accounted for in conventional GNP – large parts of transport, entertainment, household services – had disappeared from the money economy.

As I pondered the implications of this change, I realised that various other ongoing processes, often related to high personal tax rates as well as to the growing availability of domestic capital equipment, were also contributing to this flow of activity out of the conventionally measured money economy: both the wider reciprocal exchange of services between households without payment, and also what Stuart Henry (1978) called the 'hidden economy'. In 1977, and the years immediately following, this last, constituted by occupational theft and the exchange of goods and services for undeclared money payments, provided something of a cottage industry for British sociologists. Ray's Sheppey 'pirates' had a lot in common with the fiddling barkeepers, thieving bakery roundsmen and so on, described in the writings of Henry (1978), Jason Ditton (1977a, 1977b), Gerald Mars (Henry and Mars 1978), James Cornford (1978) and others.

I brought these various ideas together in a 1979 article, in the journal *Futures*, on the 'informal economy' in modern developed societies.[1] This featured a triangle diagram, consisting of three nodes, referred to variously as 'economies' or 'sectors' – respectively the underground or hidden economy, the household and communal sector, and the conventional 'formal' money economy – together with processes that might lead, in any historical era, to each of the six possible 'transformations' in the sectoral location of work, from formal to household, from household to formal, from hidden to household and so on: 'at any point in time, the particular circumstances – of technology, labour supply, and public regulation and organisation – which pertain to the production of any commodity, may lead to one of a wide range of different sorts of transformations' (Gershuny 1979: 10–11). This triangle diagram (reproduced on page 118 of *Divisions of Labour*) has been widely reused, first in an article by Ray and me in the *New Universities Quarterly* in 1980 (Gershuny and Pahl 1981), subsequently by the French economic historian Henri Mendras, and by many others with appropriate attribution.[2]

The talk I gave in that 1977 seminar in Canterbury was an early version of this 1979 article. It launched our joint attempt to puzzle out the implications of work outside the measured money nexus. Ray and I were to have a lot of fun over the following decade, as the concept of informal economic activity in modern economies took root and flowered in various international conferences, not least in relation to the hidden economies of Eastern and Southern Europe. We learned, for example, that those US economists (e.g. Guttman 1977) who attempted to estimate the size of the American hidden economy on the basis of the changing ratio of US cash in circulation to US GNP, were in fact probably estimating the size of the Polish, Czechoslovakian, Hungarian and other non-US countries whose hidden economic activity was conducted in dollars. And 'il surpasso' (the point in 1987 that Italian GNP per capita overtook that of the UK) was apparently largely occasioned by the inclusion of a large chunk of the Italian hidden economy into the ISTAT GNP estimates.

1 The origin of the 'informal economy' term, originally applied to developing economies in Africa, a concept to which I had been introduced by my colleagues in the Institute of Development studies at Sussex, is correctly identified by Pahl in *Divisions of Labour* as Hart (1973).

2 A very similar triangle is also used by Portes (2010: 153), largely unchanged from my 1979 version ('hidden' is now termed 'criminal' and the transformations 1 to 6 are redesignated A to F) but now attributed to Castells and Portes 1989 (this unabashedly justified, in a recent email to me from Portes, as 'parallel discovery'). Castells was of course a long-term collaborator of Pahl's, they together founded the *International Journal of Urban and Regional Studies*; I assume Castells first encountered the diagram in the *New Universities Quarterly* article.

But this is to get ahead of our story. In the late 1970s we were simply aware of a new field, demanding fresh empirical approaches. Strongly persuaded by Michael Young and Peter Willmott's example in their (1973) *Symmetrical Family,* I fixed on the deployment of large-scale time-use surveys that could measure both paid and unpaid work even-handedly at the household level. Ray, perhaps influenced by Sandra Wallman's mid-1970s mixed-methods social survey and ethnographic study of Battersea, *Living in South London* (Wallman 1982), decided on a local area studies approach to investigating household-level work strategies – hence Sheppey, his post-industrial laboratory, only a short drive from his academic base at the University of Kent.

Emerging divisions

Ray and I met regularly during the early 1980s, approximately midway between our respective universities in Brighton and Canterbury, over splendidly vinous dinners in one or other of the excellent restaurants in Rye, to discuss the progress of our two projects. At least once we were joined by Ray's colleague in the Sheppey project, Claire Wallace: I have a lovely photograph of her, on one of these occasions, poring over a large pile of sprocketed printout from the initial returns from their survey.

We disagreed, increasingly, on the analysis of our materials. I thought, for example that his analytic procedure for quantifying the division of domestic tasks between husbands and wives (which emerged as chapter 10 of *Divisions of Labour*) was unnecessarily complex – or perhaps I just fail to understand its finer points. And as he started to write the book, the Rye meetings abruptly stopped, and the first I saw of the text was in the printed copy he sent me immediately before its publication in 1984.

Ray summarises my then theoretical objectives (1984: 93) entirely correctly, as making 'analytical distinctions between sectors'. However, as he starts to set out the arguments in more detail, some contradictions emerge: 'Gershuny … not presenting a unilinear or evolutionary model … avoids stating any *essential* motor of change' (1984: 119). Agreed: I describe change as driven by a complex combination of technical, economic and regulatory circumstances. But in the next sentence, he claims to identify 'perhaps an unstated evolutionary tone to his work' – this reflects Ray's initial position, not mine. Then associating me with the popular US economist Scott Burns (Burns 1977) and others, he concludes that my line of argument 'during the 1970s and early 1980s' is 'more narrowly economistic than now seems reasonable to accept' (Pahl 1984: 121). The 'early 1980s' qualification here is, frankly, a bit evasive. It relates, I believe, to my 1983 book *Social Innovation and the Division of Labour* (hence, from a 1984 perspective, not *early* 1980s). This focuses unambiguously on an example of *non*-linearity in the form of a reversal of the self-servicing trend, discussing – admittedly in somewhat economics-driven terms, and certainly somewhat prematurely – the influence of the (then proto-) internet. I suggested, in high-unemployment 1983, that this would lead to a range of new formal economy jobs, ranging from the obvious software engineering, to the then less-obvious category of new paid employment substituting for unpaid informal economy work, for example the paid home delivery jobs substituting for shoppers' trips to supermarkets, which would result from a growth in computer-based home shopping.

Eleven pages later (1984: 130) he states explicitly: 'More recently Gershuny has modified what appeared to be a more deterministic stance in his earlier formulations' and then quotes extensively from my 1983 work with Ian Miles on alternative models of 'information societies', and in the same paragraph he identifies descriptions of multi-directional shifts, both into and out of the formal sector in my 1978 book. A minor, and inconsistent, misinterpretation, on Ray's part, but meaning that people introduced to my work at this time by his book may have misread my intentions. Certainly, Gosta Esping-Andersen, discussing it in his book, *Social Foundations of Postindustrial Economics* (1999), presumes to criticise my 'unidirectional developmental model' – which was in fact Ray's, and not mine. And alongside this supposed monotonic strain towards the informal economy, is the suggestion that the informal economy could be viewed not as another sector, like manufacturing or consumer services, but as a freestanding economy, like France or Germany – that, somehow, informal production was independent of the formal, so that increasingly, as this unidirectional flow in to the informal economy progressed, individual wellbeing would increasingly be promoted outside the money nexus. This may once have been part of Ray's 'post-industrial laboratory' thinking. It was never part of mine.

However, a much more important line of criticism of my work – certainly more securely based on what I had written by that time – concerns distributional issues. In the final chapter Ray neatly summarises my 'social innovation' (I would now say 'socio-technical innovation') model (Pahl 1984: 315). He explains that I discuss how public infrastructures (now I would say the internet, then it was 'switched broadband telecommunications') combined with privately owned equipment (then home desktop computers, now laptops, smartphones or smart-watches) and shopping software services, with home grocery delivery services and with unpaid household work, to produce the supper that he places on the table when she gets back from her job. Infrastructure, software, unpaid labour, domestic capital equipment: the new factors we should now add to the traditional land, paid labour and capital in order to describe fully modern modes of provision of final services. But 'the distributional consequences of this line of thought are not considered by Gershuny … [though he] … admits that any new demand for [paid] labour will be for the skilled and not for the unskilled, and that the growth of informal production is more likely to reduce women's paid work disproportionately' (1984: 316: my parentheses). This is fair comment: to this point (and as a member of Sussex University's Science Policy Research Unit) I would have been more interested in the futurological aspects of the emerging model, than in current social changes.

Nevertheless, class and gender concerns were, he admits, already present in my work by this time. In addition to the high-skill composition of new jobs, he quotes at length what I still see as the key gender issue:

> here is the inequality: precisely *because* similar sorts of men and women, *because* husbands and wives may be expected to want to work similar lengths of time, while women maintain their special responsibility for housework, women are more likely to take on part-time jobs (which are generally of inferior status) they have less energy to concentrate on their jobs, less flexibility to work longer hours when they are needed so they cannot compete on equal terms with men. (Gershuny 1983: 153, quoted by Pahl 1984: 316)

He comments, finally: 'Gershuny does not condone such attitudes, but he describes them in such a way as to imply that they are inevitable.'

Ray does have a good point. It is true that I had not published much empirical work on the distributional consequences of changes in modes of provision (though I made quite a substantial start to explore cross-sectional differences between gender divisions in different sorts of household, in Gershuny (1982). The reason is entirely straightforward. My futurological work had alerted me to the problematical nature of making inferences from cross-sectional differences about historical change. Different sorts of people behave in different ways. But particular sorts of people may behave *differently* at a later historical period than *similar* sorts of people did at an earlier one. Just because, at one historical juncture employed women maintain a disproportionate responsibility for unpaid work, we cannot conclude that an increase in unpaid work increases women's disadvantage over time.

To see the consequences of economic change, we need, at the very least, a pair of cross-sectional measurements. Ideally, to do this analysis properly we need longitudinal data (I return later in this chapter to outline Ray's vital, but almost forgotten, contribution to this area of work in the UK). But the reason that little had emerged, at the time that Ray was writing *Divisions of Labour*, from the time-use work of which Ray wrote approvingly, was really that I was just starting to do comparative historical analysis with datasets collected at successive points of historical time. These have become the essence of any serious analysis of distributional *consequences* of social change, but the evidence was still very scarce when Ray was writing. In fact, my very first national time-use survey was still in the field during the months that Ray was writing *Divisions of Labour*, and the first publication from it came out only in 1986 and 1987.[3]

3 First in Gershuny *et al.* 1986 (the ESRC case officer insisted this be in the *Quarterly Journal of Social Affairs*, a journal entirely dependent on ESRC funding, which was withdrawn

Sheppey households' divisions of labour

The empirical core of Ray's book is in chapters 8, 9 and (though I am not at all keen on this analysis and do not pursue it here) 10. Despite all the initial mistaken expectations associated with Sheppey's 'post-industrial laboratory' status, Ray's most important analytic contribution was, I now think, to clear away the undergrowth of theory and idealistic futurology in both his and my work: he realised that households' provision of final services to their members – which is the real essence of 'consumption' – could be simply described in terms of its multiplicity of sources of labour. This could be straightforwardly measured with a conventional questionnaire. On one hand the household acquires some resources indirectly by *providing labour*, either to employers or customers who would pay money for this, which could then be spent on goods or services, *or* without payment, to neighbours or friends with some expectation of reciprocal receipt of goods or services in kind. On the other hand are the three sources from which it *acquires labour*: (1) from its own members, or (2) in exchange for money, whether paid legally or illicitly, or (3) acquired through barter, or more generally as part of a network of reciprocal exchange.

Ray's survey (run by Social and Community Planning Research in London in 1981 –which later became the National Centre for Social Research, NatCen) collected extensive information on the provision and acquisition of labour, for 730 Sheppey households, a 79 per cent response rate from the from the initial sample of 923, notably high even for this period, and telling us that the survey instrument was exceptionally well designed. This evidence lies at the heart of Ray's empirical work.

The first substantive section of chapter 8 deals with *the provision of formal labour* in the form of paid employment, and hence – given the absence of an inheritor class on Sheppey – households' money incomes. He explores the social class (as indicated by the household members' own jobs) and income levels of households, in relation both to couples' joint employment status and to the overall number of employed people in the household. Two jobs are better than one, plainly, and two higher class better than two lower, though in the sample there are no men in social class I with partners in the same class – a fact straightforwardly explained by the nature of the Sheppey labour market. Then we are encouraged to consider this relationship between formal labour and household income in terms of the domestic life cycle, and it emerges that three (or more) jobs (i.e. including the earnings of grown-up children) are better than two, leading to the finding that (larger) working-class households' work strategies may eventually provide more

the following year after vol. 3, no. 4 (1987)), then with US comparisons in Gershuny and Robinson 1987. The latter shows for two countries, from the 1960s to the 1980s, very similar trends to those for 20 countries from the 1960s to the 2010s with which I conclude.

savings, or higher disposable income, than middle-class households'. (Any further analysis of this data should, however, use some form of equivalisation for household size, a course of action not pursued here.)

The really innovative contribution of the chapter however comes with the analysis of Sheppey households' acquisition of labour. Ray, together with Claire Wallace, the co-designer of the Sheppey instrument, asks household respondents whether they have at some point acquired each of 41 household tasks, including a wide range of house maintenance, home improvement, routine housework, domestic production, car maintenance and childcare activities – and whether these were obtained from outside the household, whether paid or unpaid, and who does them within the household.[4] Here the answer to the question of whether informal economic activities substitute for formal is answered in the simplest and most straightforward way. No evidence of substitution emerges. On the contrary, the greater the extent of the household involvement in the formal economy through the provision of its own labour for pay, the greater also the extent of its acquisition of labour, from that or other households, through informal sources.

Chapter 9 uses this household task evidence more intensively, to explore, at the level of the household, the various mixes of tasks that are undertaken. Three aggregate scales are developed, indicating the household's level of involvement in, respectively, *self-provisioning* constructed from food production, construction, or food preserving activity, from its own labour resources, an *informal labour* scale constructed as the level of usage of unpaid labour from other households (friends or family) to achieve a similar list of activities, and finally a *formal labour* scale, indicating the level of paid labour used.

An entirely clear pattern of combination of modes of acquisition of services emerges from this chapter: the higher the level of formal provisioning, the higher the level of self-provisioning. Entirely unsurprisingly, those best placed, by the deployment of their own skills in the labour market, to buy the labour of others, are also the most likely to be able to afford to buy the materials and domestic equipment – and also perhaps also to have more of the necessary artisanal skills – for effective domestic production. Similarly straightforward is the weak negative association between self-provisioning and informal labour. Those who do not have the skills for specific sorts of self-provisioning, but have skills in other spheres of activity and do not have the money to pay for formal labour, must perforce acquire the services by exchange, providing other households with other sorts of services. And the strong negative association between the informal labour route to the acquisition of services and the formal labour route is similarly simple to

4 I suspect that this particular instrument descends directly from a battery of questions about who in the household uses each of 40 items of household equipment, and about who carries out various domestic tasks, found in Wallman's 1978 Battersea survey (Wallman 1982: 214–15).

explain: if you have neither the equipment not the skills to produce it for yourself, or the money to buy it in, then you can acquire it only through barter.

These two chapters are clear and simply argued. Ray's conclusion: 'households still need substantial amounts of money in order to engage in self-service activity.' (1984: 317). The answer may be contrary to Ray's prior expectations, but it is nevertheless quite straightforwardly explicable. A hypothesis is overturned, and good science emerges.

Chapter 10, however is more problematical. The same data source as used in the chapters 8 and 9, allows him to look at the division of domestic labour among household members, and in particular between heterosexual partners. Does the husband, or the wife, do each task, or both, or neither? There is a simple way to construct a domestic division of labour index from this material. If the wife does it and the husband does not, score the task 1.0, if the husband does it and the wife not, score 0. If they both do it score 0.5. Sum across all the tasks and divide by the number of task that either or both do, and we arrive at a straightforward DOMDIV index, unaffected by the number of tasks undertaken (though unweighted by the frequency of, or the time devoted to, the task) with a minimum of zero and a maximum of 1. The closer to 0.5, the more egalitarian the division of the household work.

Unfortunately (in my view, at least), Ray decided not to adopt this straightforward approach (which is approximately that adopted by Gershuny 1982, and by Berk and Berk 1983). Advised by his then colleague and co-author of the chapter Spyros Missiakoulis, he opted for the much more complex formulation, set out on p. 259 and subsequently, which weights each task for gender conventionality, and the frequency of the occurrence of the task, and arrives at a single number which potentially varies from minus to plus infinity. It is hard to interpret exactly what this number tells us beyond the undoubted fact that the more positive the overall score, the more of the household's work is done by the wife. But, however hard to interpret, the results of its application nevertheless clearly demonstrate (1) that the more fully employed the wife relative to the husband, and the lower the level of childcare and other family responsibilities, the less unequal the division of unpaid work between the husband and the wife becomes; and (2) even where the wife is fully employed, she still does the majority of the unpaid work.

This latter finding, fully consistent with the mid-1970s pioneers of time-diary research in this field (Meissner *et al.* 1975, which he republished in his 1988 *On Work* reader), seems to be Ray's take-away message. To repeat his previously quoted historical-change-from-current-difference prediction, he concludes that, at least in so far as men and women will continue to want to work (paid and unpaid) approximately the same amount of time in total, 'the growth of informal production is … likely to reduce women's paid work proportionately' (Pahl 1984: 316).

I briefly bring my end of this argument up to date by adding in the current conclusions from the work I started in the 1980s – encouraged, promoted, sponsored by Ray's ambiguous though undoubted enthusiasm for it, and his then not-inconsiderable influence, both intellectual and academic-positional. But first I should mention the longer-term influence of Ray's own work on research into households and work in British social science.

Post-industrial households thirty years on

Pretty much immediately after finishing *Divisions of Labour* Ray was thrown (or perhaps launched himself) into the preparations for the UK University Grants Committee's first 'Research Assessment Exercise' (the RAE, predecessor of the present UK Universities Funding Council Research Excellence Framework, the 'REF'). Then as now, the RAE was to determine each university's specific funding for research – hugely important in both financial and reputational terms (and equally controversial) for all UK universities. Ray was the representative of British sociologists in the formulation of the procedures of this (all subsequent RAE and REF exercises followed pretty much the pattern). He also chaired the committee that carried out the first assessments for UK sociology departments, and acted as the main channel of communication between UGC and social scientists in general.

And what I consider to be his longest-lasting impact on British sociology, emerges as an indirect knight's-move consequence of the results of this first RAE. The University of Essex scored a highly-satisfactory triple: its sociology, economics and government (politics) departments were all top-ranked across the country. The then Vice-Chancellor of Essex proposed that some of the extra income deriving from this RAE result be fed back to the School of Social Sciences to contribute to planning its future research strategy. Essex University's Committee for Research in the Social Sciences decided to use this to fund an exploratory research programme on the household (with some complementary funding from Unilever Research division – note, *not* the Unilever Trust: this was genuine commercial collaboration with the social scientists). Some of the resources went to pay for Ray's year-long secondment from Kent to Essex to take the lead in this interdisciplinary exercise, working together with David Rose from the Essex Sociology Department, and with Nick Buck, a Sheppey collaborator who also soon moved to Essex. And out of this collaboration emerged what eventually became the bid for the British Household Panel Study (BHPS).

There were others involved: Tony Shorrocks from the Essex Economics department was an already experienced analyst of social inequality using panel data, Ivor Crewe from the Government department chaired the steering committee. But the initial intellectual stimulation from Ray's own research, meant that BHPS (and its successor) continues as the only one of the large national household panel studies to be led from the outset by sociologists (the Panel Study of Income Dynamics (PSID) in the USA, the Socio-Economic Panel (SOEP) in Germany have each been led largely by economists).

And the BHPS, both in design and detail, had at its heart Ray's central concerns with work and the household. The 10,000 household BHPS has now been succeeded by the nearly 40,000 household Understanding Society panel study ('US', led by Nick Buck) providing 25 waves of data, now tracking close to 80,000 UK individuals through their life course. Some new research foci have now emerged: the (to my mind rather unfortunately-named) UK US study has a substantial ethnic minority subsample, and a new interest in health, with connections to the UK Biobank. But at its core is still the concern of Ray's Sheppey study: to provide empirical evidence of how households manage their labour to get by in post-industrial society.

Ray's next book was a massive edited reader, *On Work* (1988), its 33 chapters providing an enormously valuable resource for teachers and researchers in the 1990s and into the 2000s. The editor's introduction to each of the six major sections of the book exhibit Ray's best qualities: erudition, wit, quirkiness, eloquence. His final essay 'Epilogue: on work', which uses a painting by Michel Bonvoin of a woman ironing as a pivot image for discussing alternative forms of labour, has that quality that C Wright Mills identified as 'sociological imagination' in its highest form. This piece has an elegiac feel that signals that he is now ready to move on to the next intellectual projects, *After Success*, and then two books on friendship, written as a member of the Institute for Social and Economic Research at Essex.

Time and the informal economy

Meanwhile, I had continued the work on time-diary studies that Ray discusses with such ambivalent enthusiasm in *Divisions of Labour*. After the UK study in winter 1983/84, I collected another in the summer of 1987 as part of the ESRC's Social Change and Economic Life Initiative (SCELI – an undertaking which itself was strongly influenced by Ray's early 1980s agitation for empirical work in economic sociology), which for the first time provided an empirical link between the 'longue durée' of the whole life-course in the form of individual family and work histories (their inclusion in the SCELI study forcefully championed by Peter Elias) and the seven-day time budgets of those same individuals in 1987. This was my first exposure to longitudinal data analysis, and provided the start of a definitive answer to one of the questions raised in *Divisions of Labour*. On the basis of cross-sectional evidence it appears that women in employment have much the same differential responsibility for unpaid labour as non-employed women, leading to a 'dual burden' of paid and unpaid work. The key question that allows us to make the move from sociology to futurology, which was Ray's original aim for the Sheppey work, is: how does this cross-sectional difference play out in terms of historical change?

The SCELI data provided a first chance to answer this question using the retrospective life-history data. I provided (1992, Gershuny *et al.* 1994) a new hypothesis to explain the dual burden phenomenon which I called 'lagged adaptation':

> the household's adaptation of its work strategy consequent on new employment pattern(s) is gradual; particular tasks are passed, one by one, from wives to husbands. When we look at households with employed wives as a whole, we have a view averaged across households in the various stages of adaptation. There are some households in which the wife has relatively recently returned to work, or increased paid work hours, and some where the wife has maintained a constant level of employment for a relatively long period. The adaptation model expects the former to show the dual burden effect strongly, the latter less strongly. (Gershuny 1992: 89)

My two 1990s papers on this topic used the very detailed information from the SCELI retrospective work histories, to test this hypothesis. Clear confirmation emerged. In the 1992 version, I showed that, controlling for age and family status, where the wife has less than 21 months continuous work experience, she bears on average 54 per cent of the couple's paid plus unpaid work to the husband's 46 per cent. Between 21 and 60 months of continuous work experience the husband's proportion rose to 49 per cent, and above and from 60 months couples arrive at parity. The 1994 version produces an even clearer confirmation of the hypothesis, adding an intergenerational dimension by including SCELI respondents' recollection of their parents' domestic practices in their household of origin.

But this result is vitiated by the problem, endemic to recall-based life and work history evidence, of 'survivor bias'. An alternative potential explanation for this result is not *adaptation* at all, but '*exit*'. It could be that, if she takes a job but he takes on no extra unpaid work, she then leaves him. Or she leaves the job. Either way, the *surviving* households at each point in time – which are the only ones we can observe through recall data – will show just this apparent strain towards equality.

This is where the BHPS (I took over as Principal Investigator in 1993) comes to the rescue. Prospective data from household panel surveys, which follow the same households at successive points in time, allow us to examine exit (and loyalty) processes separately from the 'voice' phenomena which correspond to adaptation in my hypothesis.[5]

Examining 'voice' alone, we get essentially the same answers from BHPS, the US PSID and the German SOEP, which have all regularly repeated questionnaire items on household members' weekly paid and unpaid work time totals. Table 2.1 is quoted from an article in *Journal of Marriage and the Family* (written with Michael Bittman and John Brice, 2005), using the three nationally representative panel surveys' evidence on change in couples' economic experiences over successive years. It shows partial regression results, modelling the determinants' of year-on-year change in the simple (women's total unpaid work divided by women's plus men's) DOMDIV index. Women and men both significantly and substantially

5 The reference here is to Hirschman's (1970) disquisition on the nature of consumer choice in the face of changing circumstances.

Table 2.1 Regression coefficients of year-on-year change: effect of spouses' annual change in employment status on change in DOMDIV
DOMDIV 0=all husband, 1.00=all wife (* p<.05 **p<.01)

	UK		Germany		US	
	BHPS		SOEP		PSID	
Wife's employment change:						
Stay full time	–0.01		0.00		0.03	*
Full time to part time	0.00		0.05	*	0.05	
Full time to not employed	**0.11**	**	**0.09**	**	**0.10**	**
Part time to full time	–0.03	*	–0.02		0.05	
Part time to part time	–0.01		0.00		0.03	
Part time to not employed	**0.03**	**	**0.05**	**	**0.08**	**
Not employed to full time	**–0.08**	**	**–0.07**	**	**–0.06**	*
Not employed to part time	**–0.03**	**	**–0.01**		**0.01**	
Stay nonemployed (ref)						
Husband's employment change:						
Stay full time	0.00		0.00		0.01	
Full time to not employed	**–0.11**	**	**–0.10**	**	**–0.01**	
other employment change	0.00		0.03		0.03	
Not employed to full time	**0.09**	**	**0.08**	**	**0.03**	*
Stay nonemployed (ref)						
N of couple-year pairs	**16044**		**14161**		**7423**	

Gershuny, Bittman and Brice, JMF 67 (August 2005) p.660

reduce their unpaid work when they move into employment, and significantly and substantially increase it when they move out of paid employment. Husbands (we show elsewhere in the paper) also increase or decrease their unpaid work as a result of *their wives' movements* into and out of paid employment. These changes in the shorter term imply only a partial adaptation, but they continue progressively (see 'stay full time' women's employment change category) – and now clearly independent of couple dissolution processes – as the new employment becomes more settled. Hence 'lagged adaptation': the relative equalisation of work burdens over an extended (five or more year) interval.

But, as we know, this extended process of equalisation of the overall work burden tells us nothing necessarily about gender equality. Figure 2.1, which brings together the very earliest nationally representative UK time use studies with the most recent, shows men and women with a long-term equality of overall work burden, but still a substantially unequal distribution among different types of leisure.[6]

6 This unique 55-year sequence of surveys exists only as a result of Economic and Social Research Council funding. The original 1961 and 1974/75 diary studies were collected by the then BBC Audience Research Department. But it was an SSRC (Social Science Research

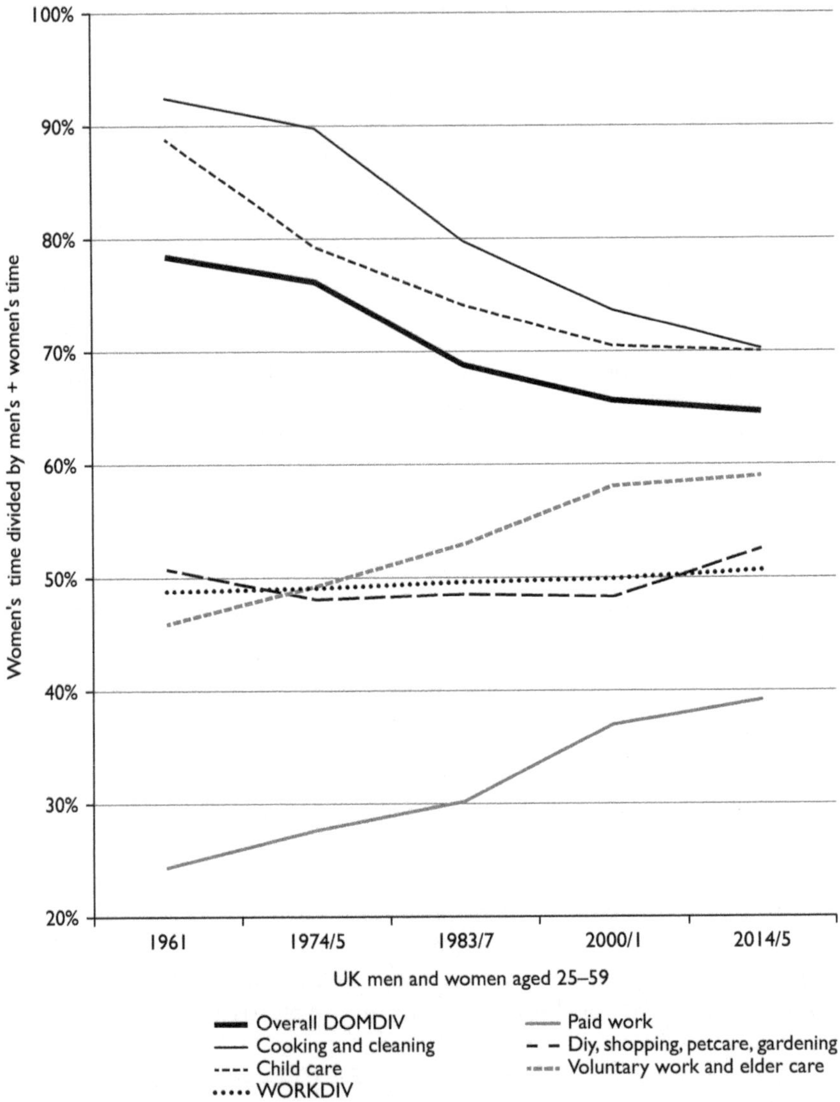

2.1 WORKDIV and DOMDIV in the UK

Council – the ESRC's previous name) grant which provided the resources to retrieve and recode the original diary materials for academic purposes. The 1983/84 (winter) survey was funded by the SSRC Social Affairs Committee on the initiative of Ray Illsley and Brian Roberts), the 1987 (summer) survey by the ESRC as part of SCELI. The 2000/1 survey was jointly funded by the ESRC and the ONS on prompting of the ESRC, and the 2014/15 study is wholly funded by the ESRC.

The overall work burden 'WORKDIV' remains largely unchanged at the 50 per cent level throughout the 55-year period covered by the surveys (a result that parallels Hamermesh *et al.* 2013's 'isowork' finding). But the unpaid work burden 'DOMDIV' remains stubbornly gendered. Less so than previously, certainly; almost 80 per cent of unpaid work in 1961, to 65 per cent in 2015, representing real social change. But it still leaves us with the same awkward gender issue: if he does substantially less unpaid work than she does, yet they both want to work the same hours in total, he necessarily does more paid work. As a consequence he accumulates more work experience, more 'human capital', and hence an increasing an advantage in the pay and promotion stakes. He gets ahead, she lags behind.

And yes, if they stay married, she may get to consume some of the financial fruits of this specialisation. But if, as we now understand happens frequently, they specialise in this way after they start to have children, then he runs off with his PA (or, though for the reasons set out here, statistically less likely, his boss), he carries away the majority of the human capital formed during the marriage, while leaving her with the babies, who as a result grow up in poverty, with all sorts of negative consequences later in their life course ....

This line of argument, the short-term elements of which Ray articulated so clearly in *Divisions of Labour*, is still entirely pertinent. The more blatantly unfair procedures of the workplace, which, though outlawed in the 1970s, still bolstered gender inequality in the 1980s, have now mostly disappeared. But at the level of households' work strategies, similarly unfair practices are apparently still thriving. Ray's research legacy, in the form of his 1980s books on work, of the household panel survey work which he partly inspired, and in the time-use research which he encouraged, is a major resource for tackling the remaining gender inequities in the distribution of work.

And finally: the informal economy? This for me transitional term has now become subsumed within a vocabulary more firmly located in established social science. That hidden sphere of economic activity which forced itself on my attention as I tried to substantiate Bell's thesis, is now firmly established within the United Nations System of National Accounts as the realm that lies between the snappily named 'System of National Accounts Production Boundary' and the 'General Production Boundary', and nations are bound by international treaty to produce 'Satellite Accounts' of their economies which include non-money production alongside the money. And these two boundaries produce in turn three regions of activity that together add up to the 'Great Day' of a society (the 24 hours of the whole population), that are simply described, in traditional sociological terms, as the realms of exchange, reciprocity and consumption.

Excerpts from *Divisions of Labour*, Part I

Past and Present Ways of Work (excerpts from pp. 54–85)

It is now time to take stock of the argument. We have seen that wage labour grew as a way of adding to the self-provisioning work of the family farm. Gradually, from the late eighteenth century through to the 1960s and 1970s, wage labour expanded, so that most households became entirely dependent upon it. Certainly, there were many households without wage earners in them, but these were largely supported by a state income in the form of returned national insurance payments, unemployment benefit, pensions or other forms of state benefit paid out of general taxation or (more recently) from North Sea oil revenues.

As wage labour grew over the period of two hundred years, so other forms of customary work declined, with one important exception: women's work inside the home expanded. Much of women's self-provisioning work done outside the home, such as rearing poultry and growing herbs and vegetables, either did not get done or was left to men who had allotments. This shift of the women into the home, doubly dependent on the wages of a male chief earner and the local shops and public services, took place at different rates among different social categories and in different parts of the country. In some towns women continued to keep hens and geese well into the twentieth century; in some rural areas the pattern has barely changed.

It is quite possible to describe households in the 1980s where the mix of work is broadly the same as it was in the thirteenth century. The man may hold some form of employment and so, too, may his wife and this may be seasonal and highly irregular. In East Kent, women pick fruit or vegetables in the summer and autumn to get more money in preparation for the winter, much as they have done for centuries. Now, instead of buying cloth or leather, they may buy their children's school uniform or some extra toys at Christmas. People still keep hens, have allotments and poach rabbits and pheasants. They still go to the local markets with honey from their hives or cherries from their trees that they have picked themselves. In the case studies in Appendix 2, a pattern is described that has a long historical pedigree. People work to get money to get by without necessarily having regular employment. There are anecdotes everywhere of people getting money in unrecorded ways: rarely are such anecdotes put into the context of a complete household work strategy. The rural household where the man is unemployed or 'early retired' but spends his time doing odd jobs for neighbours, supplying the household with vegetables and the occasional rabbit, many also include his wife earning regularly as a domestic cleaner, his son doing various labouring jobs from time to time and also, perhaps, doing a paper round or helping a local garage. His daughter may also be a cleaner – possibly in the local pub – and in addition may help out in a shop at holiday periods and other busy times. 'Earning an extra bob or two' [two shillings in pre-decimal currency] is still a current phrase. No member of the household is permanently bound by the rigid disciplines of wage labour, but some money has to be earned on a more or less regular basis.

No one would pretend that this casualized labour force is particularly privileged. It still flourishes particularly in holiday areas, where services and goods can be sold to people with money to spend, who want 'bed and breakfast', home-made jam, a row in a boat, fresh strawberries, seafood in the street, and of course, endless cups of tea. The man at the Kent seaside town who bought a ton and a half of misshapen boiled sweets – the product of a firm's misplaced confidence in youngsters taken on under a government-sponsored training scheme – will have a stall every week at the Sunday market throughout the summer, making a profit of £50 a day. All this is little different from the street traders of eighteenth or even fourteenth-century London.

Contemporary Incapacitation: The Result of Over-dependence on Wage Labour

What is unusual, exceptional and probably now in lasting decline is a situation where households in many towns are entirely dependent for regular wage labour on one or two large employers. The industrial town of the Midlands or North of England, divided like a model town plan into the shopping centre, the factory zone at one side and the residential areas on the other, is a fossil marking a particular stage in the development of industrial capitalism. Opportunities for by-employment or occupational easements may be strictly limited. The only public land is likely to be parks with rules and open space near high-rise housing on which no ball games are allowed and certainly no goats, chickens or geese. Since most of the houses may still belong to the local authority, there is little scope for home improvement, and even keeping rabbits in the back garden may be either forbidden or too risky, given the importance of maintaining good relations with neighbours.

Again because it has been mainly an industrial town, there is likely to be very little alternative employment in the service sector. Washing is done in washing machines or at the laundrette and not by local laundresses; there is negligible scope for living off private rented accommodation. Private taxis are expensive, as is the infrequent bus service connecting the housing estates to the town centre. People are caught in a number of traps. After 6 p.m. only the pubs, a few take-away food or hamburger bars and the off-licence are open. It is probably unsafe to cycle round the town as new roads to speed up the circulation of traffic do just that. In such an environment, men and women have had their capacity to do other forms of work whittled down so far that even repairing a car in the street is a cause for comment.

In retrospect, the years when it was said they never had it so good, in the period of recovery after the Second World War, were the years of incapacitation. The messy back streets with their potential for premises for small workshops were knocked down as part of slum clearance. The factories were rebuilt and rationalized. The unions got stronger and led their members to believe that collective solidaristic action would lead to a permanent position in the rising escalator of incomes. Men were pulled out of their households and, as it were, put in the block votes with other men in an all-male fraternity. It was held to be a victory when overtime was 'won', keeping the men away from home when their wives were at their busiest feeding the children and putting them to bed. Those in these expanding and flourishing unions and factories were the affluent workers. They were also those most likely to want to own their own homes – so when the factory closed or laid them off, they had little to fall back on and still had a large mortgage to pay. The physical and social infrastructure of the post-war period was developed on an assumption of smooth and continuing growth. Households with a limited and narrow view of work as factory employment were exactly as employers in the 1950s and 1960s most liked them to be. Completely socialized to the time and work disciplines of industrial capitalism, they had, perhaps for the first time in English history, lost the means of getting by with a household work strategy.

Happily, this account is overdrawn and does not apply generally across the British Isles: various alternative ways of getting by still exist, and the period of incapacitation was not, perhaps, long enough to do as much damage as it might have done. Nevertheless, many of the politicians, social scientists and journalists writing in the 1980s and 1990s grew up in this atypical period, providing them with misleading personal experience. Getting back to the way it was in the 1950s and 1960s would be as irrelevant as putting all women back to the equally atypical pattern of the 1920s and 1930s. It cannot be sufficiently stressed that a full understanding of the nature of work within a society requires a longer historical perspective than a mere thirty years.

Women's Employment 1940–1990

The employment of married women remained very stable at around 10 per cent of all married women until the start of the Second World War. By 1945 the number of married women employed was over 2.5 million, that is, more than five times the number in paid work before the war. This is probably a substantial underestimate of the number of married women workers, many of whom would have engaged in essential work on a voluntary basis. For example, there were 2,000 British Restaurants, and some of these were run by voluntary committees and some married women worked in them without pay, although these were a minority. As we have seen, many married women in employment before the war were (certainly in south-east England) 'deviants' – shaming their husbands, who felt that this demonstrated that they were not looking after them properly. However, during the war public opinion changed radically. As Gertrude Williams remarked at the time: 'War necessity has swung public opinion so far the other way that the woman who does *not* add to her household duties feels guilty and apologetic, and there is no doubt that if, after the war, society looked upon it as normal to combine home and work the majority of women should do what was expected of them.'[1]

If women were to follow all Williams's prescriptions they would stay at home with their children (which it was their natural duty to have) until they had 'launched' them – at whatever mature age that would be. Then they would look for jobs that could be undertaken 'with only the scantiest previous experience'.[2] Restaurants and personal service were two of the areas that Williams thought were likely to provide suitable employment for women, whose lives were set to a different pattern from those of men.

1 G. Williams, *Women and Work*, Nicholson and Watson, London, 1945, p. 124. Mrs Williams made no secret of what her values were, despite being a lecturer in economics herself: 'The way to express our sense of the most important work that women do in society is not to pay them to do less important work; it is to recognize the unique contribution that wives and mothers make to the community and to give them the opportunity to do it properly. ... One of the happiest innovations proposed in the Beveridge Report is the emergence of the housewife as a separate and honoured category of the population' (pp. 125–6).

2 *Ibid.*, p. 127.

These assumptions were firmly built into the post-war period of reconstruction managed by the Labour Party. Perhaps the clearest embodiment of these principles can be seen in the way New Towns were planned. Neighbourhood units were laid out some distance from the main shopping and recreational facilities in the town centre, with just a few shops within walking distance for daily needs. Men went to the industrial estates, segregated some distance from the main living areas, so that earning and consuming were kept physically separated. There was no expectation that women would want to have employment near to their homes or that opportunities for part-time work might encourage women to combine the care of small children with paid employment.

There was no absolute reduction in the number of married women working in the period immediately following the Second World War, but the female labour force as a whole did decline in the late 1940s as single women married and started their families. By the early 1950s, the proportion of married women in employment (one in four) returned to the level it had been in 1851: the rigours of married women's domestic imprisonment seemed to be abating. Despite the ideological bias in the social policies and programmes of the immediate post-war period, married women in employment began to increase both proportionately and absolutely. Numbers employed rose from 2.85 million in 1950 to 3.77 million in 1957, the latter figure being about half of the total of all female workers. Inevitably, however, conventional attitudes were maintained, even by Viola Klein, the author of a sociological survey of *Britain's Married Women Workers* published in 1965:

It is not suggested here that it is – or is likely to become so in the near future – the general practice for married women to accept employment away from their homes. Housewives without jobs, after all, still outnumber those in employment by 2 to 1; and as something like half of them have one or more children under the age of 16, the size of the reserve that can be drawn on will probably always remain limited to a minority of married women.[3]

Despite recognizing that the trends towards the greater employment of married woman would continue, Klein completely misread the situation: the middle 1960s were the beginning of an unprecedented increase in the proportion of married women in employment. By the early 1980s there were about 10.5 million women in the labour force, representing two-thirds of all women between 16 and 60. Over 60 per cent of the wives of employed men were in employment but only 32 per cent of

3 V. Klein, *Britain's Married Women Workers*, Routledge & Kegan Paul, London, 1965, p. 28.

the wives of the unemployed. While 40 per cent of the British labour force are females, 40 per cent of all female employees are part-time workers, compared with only 5 per cent of male employees. The growth in women's activity rates is related to the growth of services in the economy: service industries account for 60 per cent of all employment, but 54 per cent of all service employees are women.[4] This brief summary must now be elaborated.

The decade 1966–1977 was a period of unprecedented change in the labour force. A. R. Thatcher wrote in 1978 that the change was 'almost entirely due to the tremendous increase in the proportion of married women working, particularly the proportion who return to work after having their families. The participation rates for married women in Britain are amongst the highest in the countries of the industrial West, and so far have confounded each successive forecast by rising more than expected.'[5] Between 1951 and 1976 the number of men in the labour force remained stable at around 15.9 million; married women, on the other hand, increased from 2.7 to 6.7 million. From 1966 to 1976, in very broad terms, those employed in the 'index of production' industries declined by just under 2 million in rough proportions of three men to one woman. In the public sector, however, there was a substantial increase of 1.4 million workers, over two-thirds of whom were women. There was, therefore, a clear scissors effect: men moved out of traditional manufacturing industries and women moved into service industries, particularly in the public sector.

In 1979 the Department of Employment drew up labour force projections to 1991 in which it forecast a continuing increase in married women's activity rates from 26 per cent of the labour force in 1976 to 27.6 per cent by 1991.[6] However, it later became clear that the post-war trend of increasing female activity rates had peaked, as the overall activity rate of married women remained about 50 per cent from to 1981, in sharp contrast to the rapidly increasing rates of the preceding years.

Table 3.1 gives the age-specific activity rates for selected years. This levelling out in married women's activity rates is explained partly by increases in fertility rates between 1977 and 1981.

From the late 1960s onwards there was a substantial shift towards part-time work. By 1981 90 per cent of part-time workers were

4 Lloyds Bank, *Economic Bulletin*, 42, June 1982.

5 A. R. Thatcher, 'Labour supply and employment trends', in F. Blackaby (ed.), *De-industrialization,* Heinemann Educational Books, London, 1979, p. 27.

6 Department of Employment, 'Changing composition of the labour force, 1976–1991', *Employment Gazette*, 1979, p. 548.

Table 3.1 Activity rates of married women, 1971–1981

Age groups	Percentages employed 1971	1977	1981
16–19	42.4	54.7	48.9
20–24	46.7	59.0	56.8
25–34	38.4	52.2	51.3
35–44	54.5	67.4	66.6
45–54	57.0	65.1	66.8
60–64	25.2	24.6	23.3
65+	6.5	5.0	4.7
All	42.3	50.4	59.5
Estimated totals (thousands)	5,816	6,922	6,714

Source: Department of Employment Gazette, February 1983.

women: nearly 45 per cent of working women were in part-time employment and nearly 75 per cent of female part-time workers were aged between 25 and 55. Eighty per cent of the female part-time workers in 1981 were married, suggesting that the pattern of women's employment is related to their pattern of other work and responsibilities. The proportion of employed women who were employed part-time increased with the appearance of dependent children, from about one-third employed part-time with no children, through one-half employed part-time with one child, to two-thirds employed part-time with two children. The existence of a third dependent child did not increase the tendency to take part-time employment, while the presence of four or more dependent children somewhat reduced the tendency to be employed part-time if in employment. Nearly 90 per cent of young women without dependent children were in full-time employment, but within this group married women work shorter hours than non-married women. Indeed, the proportion of non-married young women in full-time employment is much the same as for males.[7] Older women, even without dependent children, are still more likely to be in part-time employment than younger women, indicating, perhaps, the continuing responsibilities of parenthood even after the children are grown up. A large proportion, 40 per cent, of females in part-time employment are in personal service occupations

7 It is interesting to note that employment statistics differentiate only women according to marital status. Men are not so divided, yet unmarried men in employment could, arguably, be expected to behave in qualitatively different ways from married men. Discussion of male docility or militancy rarely mentions their marital status and whether they live with their mothers or on their own.

(catering, cleaning, hairdressing and other personal services), compared with 10 per cent for full-time workers.[8]

Full-time employment consistently plays a less important part in women's work patterns: around 55 per cent of employed women were in full-time employment in 1981 and even among the non-marrieds the proportion of full-time employed women – about 75 per cent – was less than the rate for men. Women employed full-time had a median of 39 hours a week: women full-timers worked shorter hours than men within all industries and occupations, apart from managerial occupations where the proportion was much the same. This suggests that for women employment is evidently only one form of work. 'Traditionally we[9] have thought in terms of people being employed or unemployed. The position is, however, more complex; choices are made between work, non-market work and leisure: households make joint decisions with respect to the hours of work of husband and wife.'[10] How households make these decisions is, of course, not so obviously apparent: in practice, it appears that very few households have full-time employed wives with their husbands working part-time in order to take over some of their parental responsibilities.

In broad terms, therefore, women are employed part-time and in service industries. Typically, women's jobs are classified as less skilled than men's, even though they cover a wide range of skills: their employment is undervalued.[11] However, it is important to note that part-time employment has stood up well during the current recession, the unemployment rate for those seeking part-time employment remaining consistently below that for those seeking full-time employment. This may, of course, simply be a function of married women 'adjusting to a lower demand for labour', as economists put it. That is, the women perceive there are no jobs in their locality so they see little point in registering as seeking work. Evidently, married women at present unemployed could dramatically change the unemployment rate if they registered in large numbers.

Before leaving this particular issue of women's employment to up 1990, some consideration should be given to the effect of micro-electronics. What, in particular, is likely to be the impact of micro-electronics on the 1.25 million women employed as operatives in manufacturing? Clearly, the pattern will vary between industries. In the textile industry electronic

8 Department of Employment, 'Changing composition of the labour force, 1976–1991', p. 481.

9 The 'we' here is taken to be economists analysing labour force statistics.

10 Thatcher, 'Labour supply', p. 54.

11 Department of Employment, 'A changing labour force: Constants and variables', *Employment Gazette*, 91(2), 1983, pp. 49–54.

innovations have primarily affected craft skills – that is men's jobs – in the past, but in the future women's jobs are likely to be more at risk.[12] In a study of the paper, printing and publishing industries in America, micro-electronic applications increased women's job opportunities at the expense of men's. But this may not be the pattern in Britain. 'In the present climate of change, combined with redundancies, there are some indications that men, and the trade unions representing them, may be anxious to retain their traditional areas of work and may resist new technology and women workers where they can.'[13] As the authors of a recent review of the impact of micro-electronics on women's work conclude, 'women are vulnerable because they are clustered in unskilled and semi-skilled assembly work or routine white collar jobs and are failing to acquire the technical education and training necessary for the new jobs.'[14]

Paradoxically, it seems that the only way women can keep their hold on employment is through the downgrading of their work as semi-skilled and by employers preferring to have more flexible part-time employees rather than full-time male workers. In a recent detailed study of the semi-conductor industry, it has been claimed that there is a 'feminization' of the workforce as a disproportionate number of the routine jobs are taken by women. 'Thus in the assisted areas 74 per cent of all manual production workers were women, while in the non-assisted areas female production workers were 48 per cent of the total.'[15] It has been shown that there are strong grounds for thinking that many employers prefer part-time workers, since employees working less than eight hours a week, and those working up to sixteen hours if they have worked for less than five years with the same employers, are not eligible for redundancy compensation, minimum period of notice, guaranteed payments during periods of short-time working, maternity leave,

12 In a survey on *New Technology and Women's Employment* focusing on West Yorkshire by the Leeds Trade Union and Community Resource and Information Centre (published by the Equal Opportunities Commission in 1982), it was concluded that 'where new technology is introduced into mixed workplaces, women's jobs are much more likely to be affected than men's jobs. In the TUC RIC Survey, 60 per cent of workplaces employed more men than women, but in only 17 per cent of cases were more men's jobs than women's affected by automation' (p. 105).

13 E. Arnold *et al.*, 'Microelectronics and women's employment', *Employment Gazette*, September 1982, p. 380.

14 *Ibid.*, p. 384.

15 Cooke *et al.*, 'New technology and regional development in austerity Britain: The case of the semiconductor industry'. Paper prepared for SSRC Conference on Urban Change and Conflict, Department of Town Planning, UWIST, 1983 (mimeo), p. 13.

maternity pay or appeal against unfair dismissal. It has been estimated that a million part-time workers are excluded from the main provisions of employment legislation.[16] An analysis of New Earnings Survey data has demonstrated that the proportion of part-time workers falling in the unprotected categories increased between 1975 and 1979 from 20 to 30 per cent for women in manual occupations and from 18 to 23 per cent for women in non-manual occupations.[17] However, it would be premature to jump to the conclusion that part-time work is growing at the expense of full-time work; rather, it should be seen in the context of a switch in employment from manufacturing to services.

Conclusions

It is a truism to note that most of the world's work is done by women, and yet it still may cause some surprise to be reminded that the admonition urging the workers of the world to unite is logically addressed to a largely female audience. Unhappily for women, they have more to lose than their chains of servitude to employers: they also have other chains, binding them to husbands and dependent relatives. Most women's conception of work, until quite recently, has been very close to what I suggest in this book, namely a necessary and pragmatic activity essential to getting by. They have shifted between work for an employer and work on their own account. Sometimes they have worked more for the household, sometimes more for themselves; yet typically work in and around the household is always, inevitably, an essential element in their overall work-load.

Women have earned money for as long as the history of wage labour, and they have contributed this money to their families and households. Before marriage young women either handed most of their earned income to their mothers or, if they were lodging elsewhere, sent home all but a small subsistence income. Alternatively, they busily saved for their own marriages and the new homes and families that that would entail. After marriage their pattern of work was structured by the exigencies of child rearing, and their level of economic activity as employees was frequently constrained by real or imposed limitations attributable to their roles as wives and mothers. If it has become conventional to refer to the married man as the 'chief earner', it should be equally conventional to refer to his wife as the 'chief worker'.

16 C. Leicester, 'Towards a fully part-time Britain', *Personnel Management*, June 1982.

17 J. Hurstfield, 'Part-time pittance', *Low Pay Review*, no. 1, 1980.

The one-sided emphasis on employment, with the implication that this is the only significant form of work, tends also to emphasize the individual earner rather than the household as the basic economic unit. Women are perhaps more likely to perceive the household as the basic economic unit and to arrange their balance of work in terms of the needs of the household as a whole. Furthermore, in general women are more likely to manage the non-waged work of all members of the household: if anyone is to take final responsibility for the order and amount of domestic and child rearing work, it is most likely to be the woman. Women in upper-class households are in the most atypical position, and are in many ways more dependent than ordinary working women since, paradoxically, their relative economic importance in the household is less.

Evidently, it is a serious error to underestimate the importance of women's waged work as an essential element in most household work strategies. For eight hundred years women have made an essential contribution of money into the family budget. From the very early days of the industrial revolution, households needed the money that women earned before they were married in order to set them up and very often after they were married to maintain them. The notion that ordinary households can be maintained adequately with the earnings of one (male) worker is a dangerous fallacy. Some households in the labour aristocracy and in the middle classes can, of course, be adequately supported in this way. But to infer from that that most households of the ordinary working people do not need, and have not always needed, the wages of other earners is quite unwarranted. There are strong indications that such households will similarly need multiple earners in the years up to the end of the twentieth century.

The employment of married women is sometimes perceived as a novelty – a product of the growth of the service sector in the 1960s and 1970s. This too, as we have seen, is a fallacy. Women's waged work has not always been counted or, more often, has passed notice simply as women's 'money-earning activities', in Roberts's phrase quoted above. Such dilatory accounting is no good reason to make women's economic activity socially invisible. What *is* new is the large-scale employment of married women from all social classes for most of their married lives on a full-time basis. There certainly is not a historical precedent for that. But it would be unfortunate if women's waged work were perceived in too narrow and limited a way. Historically, women have been the most flexible in engaging in all forms of work: the likelihood is that that, too, will be the pattern for the future.

3 From the Isle of Sheppey to the wider world

Claire Wallace

I became involved in Ray Pahl's 'Sheppey project' (as it became known) in 1978. When I had completed my finals at the University of Kent, but did not yet know the results, I was encouraged to apply for a Social Science Research Council (now Economic and Social Research Council) studentship to do a PhD. At that stage I had not thought of doing a further degree and was at a loss as to how to proceed. I was told to 'go and talk to Ray Pahl – he is doing something interesting' and a long collaboration started from this encounter.

Ray Pahl was just at the start of his fieldwork in Sheppey and had asked school students to write essays about how they saw their future. This novel research approach had in fact first been used by Marie Jahoda and colleagues in their study of Marienthal – a small town stricken by mass unemployment in the 1930s (Jahoda *et al.* 2002). The school students saw their lives in fairly conventional ways – growing up, getting married, having children – where problems of unemployment were bypassed in their projections of a more rosy future. Since unemployment had been historically low in the decades leading up to the 1970s, the 1930s was the only obvious point of comparison. Ray Pahl saw Sheppey as his 'post-industrial laboratory' where these trends were being relived and hoped to find pointers to the consequences in more recent times. The prospect of growing up without work faced young people on Sheppey. The prospect of trying to understand this faced me as I embarked on my PhD thesis, which later became a book with the title echoing Ray Pahl's original article *For Richer, For Poorer: Growing Up In and Out of Work* (Wallace 1987). Ray Pahl's instincts as to future trends were correct and mass unemployment consequent on deindustrialisation soon confronted large parts of the UK, especially the traditional industrial areas, as well as other areas of Europe and the USA. It was a watershed in British ways of work, which had hitherto focused on the industrial work of men. This is why understanding changing patterns of work was so important at that time.

The 'Sheppey project' expanded into a more ambitious and systematic study when Ray Pahl won a Social Science Research Council grant on which I was employed as research fellow. Influenced by the ideas of Jay Gershuny (explained in more detail elsewhere in this book), the project involved a large-scale survey with in-depth interviews of sub-groups from the survey and was made public through a series of articles culminating in the book: *Divisions of Labour*. All of these sources were later deposited at the University of Essex archives for both qualitative and quantitative data, providing a rich source of material for future researchers. I have been slightly disturbed (but also honoured) to find out that my early forays into social research have been documented by others as an aspect of social history.

The research team at this point were housed in a property in Delamark Road purchased by Ray Pahl and offering a base from which to operate. The team consisted of PhD students Frances Evans and Bill Gourlay in addition to myself, all looking at different aspects of changing work patterns. Although this was practical in terms of accommodation (my previous lodgings on Sheppey had brought me into the edge of the criminal underworld), it did not turn out to be the happy intellectual community that had been hoped. Ray Pahl's role as landlord as well as project leader caused some controversy; Bill Gourlay dropped out and Frances Evans completed her PhD and went on to do other things. The overlapping and complicated divisions of labour implied by this ersatz household provoked and perhaps illustrated some of the difficulties of this approach.

One of the key concepts developed in *Divisions of Labour* is that of the 'household work strategy' and one of the key ways in which it was demonstrated in the book was through the evolution of women's work. Hitherto the focus had been on the male head of household as determining the labour market and social position of the family. Both social policies and sociologists subscribed to this fallacy even at a time when the rise in married women's labour force participation was striking and unprecedented in the post-war era, as Pahl noted (1984: 79). The refocus on household work strategies was a challenge to this conventional view and helped set the scene for a wider vision of male and female economic activity deriving from a more historical viewpoint. Hence, Pahl saw that we could better understand the future by first understanding the past.

The concept of the 'household work strategy' was based on the idea of a household negotiating the division of labour and securing sources of income as a collective unit. The concept of household was an improvement on that of family, recognising the complex ways in which households could be composed at any point in time (which might include lodgers, servants, various family members, dependent children and independent children, grandchildren, couples which may or may not be married, heterosexual and non-heterosexual relationships – not to speak of the domestic lives of researchers). In practice, Ray Pahl focused entirely on heterosexual couples and the more standard family (which was also the most common form of household at the time), but the concept nevertheless opened up new possibilities for understanding intimate relationships and their economic dimensions. The rise of single parent and a variety of other kinds of household arrangements was not acknowledged to the extent that it might have been and has been highlighted by subsequent scholarship. Work was also a broadened concept encompassing not just conventional waged employment but also domestic and childrearing work, work in the informal economy, work for friends and neighbours on a reciprocal or friendly basis, work for NGOs and charities, and so on. Pahl was a pioneer in putting all these kinds of work together into a complex whole drawn together by the idea of a household work strategy. The more emotional aspects of contemporary household relationships later developed by other authors was eschewed in favour of an economic anthropology perspective (Giddens 1991; Beck and Beck-Gernsheim 1995; Jamieson 1998). Ray Pahl's links to anthropology were developed through the linking of the departments of Social Anthropology and Sociology at the University of Kent.

Nevertheless, this was a breakthrough. Feminists had fought to have domestic or 'reproductive' work recognised as an aspect of contemporary life because it had generally been ignored by sociologists and the mass public. Ray's partner Jan Pahl was an important conduit for this feminist flow of ideas as she brought her own lens to bear on household relationships in a separate project through the domestic division of money (Pahl, J. 1989), having previously published on domestic violence as well as the earlier jointly authored *Managers and their Wives* (Pahl and Pahl 1971).

Ray Pahl took this on board and transformed it into a more complex analysis of domestic relationships encompassing all forms of work from washing up to reconstructing a house. The whole dimension of hidden labour in the activities of daily life, which were previously seen as trivial, were brought out for sociological scrutiny (Glucksman 1995). Finally, the idea of 'strategy' encompassed the way in which different household members fitted together their various contributions and portfolio of working activities to 'get by'. It assumed a rational renegotiation of income, relationships and activities. It was a clever idea, building on the thinking of others such as Sandra Wallman, which would have influence well beyond the Isle of Sheppey at the time he was writing (Crow 1989; Wallace 2002). Whether these kinds of activities added up to a rational negotiation between partners is controversial and is perhaps challenged as well as illustrated by the case study of Linda and Jim described later in this book.

Ray Pahl's aim in developing this idea was to challenge the fixation on conventional waged employment – or the lack of it – which had been a preoccupation of the 1970s for social scientists and policy-makers alike. In chapter 3 he reviews a wealth of literature going back a couple of centuries to show that cobbling together a complex portfolio of economic activities had always been the way in which households managed their fluctuating fortunes in the face of personal and historical change. The historical approach drew on a wealth of work, such as that of Tamara Hareven looking at the intersections of *Family Time and Industrial Time* across the western world, which was emerging at that time as a new way of appreciating historical change. Hareven's book was set in the USA (Hareven 1982). Reliance on waged employment, Pahl argued, had become the norm in the West over only a few decades in the twentieth century and people had adapted reluctantly. So modern Sheppey families were reflecting what had happened over a longer time scale (the case study of Linda and Jim illustrates this) but were also pointing the way towards the new era of 'getting by' with a variety of sources and activities, only some of which might be full-time waged employment. In principle, this could mean that if men lost their jobs, women could take over as breadwinners and men could move into the home through what had been called a 'revolving door' (Young and Willmott 1973). But how flexible were households really?

Chapter 10 of Pahl's book, which focuses quantitatively on on the domestic division of labour within households in the present, illustrates that the gendered interchange of work which rational choices would predict, does not in fact happen. Women were still mainly responsible for domestic work, especially when children were small, and the impact of men's contribution was negligible. 'It should be emphasized that, while employment status affects who does the task more than any other single variable, nevertheless, women being employed full-time or men being unemployed do not, as single variables, produce any significant shift away from the likelihood that the woman would do the task' (Pahl 1984: 270). In fact, hardly any of the usual variables made any difference. Neither class, nor politics nor other aspects of the work of households made much impact. The domestic division of labour remained stubbornly female-centred whatever the external conditions.

Although this was hotly debated, this remains the case in subsequent, much larger and even in international studies (see for example the work of Jackie O'Reilly using large cross-national data sets; O'Reilly *et al.* 2008). The only variable that had any significant impact on the gendered division of labour was whether women were employed full-time, part-time or not at all. The more they were employed in the labour market, the more likely it was that tasks were shared or devolved. 'The domestic division of labour is related directly to the economic activity of the female partner, the ages of the partners and their stage in the domestic cycle and to not much else' (Pahl 1984: 274). Even the ages of the partners reflected not so much a generational shift in values as the fact that the number and nature of tasks changed as people got older. One problem is that it is not clear how the direction of causality flowed in this analysis. Does bringing in an income allow women to assert themselves more in the domestic relations or does the presence of a more equal partnership allow women the opportunity to seek out and take up paid work? The results were at first rather a disappointment to the proponent of the household strategy approach: why did households not change? However, it did lead to new insights and theories.

Women were moving increasingly into paid employment as a normal extension of their roles. How can we account for the apparent lack of change in the traditional household division of labour? Some have called it the 'stalled revolution' (Hochschild 1989) and perhaps it illustrates the limitations of the view that the division of labour could be a rational calculation as economists (such as

Gary Becker) often assumed (Becker 1965). Jay Gershuny, working with larger, comparative longitudinal data sets, argues that this could also be seen as 'lagged adaptation' as women enter the workforce in greater numbers and for longer hours but value change takes place over a longer period – for men (Gershuny *et al.* 2005). Although men might be responsible for various household chores such as fixing the car or mowing the lawn, it is women who do most of the day-to-day work of reproducing the household. Paid employment for women meant taking on additional work while still having to manage the domestic sphere at the same time. Pahl's examples from Sheppey, as well ones from the past, illustrated the low wages and pitiful returns they had for their work in comparison to what men could earn. Therefore, Pahl recognised that a gendered understanding of work as part of the intersection of patriarchy and capitalism was necessary. Pahl concluded that work was more than just a set of tasks to get done. The social embeddedness of work and what it entails needs to be taken into account and this set the agenda for *Divisions of Labour*. Today we would include other aspects of this intersectionality which were not so visible at the time – ethnicity, migrant status, disability, sexuality and age might be just some of them.

The approach adopted in *Divisions of Labour* prompted a range of studies that tried to take into account the role of domestic work in relation to paid work so that nobody will be able to ever again subsume the distinction between 'work' and 'employment'. Studies included ones that attempted to further quantify these relationships as well as ones that sought to understand the meanings and negotiations behind them. A major ESRC initiative known as the Social Change and Economic Life Initiative (SCELI) sought to embed these relationships in an understanding of local labour markets and their variations, taking into account much larger regions than the Isle of Sheppey and ones intended to exemplify changes in Britain as a whole (Anderson *et al.* 1993; McEwan Scott 1994). This was a response to the criticism that Sheppey was a small and idiosyncratic island that exemplified an exceptional set of relationships rather than being the 'post-industrial laboratory' that Ray Pahl had envisaged. International studies such as the International Social Survey Programme (ISSP) adopted modules to reflect this and prominent sociologists such as Rosemary Crompton theorised these new relationships as a more relevant synthesis of patriarchy, class and capitalism (Crompton *et al.* 1996; Crompton 2006).

The key to understanding the household work strategy was therefore women's work. Pahl helped to shine a light on the many different kinds of work that women undertook both inside waged employment and out of it. The historical examples focused mostly on women and how they seized opportunities to keep themselves and their families out of poverty either as daughters or mothers. Many of his insights derived from the work of feminist historians such as Leonore Davidoff and Diana Gittins, who were keen to write the lives of working women back into history. Feminist sociologists such as Ann Oakley, Veronica Beechey and Marilyn

Porter pointed out the importance of domestic work in keeping society going. Other feminists went much further in criticising the family as a site of exploitation and a source of inequality (Barrett and McIntosh 1982). A number of debates developed as sociologists strove to make sense of this within the framework contemporary theories. Ray Pahl's work drew on these sources but also took them further in giving them contemporary relevance. Nevertheless, Pahl had quite a fraught relationship with feminism as illustrated in footnote 2 of chapter 3: 'One of the irritating aspects of some recent writing on women's work and employment is that the gender of the author is made strongly intrusive. Thus, a male reader of a book written by a female in this style is made to feel excluded and somehow at fault. This assumption by some writers that all their readers will be of the same gender is a divisive aspect in scholarship which cannot be welcomed' (1984: 63) This quotation perhaps illustrates the polarised social relations of British sociology at the time, with which Ray Pahl was struggling.

It is interesting to consider the role of irregular work that Pahl documented historically in terms of today's employment trends. It now seems more prescient than at the time. Low wages, insecurity and fragmented careers are perhaps an even stronger part of today's reality. Even in the elevated heights of the ivory tower, much of the day-to-day lecturing is done by part-time staff or people on temporary contracts. Throughout the western world the idea of full-time permanent work is seen as increasingly rare and is replaced instead by employment that is insecure and not full-time (part-time, zero hours contracts, etc.) creating a workforce of the 'precariat' (Standing 2014). This is no longer just a problem for women (although they are still often found among the precariat). The experiences of young people entering the labour force that I characterised in the 1980s as 'broken transitions' based on the Isle of Sheppey study (Wallace 1987) is now characterised by the collection of a complex basket of work opportunities which might include paid work in Costa coffee shops as well as unpaid (but greatly sought-after) internships or volunteer work to bolster citizenship and CVs. And it is no longer just a problem for the under-qualified. For graduates especially this kind of casual and non-standard work has become part of the 'normal transition' through education and into an increasingly balkanised labour market (Leccardi 2006). Constructing a finished and polished CV out of this basket of messy experiences has become a craft in itself.

The full-time work contract is less and less common for those entering the workforce, but also for those already in the workforce. While Pahl's study focused on working-class households, for whom precarity and instability might have been only a generation away, middle-class households are also increasingly faced with this kind of insecurity. Richard Sennett describes how he revisited some of the professional households involved in his earlier study of work and found that their main worries were about how secure their jobs were and trying to build careers on shifting foundations (Sennett 1998). The work on Sheppey helped to feed into debates about social class, which had come to dominate British sociology. This contributed to an understanding of the 'middle mass' based on dual incomes, distinguishing more prosperous households from those such as single parents who were associated more with an emerging 'underclass' (Murray 1984). These debates are taken up in Chapter 6 by John Holmwood. Social status, Pahl argued, was based less on traditional social cleavages between middle and working class but on households that were 'work rich' (with a number of earners) in contrast to those that were 'work poor' with one or none.

However, Pahl was perhaps too hasty to write off the achievements of what Goran Therborn has termed the 'golden age' of the welfare state (Therborn 1995). The welfare state in Europe, based on the assumption of a 'normal hetero-sexual couple family', helped to stabilise social relationships for some fifty years and gave people a sense of security and a longer-term planning horizon that had been impossible before it. The fact that it was based on the idea of a male breadwinner in most countries is precisely one of the factors that Pahl takes issue with and one that has been pointed out by feminist critics too (Lewis 1992). The 'golden age' based on the male breadwinner is increasingly replaced by more individualised welfare contracts reflecting the belated recognition of these shifts in employment relations by policy-makers and something that welfare states are still trying to come to terms with (Lewis 2001).

The idea of household work strategies and their implications for social stratification were taken up by Lydia Morris who was originally part of a study in Port Talbot working in parallel to the Sheppey study led by Chris Harris, whose work on the family formed part of the backdrop to this approach. Lydia Morris went on to look at the role of families, work and the division of labour in the North-East of England, but concluded that under some circumstances the division of labour *could* change. She drew comparisons between the UK and the USA in emphasising the way in which households were embedded in social networks, welfare systems and ethnic communities that shaped their cultural environment and the kinds of decisions they made (Morris 1990). Nevertheless, the division of household labour remained stubbornly gendered.

One factor that is clear from *Divisions of Labour* is that it is mainly a British – and in fact mainly an English – study. The examples are from England, which in some ways had quite a unique transition through de-ruralisation, to industrialisation and the modern world. How far was this typical elsewhere? In Italy, where Pahl wrote much of *Divisions of Labour*, watching the Tuscan sunsets from his aptly named cottage *D'Autore* (in English – 'of the author'), transformations in the division of labour were also taking place, but from different beginnings. The large, extended, traditional patriarchal family based on stay-at-home mothers was being eroded as he wrote, with dramatic falls in the number of children being born. In order to 'get by' households needed two earners, preferably two full-time ones, so Italian households had to develop new strategies for raising children – if they had any.

Although family help might still be important, the geographical mobility associated with modern employment regimes meant that they might not live close to relatives and were therefore forced to find alternatives (Abbott *et al.* 2013; Gstrein *et al.* 2014). Much of the domestic work of caring for relatives left behind, traditionally undertaken by non-employed women, was now outsourced to immigrant workers in the informal economy. While modern Italian women quickly adapted to these changing roles, at least some Italian men (like those in Sheppey) remained more traditional, refusing to leave the maternal nest and continuing to live large parts of their lives being serviced by 'Mama'. Household work strategies were important for understanding these changes, but perhaps in a different way to ones originally envisaged by Pahl. Much of this shift was documented by Ray Pahl's old friend in Milan: Enzo Mingione.

In the Soviet Union these transitions were even more extreme. For several decades, the countries dominated by Soviet communism had developed a work–gender–welfare contract which involved the full-time employment of both men and women but supported by extensive childcare facilities, at least in the later years of the regime. Men's and women's roles were nevertheless heavily gendered and there were no feminist challenges to these popular assumptions (Corrin 1992; Wallace 2000). The collapse of this system, which happened within a decade of the publication of *Divisions of Labour*, meant a renegotiation of gender roles in the context of economic collapse even more stark than that on the Isle of Sheppey. The Soviet communist system was able to survive for a long period partly due to a thriving informal sector which had kept the wheels of the economy turning and helped to preserve the livelihood and mental health of the population. Ray Pahl's awareness of this had stemmed from his friendship with colleagues in Czechoslovakia (now the Czech and Slovak republics) such as Jiří Musil and in Hungary with Endre Sik and Iván Szelényi, where the informal economy was most developed and most researched (see Pahl 1988 and Szelényi 1988). His interests in these changing divisions of labour helped him to look eastward to understand what was happening there. However, the inability of people to adjust quickly to these changes took their toll in the form of an escalating health crisis accompanying the economic one. Men literally died when they were not able to adapt. They died of suicide, alcoholism, accidents and cardio-vascular disease, all of which spiralled from the 1980s onwards and especially after the collapse of communism (Haerpfer *et al.* 2013). Women, like the ones in Pahl's historical studies, showed their flexibility as well as their low aspirations by trying to get by as best they could and thus ensuring the survival of their families (Abbott and Wallace 2007).

These illustrations from different parts of the world show the power of understanding social change through the prism of all forms of work and their gendered implications embodied in the idea of 'household work strategy'. This awareness was reflected in the publication of the edited collection *On Work* which included chapters from these broader contexts and international studies (Pahl 1988).

It is also relevant in other non-western contexts. In much of the global South, paid employment is the exception rather than the rule and the way in which households, as the basic units of production, are able to get by depends on an understanding of household work strategies. These can include non-resident kin who might be responsible for subsidising households through remittances, illustrating that the household work strategy could be a transnational one too. Arlie Hochschild and Barbara Ehrenreich's influential work on 'care chains' illustrated how domestic work and caring for dependent relatives can take place on a transnational basis and form the reason for migration, which has become increasingly feminised (Ehrenreich and Hochschild 2003). Thus, Filipino immigrant women would care for children as 'nannies' in New York while, back home, someone else was caring for their own children.

Miriam Glucksmann further developed this theme by arguing more recently for a re-invigoration of the understanding of work, taking into account the Total Social Organisation of Labour (Glucksmann 2009). This would break down barriers between consumption and production, public and private, work and employment, paid and unpaid, domestic and global by bringing a more comprehensive model to bear which would take account of different scales and different dimensions of work. Building on Pahl and Gershuny's earlier work she ambitiously points the way towards understanding social relations in the twenty-first century. From this perspective it is not simply a case of finding different case studies from around the world to exemplify variations in divisions of labour, but of understanding their essential interconnections.

The various arms of the debates that stretched in new directions and connected with other issues and discussions illustrate the continuing relevance of *Divisions of Labour* for understanding contemporary social life. Many of the insights derived from intensive study of a small island in the Thames Estuary had ramifications far wider than could ever have been initially envisaged.

4 Time and place in memory and imagination on the Isle of Sheppey

Dawn Lyon

Introduction

Much has been said already about the influential sociological text, *Divisions of Labour*, published by Ray Pahl in 1984, and the research that led up to it from the late 1970s. It has been read as an unintended community study, as a site for the study of social change, for its significant conceptual contribution to the sociology of work and the relationship between formal, informal, paid and unpaid socio-economic modes, and for its careful empirical documentation and analysis of social polarisation between work-rich and work-poor households. It is a strange task to return to such a text and its associated materials and to feel the ways they stir the imagination in the search for new insights and fresh analyses. The stance I take here as a 'restudy researcher' is to look again at Pahl's writing and archive – along with additional material that his work has since inspired – and draw into the foreground some elements and themes which did not take centre stage in *Divisions of Labour*. Rather than aiming to fill any explicit gaps (cf. Lassiter 2012) or take issue with Pahl's earlier analysis, this is intended as a complement to his work and one that works with his ethnographic sensibility. In particular, I seek to demonstrate the gain of bringing our sociological attention to the temporal and spatial texture of everyday life in the Sheppey materials, something which can easily slip from view when we focus on broader sociological themes and arguments.

In what follows, I discuss Pahl's approach to doing sociology, something about which he is explicit in his comments on the sociologist's tools and tasks, and something which is felt between the lines of his work. I then explain the reused and replicated data on which this chapter is based. The discussion that follows is in two parts. In the first, I explore the ways in which place is a site of affective attachment, produced through the rhythms and routines of everyday life, with particular reference to the atmosphere of the 'bike rush' of dockyard workers as recalled in oral history interviews. In the second, I make use of young people's imagined futures to explore time, space and the operation of class.

Doing sociology: Ray Pahl in Sheppey

Pahl spent the best part of a decade on the Isle of Sheppey in Kent, as a setting for his investigations into the different configurations of 'forms' and 'sources' of labour used by the household to get work done, and the divisions of labour within the household to settle the allocation of tasks (Pahl 1984: 148). While he was keen to identify the 'household strategies' associated with these configurations, he was also profoundly interested in the lived experience of sorting out 'who does what'. His approach was a broad and deep engagement with the reach of the economic, social and cultural into the inner worlds of people's lives and the micro-level arrangements and conditions in which these lives took shape, through time and in the everyday.

If Pahl sought out how the connections between 'public issues' and 'private troubles' were lived through time (1984: 7), he made a calculated judgement to foreground two types of data in the analysis he developed in *Divisions of Labour*. Despite being wary of the 'snapshot approach of the survey' and habitually 'bemoaning the lack of detailed ethnography of ordinary people's lives' (1984: 7), in the bulk of his empirical chapters, he opted for the power of quantitative analysis of the household survey data he had collected. At the same time, he emphasised that his arguments were also 'based on years of informal and qualitative interviewing and observation' (1984: 13), explaining that 'in the early years' he concentrated on 'a relatively small number of households and built up a picture in each case of all the forms of work in which members of those households were engaged' (1984: 148). He pursued an 'anthropological' style of research (1984: 198, 213), recalling many evenings spent 'simply talking generally to people about the Island' (1984: 185) (often in the pub) and going as far as to buy a house in Sheerness in 1980 as a base for the research team (1984: 214) pictured in Figure 4.1. While recognising the value of his approach for understanding the forms of work in which people engaged and gaining direct experience of 'forming social relationships with one section of the Island's population' (1984: 214), at times he lamented the consequences of such extensive data collection: 'Having spent six years visiting and doing fieldwork on the Island and spending time in particular factories, streets and communities, I feel daunted at times by the overwhelming wealth of information' (1984: 155).

In addition to the quantitative analysis in Part II of the book, Pahl devotes one chapter (chapter 11) to two case studies of particular households and their contrasting – indeed *polarised* – experiences and strategies: Linda and Jim (discussed by Jane Elliott and Jon Lawrence in Chapter 5 in this volume), and Beryl and George. Despite having conducted one or more 'extensive interviews' with 'thirty-two selected households', quotations from which were 'laboriously coded and filed' (1984: 277), Pahl is open about his deliberate decision 'to deny the reader these expected aids to empathetic understanding', arising from his ethical and methodological commitment to avoid doing 'violence to the complexity that the interviews revealed', in a way that would have 'simplified and insulted' their 'humanity' (1984: 278).

4.1 Pahl's house, 'The Olives', Delamark Road

More generally, Pahl was not satisfied with the 'tools of sociological investigation', which he described as 'coming between me and the people whose everyday lives I was trying to understand' (1984: 8). He was further sceptical about the adequacy of sociological forms of representation of work and community, and wondered if his Sheppey research would be better explored in the form of a novel, film or TV script (cf. Ronald Blythe's 1969 account of *Akenfield*) (Pahl 1984: 2). In the Introduction to *Divisions of Labour*, he reflects on whether and how to use images in the book, and the place of the visual more generally in his research. The final publication does include some general historical images of work in Part I, and ten contemporary photographs in Part II of everyday spaces and activities on Sheppey which resonate with his arguments and help convey a sense of place to the reader. In the introduction to 'Portrait of an Industrial Island', he powerfully evokes scenes of Sheerness streets: 'In summer elderly women put wooden chairs on the pavement to sit and chat and a group of lads strip a motorbike on the pavement'; and later in the same paragraph: 'A large Ford van with a "J" registration, painted entirely black, has the words "Funeral Service" on the side.' We see just these things in the photographs selected for inclusion in the original book. In addition there is a map of the Island included in the book (see Figure 4.2), annotated in relation to the use and character of the space, notably including several holiday camps, a prison complex and extensive car parking (for newly imported vehicles).

We can see clearly the 'geographer turned sociologist' (Savage 2010: 5) in this representation. Pahl had long been interested in the 'reciprocal relationship between the social structure and the spatial structure' (Pahl 1970: 53), between space and class, and he sought 'to develop a spatialized conception of social change' (Savage 2010: 159). In his work on Sheppey and elsewhere, he was 'consistently mindful of the importance of the spatial context in which social processes of polarization were working themselves out' (Crow and Takeda 2011: 2.1). Space, it seems, rereading his work today, was more than a material setting for social relations, it was a 'way of understanding' the 'interplay of people and the environment' (Creswell 2004: 11) and recognised as produced through those social relations.

Divisions of Labour also demonstrates Pahl's interest and thinking in different coexisting temporalities. The longevity of the project itself is felt in the depth of engagement with the people and place through time. It is also a reflection that takes temporality seriously, reaching back and forth to explore the sad momentum of trajectories of decline (as in the case of Linda and Jim), and the 'impressive and alarming' (Pahl 1978) maturity of young people facing an uncertain future. He is interested in the emergence of Sheppey as the place it became in the 1980s, connected to histories and traditions that might no longer be held in conscious awareness, but made themselves felt through people's 'latent beliefs and values that have emerged out of their own and their parents', and perhaps grandparents', experiences' (Pahl 1984: 185). And he is attuned to an anticipatory mode of sociological analysis developing an 'unusual temporal device of projecting forward' (Strangleman, Chapter 1 in this volume).

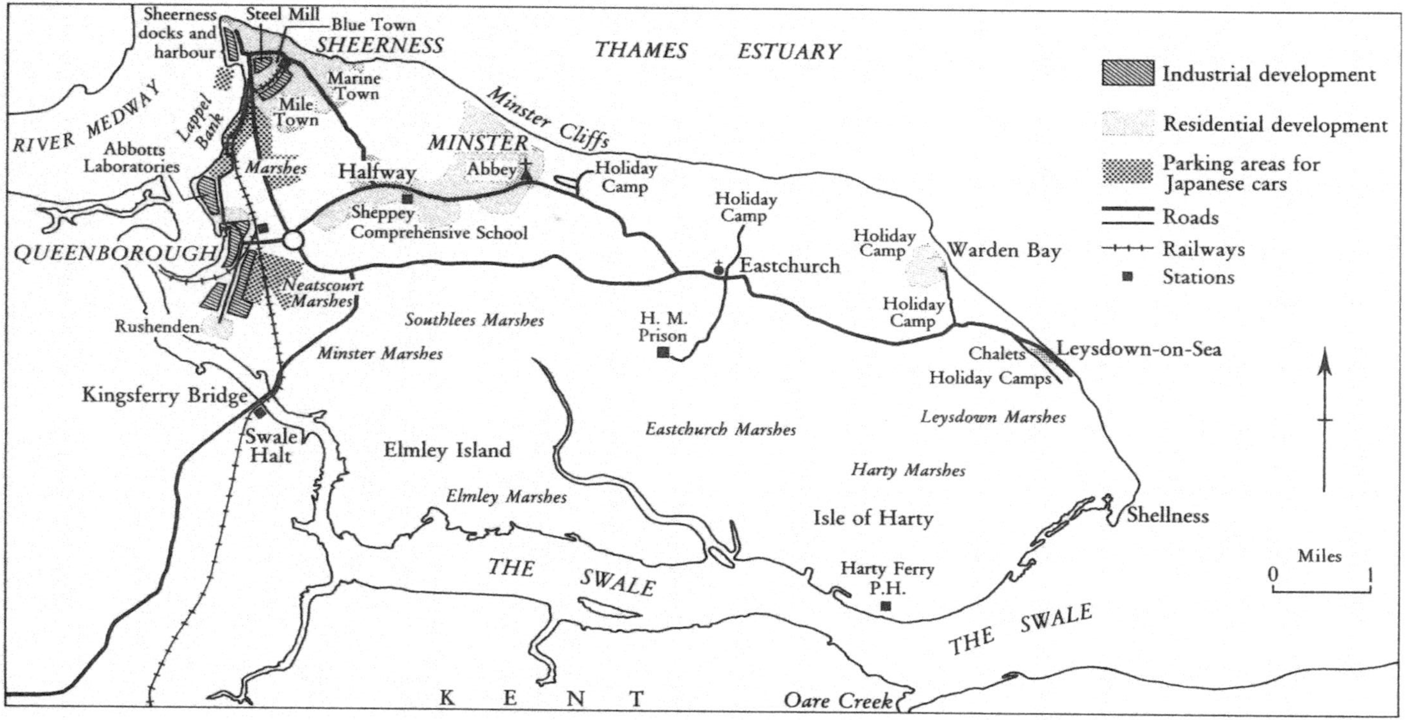

4.2 Map of the Isle of Sheppey published in *Divisions of Labour*

Revisiting and replicating Pahl's work

In recent years, together with colleagues,[1] I have 'revisited' Sheppey, exploring through secondary analysis some of the data that indirectly shaped *Divisions of Labour*, and conducting new research replicating and extending a small portion of those data (Crow and Lyon 2011; Lyon and Crow 2012; Lyon, Morgan and Crow 2012). In two projects *Living and Working on Sheppey* (2009–11)[2] and *Imagine Sheppey* (2013–14),[3] we collected oral history interviews, 'imagined futures' essays and produced new visual documents about the past, present and future of selected sites and people in Sheppey.

The different strands of these new projects have positioned us in various ways in relation to the original material, Pahl himself and his team of researchers, as well as the setting of the research on the Isle of Sheppey. We had access to archived material that included 'behind the scenes' (McLeod and Thomson 2009: 125) memos among the research team, 'marginalia' such as notes and comments on the data, odds and ends gathered in ways that can no longer be traced such as photos and small objects, and the data itself in the form of tapes, transcripts, and hand-written essays. This additional archive material was too fragmentary to be amenable to the same analysis as the main data set, as Goodwin and O'Connor (2015) argue they should be. However, it did give us glimpses into the methodological inspiration of these strands of the original project and the thinking and interests of the research team as the study developed. This was complemented by the informal discussions and interviews we (Graham Crow and I) were able to conduct with members of the original research team, especially with Pahl himself (July 2009), which added further context about the research process.

While the data we selected for the new projects – oral histories and imagined futures essays – had already been analysed (Pahl 1978; Buck 1981) and used to inform *Divisions of Labour*, there was more to say, both about these data, and how they inspired us to collect new data in a similar way. We brought some different questions to the study, for instance about attachment to place and attention

1 Giulia Carabelli, Graham Crow, Peter Hatton, Jenny Hurkett, Bethany Morgan Brett, Tim Strangleman, Alice Young, and the artists group 'Tea'.

2 The *Living and Working on Sheppey* project was funded by the HEFCE-financed South East Coastal Communities Programme: www.coastalcommunities.org.uk/. The project team included academics from sociology and arts at the universities of Kent and Southampton, staff from the UK Data Archive, University of Essex, the artists group Tea, and members (staff and community volunteers) of the Blue Town Heritage Centre, an information, resource and visitor centre on the history of Blue Town and the Isle of Sheppey. Until his death in June 2011, Ray Pahl was an informal consultant to the project.

3 *Imagine Sheppey* was part of a large Connected Communities research grant from an AHRC/ESRC joint initiative on Community Engagement and Mobilisation. The larger project is 'The social, historical, cultural and democratic context of civic engagement: imagining different communities and making them happen' – or *Imagine* for short – grant no ES/K002686/1.

to atmosphere, embodiment and notions of destiny, fate and luck, informed by present-day debates that were not prominent at the time of the original research. This meant that our reanalysis was able to lead to new insights about old data, to making different sense, something which delighted Pahl as we discussed our emergent thinking with him (interview with Pahl, July 2009). As our own work has developed, we have become more interested, following Mische (2009), in future orientations and projectivity as an aspect of agency in particular among young people, further demonstrating the mutability of a set of projects through time.

In *Living and Working on Sheppey*, one starting point was the eight interviews conducted by Pahl and colleague Nick Buck in the early 1980s with former workers at the Royal Sheerness Naval Dockyard on the creation and collapse of an occupational community (Buck 1981). We sought to extend this collection and working with community interviewers collected 33 additional oral history interviews (25 men, 8 women) with older people who had either a direct or indirect experience of working in the dockyard (which closed in 1960). We took inspiration from themes that cut across *Divisions of Labour* and asked people about their experiences of growing up – family life, education and looking to the future; working life; family formation and housing; Blue Town (the residential area immediately adjacent to the dockyard) and Sheppey; geographical mobility; social life and leisure; and retirement, past and future. This group of interviewees, identified through snowball sampling from contacts at the Blue Town Heritage Centre, included people whose early lives or experiences of work were bound up with the dockyard, either through formal employment or in the informal economy that was connected to it, for instance, their associations with the bakery, launderette and newsagents close by.

A second strand of the *Living and Working on Sheppey* project was a direct replication of an exercise undertaken by Pahl in 1978: the collection of essays written by school leavers imagining themselves towards the end of their lives and looking back. Fascinated by the essay-writing technique (Himmelweit *et al.* 1952; Veness 1962; Jahoda *et al.* 2002), Pahl undertook this sub-project early on during his time on Sheppey as part of his efforts to understand how the chronic economic challenges of the period were affecting ordinary people's everyday lives locally. It was one of his exploratory projects – 'sort of a pilot thing' (interview with Pahl, July 2009). Inspired by this material, and by other research using similar techniques to explore young people's aspirations, hopes and dreams (Rex and Moore 1967; Thomson and Holland 2002; Bulbeck 2005; Elliott 2010; McDonald *et al.* 2011), we replicated this exercise in 2009–10.[4] In a similar strategy to that used by Pahl, we approached teachers as collaborators to set the essay-writing task, and asked young people: 'Imagine that you are towards the end of your life. Look back over your life and say what happened to you.' We now have two sets of young

4 For simplicity, from now on, we refer to the 2010 essay writers instead of 2009–10.

people's accounts,[5] set thirty years apart but marked by similar circumstances of global economic crisis and recession.

We conceptualise the future not as a distinct and disconnected temporality but a horizon that is 'the assemblage of past and present temporalities' (Coleman 2008). Mische (2009) calls for an understanding of human action that 'is constructed within an imaginative horizon of multiple plans and possibilities' (2009: 696); experience is therefore inherently experimental, and characterised by projection (2009: 697). The present-future connection – projectivity – is therefore central to social being and social action. Although we do not read the imagined futures written by young people as 'predictive, or constituting a type of plan that they expected to work towards', we do see their narratives, following Sanders and Munford, 'as expressing their understanding of their present time worlds and the possibilities they see for girls and young women [as well as boys and young men] like themselves' (Sanders and Munford 2008: 331). This may well be significant for how they go on to live. As such, these reflective essays are a 'questioning exploration' which shed light on how young people may make their way through the world (Archer 2007: 73, 65).

Among the archived material of the original project, we came across handwritten notes by Pahl, recorded on cards in the box with the 1978 essays. 'Total fantasy', says one (about essay 8); 'totally unrealistic idea of what he earns and what he gets – own house, car etc.' says another (about essay 38). These are fascinating insights into Pahl's thinking through the data, both in terms of his authoritative stance based on his 'superior' socio-economic knowledge and understanding of the allocation of opportunities, and in terms of themes that sparked his interest. Certainly the theme of fantasy in the lives of young people stayed with him (e.g. Pahl 1995: 150–1).

The Isle of Sheppey was a case study for Pahl's interest in households' and individuals' practices and strategies for 'getting by'. While he makes no claim to the 'typicality' of Sheppey,[6] his analysis was attentive to the particularity of place. In sympathy with this approach, taking a single street on the Isle of Sheppey, Blue Town High Street, the artists Tea[7] worked with both younger and older people (including some of those involved in the other strands of the project) to record memories and imaginations of the past and future. From this they produced a visual and aural montage of a journey along the high street through time,[8] which is also an exploration of the past, present and future of life and work on Sheppey.

5 In the 1978 collection, n=141 (89 boys, 52 girls); in 2009–10, n=110 (52 girls, 55 boys, 3 unknown).

6 Pahl was attracted to Sheppey for its self-contained character, distinctiveness, reputation for informal work, pattern of unemployment and marginality (1984: 144–6).

7 www.teaweb.org/.

8 *Back and Forth on High Street Blue Town* at: www.livingandworkingonsheppey.co.uk/blue-town-high-street-a-video-by-tea/.

In our follow-on project, *Imagine Sheppey,* we extended our work with young people using arts practice to further explore how they are 'oriented' (Ahmed 2006) towards the future. In a series of arts-based workshops led by Tea, we intervened in selected sites on the Island to alter the space as an experience of change – temporal, material and symbolic. We recorded improvised performances that captured stances towards the future that could not be articulated in language alone, and made use of these images for elicitation in focus groups with a wider group of young people (Lyon and Carabelli 2015; Carabelli and Lyon 2016).

Remembering place and atmosphere

Sheppey evokes strong feelings of both affection and disgust on the part of Islanders and others, and it remains a stigmatised place within and beyond Kent. Both sets of oral history interviews with Sheppey dockyard workers and those associated with it (from 1981 and 2010) reveal strong forms of attachment to the Island, for instance: 'Where do I belong? On Sheppey, no doubt', comments Norman Folds;[9] 'Oh yeah, proud I'm an Islander, I'm a Sheppeyite, yeah', asserts Barry Alba; and simply, 'I love the Island', states Louise Marsden.

Sheppey is often described as a place that 'feels like home' – an affective attachment also reported by Pahl (1984: 189). This is interesting as according to Pahl's survey, two-fifths of all households had come to the Island since the closure of the dockyard in 1960, yet 'the *traditions* of the Island to which they perforce subscribe are those myths based on the pre-closure world' (1984: 193, emphasis in original). At the same time, distinctions persist. There are those who are 'proud … to have been born on the island' (1984: 193) in relation to whom contrasts are drawn with 'people from abroad, they call us', from 'across the bridge' (Harry Coombes) 'foreigners' (Stewart Anderson) – albeit a characterisation reportedly made with humour. These are distinctions that have persisted since the 'borders' that were enforced earlier in the twentieth century. As a strategically important location in defence terms and designated a Special Military Area in the First World War, passports were required to move on and off the Island. This was repeated during the Second World War, and is clearly still alive in the local imagination.

Others explain the spatial and social composition and contrasts *within* the Island, for instance between a Queenborium, a Blue Towner, or Swampy 'who used to be called Wessies [from West Minster]'; 'there's no room for anybody else' (Harry Coombes); and between Blue Town and the rest of Sheerness (Harvey Jones): 'Blue Town, oh that dump' (Charlie Arnolds) it was 'the poor end of the Island' (Gavin Frinstead) 'the poor end of Sheerness' but 'where most of the work was' (George James). 'I look on Sheppey as three different places, to be

9 All names are pseudonyms.

honest with you', comments Oscar Thomas. He goes on to make a distinction between the 'top end' referring to Leysdown and the beach, from Eastchurch to Warden Bay and Harty, then Minster and Queenborough.

There are finer-grained distinctions still around the site of the Dockyard itself. As Pahl reports:

> The main outlines of the town of Sheerness were determined in the nineteenth century … The houses in Marine Town were of considerably better quality than in Blue Town or Mile Town and attracted the better paid dockyard workers. Shipwrights and metalworkers in particular were concentrated in Mile Town. Segregation by social status existed at a very local level. (Pahl 1984: 162)

Beyond Sheerness, towards the centre of the Island, Minster is composed of privately owned, individually built houses inhabited by more prosperous local people. Between the two – Sheerness and Minster – lies the aptly named Halfway, where newly built estates have attracted commuters (Wallace 1987: 13). To the south of Sheerness, the faded prosperity of Queenborough is evident in period architecture whereas the Rushenden Road Estate is 'an all too obvious machine for workers to reproduce themselves in' (Pahl 1984: 153).

'Outsiders' who did not pass the dockyard entrance exams could nevertheless work there as semi-skilled workers or labourers (Buck 1981: 77) but did not benefit from the same conditions as the key tradespeople. Life was further divided between those who had access to the other side of the wall, and those who did not. While there were women workers in the dockyard, 'there was an awful lot of women in the [town], and wives in Blue Town [who] had never been over the other side of the wall', reports Harry Coombes, despite family access on Navy Days. He continues:

> Their husbands came out every day and they never knew where they worked, and they never said much, and I find that quite extraordinary, and I didn't want to be one of them who wondered what was [there], because it was right opposite my house. There was a great big wall, we couldn't see over it …

As a child, he was determined not to be excluded and repeatedly found his way into the dockyard to deliver newspapers in person, despite the challenges of getting through the police security at the South Gate, where 'every day they, they treated you like you were a stranger'.

Attachment to place is often articulated in the interviews through the evocation of the atmospheres, rhythms and routines of everyday life. A prominent episode recounted by interviewees is the so-called 'bike rush'. Interestingly, this was not explicitly mentioned by Pahl in *Divisions of Labour* which shows the ways in which our questioning – both to generate data and in the questions we ask of the data – opens up or closes down different areas of discussion. Many of those working at the dockyard travelled to and fro by bike and since they often lived

4.3 Dockyard workers, 1959

close by, also left the dockyard to return home for lunch (one and a quarter hours).[10] This was a collective routine that marked time and place and was a visual and sensory spectacle for those who took part in it or witnessed it. Christian Day and Kevin Riley talk about the sound that signalled the start of the exodus and the congestion that followed when the bikes 'used to cover the whole road … the whole width of the road' (Oliver Tide).

> I used to cycle to work, and going down the Blue Town Road, towards the, the South Gate, the one that's bricked up now, err, just inside the South Gate there they used to have a bell, and they used to ring the bell at ten to seven, just two or three times, and then when it got to two minutes to seven they used to ring it continuously, so you would hear the ding, ding [*laughter*] and you knew … The dockyard sort of tended to dominate the town to a certain extent, because particularly at knocking off time there just used to be a mass of bikes used to come up that Blue Town Road, and up the High Street to the town clock … you know, it was like an invasion really, and the same going the other way. (Christian Day)

> You can imagine the first hooter going coming out and if you stood there you'll get crushed with the bikes coming out and people coming out. It was just like the Tour de France, everybody was hurtling up the High Street here, getting out on their bikes. (Kevin Riley)

Harriet Esham recalls a second-hand account of the lunchtime 'rush' and marvels at the mental image it conjures up for her.

10 When lunch was reduced to one hour, it was no longer possible to return home (Clive Linders).

> He said, 'You wouldn't dare set foot out of, of the shop when the men were coming home for lunch', and he said, 'Anyone on a bike would never fall off', because, you know, the road was just congested, everyone just kept out of the way when the men were coming home and going back to work.' It must have been a sight … it really must.

There is both fascination and fear in these accounts that suggest onlookers both enjoyed the speed of the crowd while being mindful of warnings to 'steer clear'. 'It wasn't everybody who could afford even, even afford a bike then', Marjorie Jenkins points out, and buses also competed for space close to the South Gate. Not everyone had to contend with the masses either. 'That's another thing that annoyed the workmen', Kevin Jones reports, 'you see, the clerks, the pen pushers, they used to come out five minutes early – so that they were away before the bell rung for us you see.' Still, Oliver Tide wonders now 'why was we [in] such a mad panic you know', but at the time 'it was like you had to get home … and I remember head down, coming round near the, the railway station, and I ploughed into the back of someone [*laughter*] knocked this chap flying and I went flying!'

The ways in which the bike rush is recounted draw our attention to 'the production of atmospheres' (Böhme 1993: 116) through specific forms of interaction and movement. An atmosphere 'proceeds from and is created by things, persons, or their constellations' (1993: 122), in this case the collective movement of the bikes along and beyond Blue Town High Street. The presence of the dockyard shaped the structure of the High Street quite literally with the wall that separated the space of work from other spheres of life, the shops and services that lined the high street (a post office, tailors, cobblers, launderette, more than one butchers, bakers and newsagents, as well as numerous pubs and social clubs and densely packed housing). In addition, it set the tone of the patterns of the day, and the interactions that took place in the street. The bike rush produced a sense of belonging, experienced as a 'spatially extended quality of feeling' and felt as a 'bodily state of being' (Böhme 1993: 118) whether on a bike itself or as an onlooker on the pavement.

For Harry Coombes, recalling his memories of the bike rush as a 10-year-old boy, the passage of the bikes, 'the hundreds and hundreds of bicycles each day which came from West Minster and all the towns beyond and Queenborough' was bound up with the economy of his father's newsagents shop where he used to work:

> It was a goldmine, that little shop was on the bike run for the dockyard workers … Around about seven o'clock you'd hear the hooter go and my dad would say 'right, you go and do the bike run'. And I had to go out and stand on the kerbside outside my dad's shop and we would have newspapers rolled up with ten Weights or ten Woodbines [cigarettes] in there and you'd hand them out.

The young Harry who 'did this for years' understood the routines of the dockyard workers, including the alternative paths taken by those who 'had put money on a horse' and so 'would cycle round the other way, and round the back of the shop'. This produced an additional form of work:

> So my father and I then on Saturdays had to go debt collecting [*laughter*] to collect the money for ciggies and newspapers over in West Minster mainly. Always got paid eventually, because it was such a closed community on an island if anybody owed you money they would all lobby to make sure that you got paid, and there had to be a really good reason not to pay.

When the dockyard closed, the absence of these workers and their everyday routines transformed the social and sensory environment of Blue Town and Sheerness in particular. While many left the area once characterised as 'full of people' (Dennis Kew), those who witnessed its 'sad' (Oliver Tide) and 'ugly' (Pahl 1984: 152) decline and the 'neglect' (Harriet Esham) that followed recall the contrast between the liveliness of the everyday in the time of the dockyard and post-closure stillness.

> It was just like a load of cattle all coming out on bikes. You couldn't walk, you know, it was about five adrift all up the High Street, the whole lot for about five or ten minutes they all came out. Yeah, so it is quite considerable the way life has changed, yeah. (Gavin Frinstead)

> I used to like watching all the men coming out on their bikes at lunchtime. I used to stand in the town near the clock sometimes … and when that went the town seemed bereft, um, it was so quiet, and then of course everything started to fold up after that, and that's when I first noticed the disintegration of the town. (Olga Biggins)

With reference to the 'two or three places on Blue Town High Street' that were storage spaces for the '4700 or something like that' dockyard workers' push-bikes (George James) – it was necessary to have a permit to take a bike onto the dockyard itself – Kevin Riley remembers the change in the physical and material

4.4a and 4.4b The dockyard wall and former South Gate

space of the town in a relatively short space of time: 'Then you could look a year later and look up there and there was nothing'. This extended to the commercial life of the street too: 'Shops closed, it was just absolutely awful'.

Interviewees also remark on what happened to the physical infrastructure of the dockyard itself. 'The Dockyard was just flattened more or less', claims Sam Morris, making the comparison with Chatham which closed later in 1984 and was retained as a heritage site. Key markers on the landscape that sustain memory have themselves disappeared: 'I – it's nothing actually as I remember it, not really'. Confronted with the idea of being able to move now however, there are different views: 'If I come into money, I would seriously think of leaving the Island … Because it's not the Island anymore', Marvin Ramsey asserts. At the other end of the spectrum, Charlie Arnolds's attachment to place is enduring: 'I think if I was to win the bloody lottery tomorrow, I wouldn't move off the Island.'

Space, time and class in future-imagining

In contrast to the focus on memory in this chapter so far, I now want to turn attention to the temporal and spatial imagination of younger Sheppey residents. Lisa, a workshop participant in the *Imagine Sheppey* project, produced a collage representing her sense of time and locatedness. In this collage (Figure 4.5) at first the viewer is struck by the linearity between past, present and future, all anchored in place, and a specific place at that, using twentieth-century images of Sheerness. However, on closer inspection, the picture fragments. In contrast to the legible representations of a knowable past, the future cannot come into view. There is 'hope' and even 'love' which may or may not be read as directly linked to 'your path'. But there is no clear temporal direction as slivers of images send the viewer's gaze up, along, down and around. There is no 'pre-composed plot' that can be foreseen (Ingold 2007: 78, 75).

Similarly, when we replicated the task that had been set by Pahl more than thirty years earlier, asking young people to write from the present about a future that is past, the exercise revealed the different ways they were grappling with the unknown, the uncertain and the unpredictable. Nevertheless, their future-as-past accounts reveal the transmission of everyday cultures of life, work and community and a sense of one's place in the world, geographically, socially and symbolically. Hearing directly from young people about their hopes, dreams and fears also highlights the contrast of myth – of Islanders having low aspirations – with reality, as noted in the original studies (Pahl 1984: chapter 7; Wallace 1987: 14 and Chapter 3 this volume). At the same time, the essays are 'multi-voiced texts' hinting at others' values and aspirations for the essay writer as repertoires and resources for sense-making. In the context of the closure of the dockyard as the sole significant and centuries-old employer, we can glean the workings of the 'half-life of deindustrialisation' (Strangleman, Chapter 1, drawing on Linkon 2014) in

4.5 Collage: 'The future is unclear' (Lisa, *Imagine Sheppey*)

the psyches of young islanders who have grown up in the shadow of the former dockyard and the ruins of associated industries.

One of Mische's dimensions of projectivity is 'reach' which refers to the 'degree of extension that imagined futures have into the short, middle and long term, along with the future scenarios imagined at each stage' (2009: 699). Reading the essays for their temporal landscapes, it was clear that across the two cohorts (1978 and 2010), the near future was widely experienced as being 'at the threshold of my life' (F117/1978), 'it was like turning into a new world' (F124/1978), being 'released from prison' (M7/1978). 'The path seemed longer than usual' wrote one young man in 1978, 'as soon as I walked out of the gate I felt free' (M86/1978); leaving school was 'one of the saddest days of my life' (M28/1978), wrote another, for the loss of friends. This transition required courage: 'I'm holding the key, but dare I open the door?' (F51/2010). In the following excerpt, the realisation of transition is recounted in retrospect but is already anticipated in the present at the time of writing.

> I left school in 1979 with five CSE all of average grades and qualifications in commercial studies. I found my first job as a copy typist in the local factory in a tiny office with old tables as the desk. The pay wasn't particularly good but it was the expiereance[11] that I was after not the money. That job however lasted 3 months

11 Spellings retained as in the original essays.

> and I found myself looking very hard for another which I feel was the first real stop in my life. It was then that I realised that I had truly left school and all its security and I was now to face the big outside world and take life and its problems as a mature adult. (F97/1978)

End points are imagined in a variety of ways among which there are several dominant forms. These include being in retirement – usually from between 60 and 80; or close to death, at times in a state of satisfaction, at others in despair. In addition, many young essay writers situated themselves as under 50, a life marker beyond which it was impossible to imagine. 'At forty, I can safely say my life had ended' (M4/1978) writes one young man in 1978. Another emphasises the unchanging character of time once certain milestones were achieved: 'Not much happened after that, it was just day in day out routine' (M42/1978). We can make

4.6 Child in alleyway

4.7 The Sheppey Bridge viewed from the Island

sense of this in multiple ways, for instance as an 'extended present' (Brannen and Nilsen 2002), or the impossibility of life projects as an instance of 'fragmented reflexivity' (Archer 2007). Furthermore, although there is less emphasis on 'chronologised milestones' in 2010 compared to 1978, we do find evidence of considerable 'clarity' (Mische 2009), that is the degree of detail in which young people imagine their lives, including 'hyper-planning' (Hockey 2009: 228) in the face of uncertainty. This supports the argument that young people from less-privileged backgrounds are more reflexive in their planning than their middle-class peers (Laughland-Booÿ, Mayall and Skrbiš 2014; Bryant and Ellard 2015).

Turning to the presence of place in the young people's accounts, approximately half of the young essay writers in each cohort made reference to the locations in which they might live and work. This included the reproduction of negative local images and seeking an improved life setting: wanting to leave 'this domp of a place' (M64/1978), 'a dump like Sheppey' (M71/1978), albeit perhaps in recognition that 'there weren't enough opportunities on the Island' (F72/2010). Life is imagined to be better elsewhere: 'I would also dream of the day that I would leave the island for good' (F110/1978); and 'I hope to have a reasonably big house that is preferably off the island' (F38/2010). Others, however, reject negative representations of Sheppey and talk about the value of the Island in relation to family and a sense of 'home' and belonging, for instance: 'I live on the Isle of Sheppey and I quite like it here actually. It is a nice place to live, and if I ever moved away I would be leaving so many friends behind' (M45/2010). 'The Isle of Sheppey is the place I grew up … I loved every minute of it. A lot of things have changed since then, the people, the streets and also me! I will miss my life hear in Sheppey but I will cherish the time I had for as long as I have left' (F82/2010). And with explicit reference to her 'aspirations': 'Finally, [I want to] make people proud to grow up here on the Island' (F51/2010).

There is a shift in the mobility that is imagined between 1978 and 2010, from living elsewhere in the UK to moving abroad (Lyon and Crow 2012). One quarter of the 2010 cohort (compared to one-tenth of the 1978 essay writers) write of setting up home in an international context: close to NASA, in Alaska or in a 'mansion in Florida' (M96/2010), being drawn to 'the forests of Tasmania' (M62/1978), moving to Africa, or 'retiring to a villa in Cyprus' (M50/1978), or Spain (multiple references). These figures are higher still if we include holidays and 'seeing the world' (they rise to 60 per cent). One writer imagines having a 'dream home in Australia but to be honest … I live everywhere on the globe' (M95/2010).

The impetus to leave is tempered by a strong attachment to place and relationships: 'I did think of London but it was too far to travel' (F93/1978); 'I thought about moving to Australia but could not bring myself to leave my family' (M6/2010); 'I would like to go to New Zealand at one point in my life … I would also like to stay on the Isle of Sheppey' (F62/2010); and 'I would like to move away from the Island but, stay close to my family' (F59/2010). However, some anticipate the possibility of achieving belonging elsewhere despite the loss associated with a move: 'I had a flat I rent out in Sheerness as a way to keep me connected and my best friends are from the Island' (F72/2010); and 'I cryed my eyes out when we left as I saw leaving all my friends and old secret hiding places behind, but when I got to Dorset I made new friends and I loved it' (F111/1978).

Overall these accounts highlight both cosmopolitan and local connections and the changing balance between them (Henderson *et al.* 2007: 106). The tension between wishing to experience life 'off the Island' and remaining in a space of social and symbolic belonging itself constitutes Sheppey as a place in relation to which young people imaginatively explore their aesthetic, affective and instrumental attachments (Savage 2010: 27).

A device for story-telling that is striking in the essays is the young writers' use of a third person through which to emphasise their 'escape' from class destiny. Interestingly, this type of comparison is echoed in the chapter Pahl devotes to contrasting the fates of Linda and Jim (see Chapter 5, this volume) and Beryl and George. In the next two examples from young men, one in 1978 and one in 2010, both juxtapose their success with the struggles of a peer, already recognising how 'little actions affect you in time' (M57/2010), and the burden of decisions and directions they face at their stage of life. In imagination they can already feel the fragility of their own trajectories expressing how else life might be.

> But now, I've made a lot of money and I've no need to work for the rest of my days, but money isn't everything, sometimes I wonder what would've happened if I hadn't been lucky in business, if I didn't make the money I had now. Would I be like my school friend Mark who is still working at the factory job he found when he was sixteen, and how lucky I thought he was to take home £40 a week although we're probably equally as happy now. … But my children will never have to graft like I did, at least I've got the money to give them and thats one thing Marks children will never have. (M15/1978)

> My friend rodger was one of those pieces [treasures] left uncovered, left in the dark, forgotten with no education, no job, nothing … Just writing about him makes me feel sad, but that was his own faultality not mine, I could not change the way he thought and behaved, yes, I helped hime, yes I did, but he ignored and I was left shocked. If Rodger had listened to his family, teacher and even me he could of improved how he lives now, but he chose to ignore me and now I'm retired and living right, with my grandchildren and family, while rodger chose to blow away his future to drugs and is now in sheltered accommodation. Strange how little actions affect you in time and in which become drastic. (M57/2010)

Finally, the future is lived in the present through imagined forms of intergenerational transmission. While the essay writers recognise some of the constraints they face in their own lives, they envisage different trajectories for their children: 'My three children have all been married and are living in Manchester, Sheffield and Bristol' (M48/1978); 'There's only me here now. John and his wife and three kids live in Australia, and Jayne is divorced living in London with her son' (F124/1978); and 'Now some of them [children] are living abroad and having an amazing time' (F98/2010). Some express their ambivalence about such mobile lives, however: 'it was a bit of a shock … but we respected his wish and so he left and went up London […] my son visits me once every year' (F99/1978).

Conclusions

This chapter revisits two sub-projects – oral history interviews and imagined futures essays – of the programme of research pursued by Ray Pahl on the Isle of Sheppey in the late 1970s and early 1980s. The first contribution of the chapter is to demonstrate the value of revisiting previous data and its associated materials. The relevance of the intellectual context and debates through which thinking takes shape means that different questions get asked in different times and places. Revisiting earlier studies allows new researchers to make different sense of the same material several decades on. I have sought to do that here through questions about place-based identity and affective attachment to place in memory and imagination. Second, Pahl's work was a springboard for a new engagement not only with data from his original studies, but new data collection. The analysis presented here also shows how there can be a dialogue through time, both across

4.8 Ray Pahl, Dawn Lyon and Graham Crow, Workshop: *Re-using the ESDS Qualidata Pioneers of Qualitative Research Collection*, University of Essex, 10 December 2009

distinct sets of research materials, and between researchers themselves (as at the event pictured in Figure 4.8). Finally, the chapter is an example of how 'micro social life, the banal and the familiar are co-constitutive of the wider complexities, structures and processes of historical and contemporary social worlds' (Neal and Murji 2015: 812). In bringing a different focus and form of attention to the material than was prominent in *Divisions of Labour*, it is possible to see how data may be revitalised by the diverse workings of the sociological imaginations of different researchers.

Photographs: Sheppey today

The now closed steel mill at Sheerness, part of Sheppey's deindustrialisation story

A car transporter leaves Sheerness docks, passing the disused Dockyard Church

A faded advertisement for the Co-op, a reminder of Sheerness's Co-operative past

An assortment of vessels in Queenborough Creek at low tide

Holiday chalets still form an important part of Sheppey's tourism economy

Supermarkets are one area of growth in the Sheppey economy

A mural adorns the sea wall next to the slipway at Queenborough

A typical Sheerness street with houses fronting onto the pavement

Alleys running behind houses provide short cuts between streets in Sheerness

The high wall that marks the boundary between the dockyard and Blue Town

Looking across the River Medway from Sheppey to the Isle of Grain

Excerpts from *Divisions of Labour*, chapter 11

'The Story of Linda and Jim'[1] (excerpts from pp. 277–304)

On the problems of description

I do not imagine that my descriptions of the division of labour in the last three chapters have been consistently easy reading. Given the size of the Sheppey survey, I felt that the overwhelming priority was to be precise, and, in presenting cross-tabulations, scales and complex statistical procedures, I have deliberately eschewed quotation and anecdote that might have brought them alive.

[...]

If I had attempted to demonstrate the divisions of labour by using single quotations from the many different and diverse households that were studied, it would have done violence to the complexity that the interviews revealed. There would, I felt, have been a danger that such quotations would have both simplified and insulted the humanity that the figures, on inspection, soon reveal. I decided instead to give some perspective to the themes and arguments of the preceding chapters [through a case study] [...] I have tried to present the case of Linda and Jim more or less chronologically so that the reader moves through five years of the household's life. I have also allowed the respondents to say as much as possible in their own words. Towards the end, when readers are more familiar with the way Linda and Jim speak, I put in more commentary and summarize events, largely to speed up the story. The way Linda expresses herself is as important as the content of what she says. My hope is that the reader will get some understanding of process from this account.

[...]

Linda and Jim live in a council house in what is held to be one of the rougher parts of Sheerness. The front room is comfortable and well-furnished and Jim has now built a bar in the corner. The room behind is warm, friendly, with piles of newly-washed clothes and other signs of

1 Extracts taken from chapter 11: 'Polarization of Workers' Lives: Jim and Linda; Beryl and George'. Throughout the names used are Pahl's original pseudonyms. Original ellipsis indicated by '...'; omitted sections from original text by '[...]'.

an orderly domestic routine. The kitchen leads off this, jutting into the garden. Jim parks his car in the front garden. The house is cluttered with a superfluity of stuff of one sort or another – but this gives a friendly and welcoming impression. A cup of tea appears at any time of the day or evening. Linda is a jolly, rather stout woman with a ready grin and a rather husky laugh. When things are treating her well her hair is blonde and she is forever laughing, chatting and cracking jokes. She loves to talk and is very quick to pick up a line of questioning and to add her interpretation of events and circumstances. [...]

Her husband Jim is much less articulate. He does not really like talking about himself and is much more ill at ease. Stocky, well built and with dark hair beginning to turn grey, it is clear that he has spent much of his life in the open air. Gentle, quiet and good natured, he tends to sit quietly while Linda gives forth. However, there always seems to be a close and understanding relationship between them and, as opposites, they appear to complement each other.

Linda's story: 1978

Linda was born in 1944; she was one of twelve children. By 1960, at the age of 16, she had married. Her family had always struggled to get by – even in years of so-called affluence in the 1950s. ... At weekends, as soon as she was 14, Linda took casual employment at the holiday camps in Leysdown on Saturdays and Sundays. ... [This was when] she met Jim, who was in the Merchant Navy and was some eight years older. 'You know, when we went to see the vicar in the beginning he thought my husband was marrying me out of pity, you know. He thought I was, sort of, in a bad place: he wanted to get me out of it and, you know, he tried to talk us out of it. You know, the first thing my Mum said? "Well I don't know about that: I'm going to lose her two pound a week housekeeping money." Because we used to have to give her two pound a week. Even if you only earnt two pound and a couple of pennies over, you still have to owe her two pound.'

[...]

In the mid-1960s Linda had started her family and she joined the casualized wage-labour force of East Kent, used by the local farmers to harvest their produce in the way they have done for centuries. ... Linda's informal wages went, traditionally, towards kitting out the children for the new term. 'I don't know why, but it's just a thing we've been brought up that way, after September all the kids have to be rigged out from shoes and coats to everything, you know, for the winter season. I do them one at a time, you know, one week at a time and then, after that, then everything goes into Christmas money for the kids and for the food.' The family has never had a holiday.

[...]

Coming from a large family, Linda has many relatives on the Island and some of them benefited from the [Island's] greater prosperity in the 1970s. Some, indeed, were stevedores or steel mill workers. Some had wives in full-time employment and lived in luxury in their own homes in Minster or Halfway. Others had grown-up children living at home and collectively acquired substantial household incomes. Linda was conscious of being the poor, rather struggling one and she was reluctant to own up to her difficulties. 'If I needed money, I was in trouble with a debt or something, I could go to any of my brothers then but, you know, I've been near enough that situation at times but I wouldn't go and ask them, although I know I could, but we've always managed to get out of it, you know.' [...]

The pendulum swings: 1980

Between 1978 and 1980 Linda and her family flourished. At the time of my previous visit, Linda had been to her doctor who diagnosed that she had an arthritic hip and would not be able to work in the fields anymore. As she put it: 'I'd always had it in the spine, but then they found out the hip and he said "no more spud-bashing for you, you know, that's your lot".' But that was only a short-term setback and Linda was extremely fortunate in getting a job with the home help service cleaning in old people's houses, for which, working in the mornings only, she got 'about £32 after stoppages. Well, the most I had was about £54. That's going till about 3 o'clock in the afternoon or starting off early in the morning. That makes a lot of difference.'

As a result of having two regular incomes in the household, there was, for the first time since the household was formed, a degree of financial security. As Jim, her husband, was now getting about £85 a week net, their combined income enabled them to get by quite well. As Linda said with some pride, 'last year we got on our feet, you know, paid all our bills and things and bought all the kids clothes and things for school, that type of thing, then you don't have to worry. And then when a big bill comes in, like after Christmas last year, I could help him pay the bills off and we still had a few quid.' Things were so good for the household that they decided to have a holiday – for the first time ever – and they went to a Butlins holiday camp for a week, which was a great success. [...]

Two weeks before Linda told me this her husband learned that, at the age of 43, he had been made redundant. This catastrophe hit the household most cruelly just when everything seemed to be working out well and they had reached some degree of modest prosperity on between £120 and £140 a week. They had a few weeks to think through the implications. Their eldest daughter was leaving school in the spring and the hope was that she would find employment, and Jim was at that stage hopeful of finding something else soon. [...]

How the household gets the work done

Linda's eldest daughter, Kim, does her share of the domestic work [...] Linda is fortunate in that Jim too does substantial cooking and cleaning and child care. 'He doesn't think there's any jobs that he won't do because it's women's work. If it needs doing and I'm out at work, he'll do it anyway. It's like the oven – I hate cleaning the oven but he'll do the oven because he knows I detest doing it ...' Jim is a good cook, he learnt this in the Merchant Navy, and he also spends a lot of time with the children [...]

'Oh yes, we've always shared jobs. He's always been like that, good. He's not changed at all over the years.' No matter how hard I questioned Linda it seemed there was nothing that Jim could not or would not do around the house. I suggested that when he became unemployed he might do even more but she doubted that it was possible. He couldn't do more 'Not to what he does now [...]'

The transition from school to ...

Linda admitted that she was worried about the future. The few short months of security were over. She was more worried about whether her elder daughter, Kim, about to leave school in the spring of 1981, would find employment. 'If I could see a way of Kim getting a job and being settled, I'd be all right; I'd concentrate more on what we're going to do, but I want to get her sorted out first.' [...]

Finding a job when her father had just been made redundant added a burden on a young girl's shoulders when she was only just 16. Linda reported how she felt. 'She said, "Oh, you know, they can't do that to you, Dad, can they?" And he said, "Yes, they can," and she said, "But that's not fair. You've been there a long time. Why is it you? Why don't they ..." And he said, "Well, it's not only me, there's ten ...". She said, "Yes, but why have you got to be one of them? You always go to work. You don't take time off." You know. Why should her Dad get it because he always goes, he never mucks them about.' [...]

Kim is a willing girl, who doesn't mind hard work, and so, as Linda says, 'You'd think it wouldn't be too hard to get a job – but on the Island it's going to be. And I wouldn't like to think she'd have to go off the Island 'cos I think I've never gone off the Island much. I think I'd worry what was happening to her.'

[…]

She and Jim spent many hours talking over the future. 'We decided like whereas before we weren't that well off – before I went out to work regularly – we only, sort of, we had his money, and it wasn't all that great, but it was enough to keep going. But you know what we were saying is, it's easier for us to come down to not having much again than it is for somebody who's had big money all the time.'

Nevertheless, in contrast to our talks in 1978, Linda was, in 1980, rather more resentful of the labour aristocracy on the Island. 'I don't think it's right, 'cos even now in this dock if there's not many ships in you see the dockers go down to work and you see them come home just after 9 but then they're on pay all that time. They're home and then you've got other men that've got to work solid eight hours, you know, do a really hard day's work, and don't get as much money as they do for it. Well, I think, you know, people like me around the Island are getting a bit bitter about it, 'cos, you know, well, they think they're the untouchables, they are.'

[…]

Despite the ups and downs of the struggle to get by, under reasonably stable circumstances Linda could keep the house together: the work got done and they could achieve some modest comfort and happiness. The members of the household were not afraid of hard work, they liked to help others and they were generous with their time and emotions. Their standards of honesty and decency shone through and there was a considerable concern for the troubles of others. They liked being together. Linda says, 'I like it in the winter more than anything 'cos when they're all in and it's dark at 6, I know everyone's in and I feel sort of locked in and secure and safe. You know, we're all right, nothing can happen to us, we're all in together.'

Then Jim was made redundant. In October 1980 he was still in employment, but his days were numbered: I talked to him about how he felt and how he'd managed his life so far.

Jim's story: Autumn 1980

[…]

Jim was 43 when he became redundant and had been with that employer for eight years. Before that he had done a variety of jobs, in addition to the period of self-employment described by Linda. He had worked on the dredgers at Greenwich, and had had a number of tasks in the building trade – including work on constructing the M2 motorway. During his six years of self-employment in the 1960s, he did general repairs, window cleaning and so forth. For a time he worked for Sheppey Fertilizers, popularly known as the glue factory: 'That wasn't very nice, you know. First job they gave me when I went there was cutting up dead carcasses with an axe and I wasn't very keen, but I saved it until I got another job – which is the way things went, from one job to another.' For Jim a good job is an interesting job. 'I don't like doing the same thing all the time – well, the same as everyone. I don't think anyone likes doing repetitious work – assembly line or something like this. I don't think anyone likes this very much. But I'd say I like to be outside – I like to work on the water. I'd go on the water anywhere – even in winter. I'd sooner go there than in a factory all the time.' But would he go back to the glue factory rather than go on the dole? He remembers how hard it was: 'I've been humping for 12-hour shifts and you had to sling about 90-ton bags over a period of twelve hours. You come home and sit down and go to sleep. I think it would be better to be on the dole than that.

[...]

As we spoke, Jim knew there was no escape from the inevitable: 'If nothing changes I should be redundant by Friday and then we get two months' pay in lieu of notice.' Now, whose fault was that? How had he lost his employment? Bad management? Declining profits? World recession? Greedy workers? Very slowly, Jim and I pieced the story together – the events, the arguments and his feelings about it all.

[...]

'Well, I'm a bit angry. I'm not bitter but I am a bit angry – not so much with my employer, although I am a bit angry about it – but with the chaps at work, you know, at the moment. That'll probably wear off, you know, but it's when you've more or less lived with somebody for eight years, you know, you expect them to give you a bit of support when something comes along, you know. Not to consider themselves, as they are doing. I know a few of them are more concerned with keeping a shift system rather than a day-work system because they want to carry on with their part-time work as well. You see, we work 24 hours on at the moment and we're 48 hours off – and all of them do part-time work – I think they earn more at that than they do at work. Mostly in the building trade. I know a few are more concerned at losing that than changing the system to try and help alleviate the redundancies. Well, this is my feeling, anyway. This is what it appears. When the question of redundancies first came up, the first thing I heard people talking about at work were – not redundancies – but what they were going to do if they were going to go on the day-work system. How are they going to do their other jobs. And it surprised me, you know.'

[…]

Paradoxically, the union was being used to protect the interests of the men with second jobs rather than those like Jim who just happened to be one of the two last in who were being forced into redundancy. Worst of all, the shop steward seemed to be almost a willing accomplice to the management's plans. 'They don't like him very much but the trouble is when you're in a situation like we are, you're in a minority. When it comes to voting for anything, like, see we're in a difficult situation. […]

Surprisingly, you don't know people until something comes up, do you? It was suggested that they took a cut in pay to help things along, you know, but the majority of them did not want to know… It's surprising really – you've been with men – we've practically lived together. We're with each other all the time for 24 hours a day. Oh yes, I think they've let us down. Even if they had to go, I'd like to see a bit more of a fight about it, you know.' […]

Facing life on the dole

I asked Jim how he would feel if Linda became the main earner; if he failed to find a job and she went full-time in hers. He was quite cheerful about that prospect. 'Oh well, I wouldn't mind changing roles – I do some of the housework now, you know. We work together and all this and I don't think I'd really mind if *she* didn't mind. I'd have to do the washing, which I don't do at the moment. I help clean up and I cook the meals, but I suppose I'd have to take over the whole lot. I don't mind doing housework. I've done the washing but I never seem to get it the same as my wife does – I seem to associate that more with women, I don't know why but I do.

'I'd look at it this way: if my wife was able to earn more money than me by going out to work, I'd say, well, you go out to work and I'll stay at home! I'd end up a male housewife! It wouldn't affect me at all really. Mind you, I think I'd be a lot more clockwork than a woman. Because I've been to sea, in the services. I'd have days for things, where my wife doesn't seem to. You know, she'll do things when she feels like it, but I'd be more inclined to work to a timetable. I think it is easier in some ways. We both cook (my wife does cook sometimes), but I think it would be easier somehow – if you were in sole charge you'd know what you were doing, and what you'd got, and things like that.'

However, it was important for Jim that this role reversal depended on the *household* as a unit earning its keep. It was important that Linda should *earn* her money, and then he would play his part in a natural (though reversed) division of labour. 'To me that would still be a job – still *someone* earning money. *If it's my wife or me, it would be the same as having a job really* [my emphasis]. I wouldn't be living off the state, in other words.'

[...]

Jim was a thoughtful man with considerable talents. But at 43 he was out. 'I'll miss going to work: I enjoy my job. I think I'll miss this more than anything else really. It's the first job I've ever had that I could say "I like going to work".'

And he lost it. At the end of October 1980 he was made redundant. Three years later he was still unemployed. During that period I kept in touch with Jim and Linda and had many formal and informal chats with them. How they coped in those three years is the focus of the next section.

After redundancy

Halfway through January 1981, I talked again with Jim and Linda. They had had a good Christmas. They had been using the redundancy money and morale was quite high. 'We bought new furniture for here, something we've never had in the twenty years we've been married. We could really only afford to do this room out of it. And we gave the kids a good Christmas, and he paid his car up and we paid a couple of bills and things up.' But, Linda ruefully remarked, 'I honestly thought ours would go further or last longer than it did.'

[...]

The family was clearly closely bound together, and the household of six – parents, three children and a lodger – were just about surviving on a little over £80 a week in 1981. But it could not last and they knew it: they had been subsidizing income with the meagre capital of the redundancy money. And it was not simply a matter of crude survival. Expenditure is related to cultural practices: as the ever-perceptive Linda observed, 'it's all the working class but it affects people differently 'cos we've all got different ways of life. I mean, I smoke: I'd hate to give that up.'

[...]

A collective strategy to be a household business

A week or so before I arrived for this conversation in March 1982, there had been a great state of excitement. They had got the idea that they could run a private meals-on-wheels service for the elderly. Jim would do the cooking and both Linda and Kim would join the business, helping, delivering and so forth. When I arrived they were both sitting at a table banging away at a calculator working out their costs. Jim had got a van from his father and was working out how to convert it, installing calor gas cookers and so on. They were wildly excited. Jim had been to see his bank manager who had agreed to a loan and he had found a source of second-hand catering equipment. His brother-in-law got him a card to go to the cash-and-carry and he'd been round the morning of the day I came, gathering the prices of food in bulk. He was bursting to talk figures with me – relative cost of meat and vegetables, propane *v.* calor gas, special insurance schemes, how much he would pay Kim as an employee. The basic plan was to provide forty hot meals every day, including Christmas Day and Boxing Day, to elderly people on the Island.

At last there seemed to be real hope of everyone getting to work: they were bursting with eagerness to work hard. They did not care how many hours they might have to work. They would be working together. They were desperate not to make any mistakes, to get their costings right, and they seemed to have a remarkable capacity to grasp the details and complexities of the operation they hoped to start.

There was a very good reason to expect the scheme to work, since all that was required was for Kent County Council to subsidize the service to a modest extent. [...] But Linda and Jim didn't get their support. Jim went to see the group organizing activities for young people in the area and some KCC employees thought that the scheme was going ahead under this other organization's auspices. All was muddle and confusion. It was a terrible blow to them both. They were so sure that it was going to work, and had had so much support from the social workers. It was almost as big a blow as being made redundant. They were being hit alternately by the private sector and the public sector. How could they get their household satisfactorily through life when there was no formal employment and they were legally prohibited from doing odd-jobs?

Linda had to borrow money from her brother to pay the electricity bill. Sometimes she did not have to pay it back. Her parents-in-law paid the telephone. The household was dependent on friends and relatives, but there was something undignified and shaming about it all.

A year later, at the end of February 1983, Linda was clearly struggling. 'You lose a lot of your fight. You're inclined to think is it worth it?' And Jim admits he's disappointed and wonders who to blame – 'Is it me? You think, are you doing enough? But there's not much you can do, you know. I mean, years ago I used to go round all the factories, but now you can't get past the gate. Now they've got a man at the gate, which they never used to have years ago. You just walked in the door.'

[...]

There's much more that could be said about Linda and Jim and in some ways they deserve a book to themselves. Their story is continuing.[2] They are living through the worst time of their lives. Linda will have the last word:

'I think it should have been a time when we should have been on our feet, and sort of sitting back a bit. And you can't do that. All the worry. Marilyn's got a trip going to France. Well, I just couldn't do it. Marilyn's school you can pay in bit by bit; they give you time. But Trevor, though he's the youngest one, he's more caring and, well, "It doesn't matter to me she's going to France, it doesn't matter about me, I don't want to go". So I've been paying for her. I paid the last £5 today because I worked last night. The trip's paid for, but if I don't get any more work like that, she's still going to want something to spend when she goes ... Oh, that does make me bitter. I'm very bitter about that 'cos I feel that we're wasted, that we've got something to offer and nobody wants it.'

2 In March 1984, as the book goes to press, Jim is starting a small business, providing his own meals-on-wheels service to elderly people on the Island. Linda phoned me in February 1984 to tell me the news that at last Jim had got the support he needed. They are both eager that I follow their story into the better life that they can now see opening up in front of them.

5 Narrative, time and intimacy in social research: Linda and Jim revisited

Jane Elliott and Jon Lawrence

We begin our chapter with the same material[1] with which the previous excerpt concluded but present it here as it appears in the archived transcript of the interview rather than as it appears in the original book (where Pahl's role in helping Linda voice her frustrations is edited out):

> *Pahl*: Do you think this is probably one of the toughest times of your life?
> *I think this is the worst time because* I think it should have been a time – *'Trevor', the youngest one is 11 now and 'Marilyn' will be 13, and I think it's a time* when we should have been on our feet, and sort of sitting back a bit. And you can't do that; all the worry. Marilyn's got a trip going to France. *Well they both brought home a letter within a day of each other from both schools, a trip to France*. Well, I just couldn't do it. Marilyn's school you can pay in bit by bit; they give you time. But Trevor, though he's the youngest one, he's more caring, and, well, *it doesn't matter, she's going to go to France*, 'It doesn't matter to me she's going to France, it doesn't matter about me, I don't want to go. *I'll go when I go up to the next school*.' So I've been paying for her. I paid the last £5 today because I worked last night. *And I'll make it up to him in other ways because he's not really bothered*. The trip's paid for, but if I don't get any more work like that, she's still going to want something to spend when she goes.
> *Pahl: Does it make you feel angry though, because there you are, made to work?*
> Oh, that does make me *very* bitter. I'm very bitter about that 'cos I feel that we're wasted, that we've got something to offer and nobody wants it.
> (Linda, February 1983)[2]

So ended Pahl's powerful case study of Linda and Jim, a middle-aged couple with three children he had come to know well over the preceding five years as they struggled to cope with economic hardship, especially after Jim lost his job in autumn 1980 and Linda found her own efforts to become the main breadwinner thwarted at every turn. The story of Linda and Jim dominates chapter 11 of *Divisions of Labour*, in which Pahl explores two of the book's key themes: the

1 Material from Ray Pahl's papers is quoted by permission of the UK Data Service, University of Essex. All names are pseudonyms.

2 Text in italics appears in the archived transcript of Interview 6 (p. 5) but was omitted from the published volume (Pahl 1984: 304). It is notable that Pahl's determination to give Linda the last word means we miss how he helped her express her bitterness about their 'wasted' lives.

'polarization of workers' lives', and the ways in which couples share the domestic division of labour over the life course. Pahl pairs the story of Linda and Jim with a much shorter case study of Beryl and George, a couple untouched by unemployment and living a life of 'modest affluence' (George was a docker, Beryl a part-time cook). George and Beryl are used as a device to highlight the arbitrariness of Linda and Jim's fate. Pahl comments,

> They [Beryl and George] are like Jim and Linda might have been if Jim had been in the docks instead of on the water. The contrast between the contented, relaxed style of Beryl and George and the tense, anxious and struggling life of Linda and Jim could hardly be greater. In many ways, the latter couple had more enterprise, initiative and determination to achieve, yet they were oppressed by circumstances they could not control. (Pahl 1984: 309)

In *Divisions of Labour* Pahl struggled with the dilemma of how to integrate quantitative and qualitative research. He argued that 'using single quotations from the many different and diverse households that were studied … would have done violence to the complexity that the interviews revealed … quotations would have both simplified and insulted the humanity that the figures, on inspection, soon reveal' (Pahl 1984: 278). But Pahl recognised that readers would miss 'the expected aids to empathetic understanding'; his solution was to close Part II's exploration of household divisions of labour with the two stories of Linda and Jim, and Beryl and George.[3]

It is immediately striking that the case study of Beryl and George is not only much shorter than that of Linda and Jim (covering barely five sides compared with the 24 devoted to Linda and Jim), but also that it does not have the same narrative form. The focus is on leisure activities, domestic responsibilities and current plans and projects rather than on how they have come to be where they are today. For example, the couple regularly visit their adult married children and George is helping each to renovate their house. Pahl provides a limited back story for George – he comes from a Sheppey family, left school at 14 and joined the Royal Air Force (RAF) before becoming a stevedore in the docks; while we only learn that Beryl has a part-time job as a cook from 8.30 a.m. to 3.45 p.m. After providing a short summary of their housing career – how they began in a council house, got onto the property ladder relatively early and have now been able to buy a newly-built house, Pahl writes: 'They have reached the peak of their household housing strategy and both feel completely contented and satisfied; they have no wish to move elsewhere' (Pahl 1984: 305).

3 Later, in his work with Liz Spencer on friendship, Pahl would champion the 'rigorous analytical' methods of thematic plotting as an antidote to the temptation to rely on '"cherry-picked" anecdotes' (Spencer and Pahl 2006: 221).

In the case of Beryl and George there is no sense of a life story unfolding, or a couple struggling with external difficulties, in part because unlike Linda and Jim they were interviewed only once, as a follow-up to the main questionnaire. Indeed, perhaps what is lacking is any sense of narrative 'trouble' to help structure an engaging story. In contrast, the case study of Linda and Jim is carefully constructed so that Pahl separately presents 'Linda's story', and 'Jim's story' and provides an account of the difficulties they have encountered since Jim's redundancy at the end of 1980. This was possible because Linda and Jim were not part of the main sample at all, but rather a pilot case that he kept returning to almost as an experiment in longitudinal qualitative research.

By providing this detailed qualitative material Pahl brings to life the starkly contrasting experiences of two couples on the Isle of Sheppey. He underlines the seemingly arbitrary factors that have shaped the life chances of Linda and Jim, and Beryl and George and given them such unequal rewards for their labours. But, by presenting these contrasting couples Pahl also deftly illustrates the findings from the quantitative survey on the domestic division of labour, reported in the preceding chapters. Despite sharp economic differences, now that their children are older there is an extensive and habitual sharing of domestic labour, which both couples are happy (even proud) to discuss with him. As he explains at the beginning of chapter 11, his aim has been 'to give some perspective to the themes and arguments of the preceding chapters by two case studies' (Pahl 1984: 278). Whereas the survey material has allowed Pahl to provide only a 'snapshot' of what people reported about their employment and domestic division of labour, so that process and change can only be 'inferred', he hopes this weakness can be 'partially overcome with more intensive analysis of a small number of households' (Pahl 1984: 279).[4]

In both case studies, Pahl is skilful in demonstrating the interdependence of experiences in formal and informal employment and experiences of domestic life and domestic work. For example we hear that Beryl does less of the cooking than George because she is busy working as a part-time cook and therefore is less inclined to cook at home. Conversely, George learned to cook while he was in the RAF (but also learned to iron which he dislikes and now avoids if possible). We also learn that Jim does substantial childcare, cooking and cleaning – he is a good cook, a skill learned in the Merchant Navy. In addition to making a bathroom

4 It is perhaps ironic that in moving to the University of Essex Pahl became one of the main architects of the British Household Panel Study (now expanded into an even larger household panel and known as 'Understanding Society'). By following a huge sample of households over time these studies now enable analysts to conduct multivariate statistical analysis that tries to capture the processes by which individuals move into and out of employment, the dynamics of households and changes in domestic divisions of labour over time and over the life-course.

cabinet and a bar for their home, Jim likes to show their children how to do this type of woodwork and has the patience to sit and make things with them.

The detailed case studies allow Pahl to give some indication of how the domestic division of labour, and indeed the intensity of domestic labour, changes over time. For example, we hear how Linda's eldest daughter Kim is now old enough to help with washing up, looking after the younger children and occasionally cooking a meal. We are also told that, 'During the school holidays the younger children presented a problem when both parents were in employment.' The story of Jim's redundancy reminds the reader that the employment categories presented in the tables of chapter 10 are far from fixed and that as children get older and individuals move in and out of full-time and part-time employment the needs of the household, and the time available to meet those needs, change.

Speaking in 1998, Pahl acknowledged that it was through human stories, not through statistics, that the findings from Sheppey reached people. Describing a presentation he gave at 10 Downing Street, Pahl recalled that 'the interesting thing was that all my clever social science – they didn't really pay much attention to. But when I told them one or two anecdotes, they completely believed it' (Pahl Interview 1998: 108).

Partly because it had such depth and narrative richness, it was the story of Linda and Jim which had particular power to move. Speaking in 2006, Pahl recalled 'people have told me that this story moved them to tears'. Crucially, he acknowledged that it had also affected him profoundly, commenting that, 'it created within me a tension which I have wrestled with ever since'. Pahl spoke of feeling both empathy and responsibility for Linda and Jim, and asked: 'How does one balance the sociological head with the human heart?' (Pahl Interview 2006: 8). During the pilot phase of his Sheppey research, in 1978–79, it was Linda who did most to introduce Pahl to friends and family, greatly facilitating his initial orientation to the Island.[5] Later he would describe Linda as his 'key informant' and 'my sort of guide from the very early time' (Pahl Interview 1998: 106).

For the case study of Linda and Jim Pahl drew on six interviews held between May 1978 and February 1983, and in the book he signalled his intention to continue the series of interviews 'over the years ahead'. In fact he had already conducted a seventh lengthy interview in December 1983, immediately after Linda and Jim had read a draft of chapter 11. A few years later he organised a research project on kinship patterns based entirely on interviews with Linda's extended family (Wilson and Pahl 1988), and we know that he subsequently conducted at least two further in-depth interviews with the couple, one in March 1989, and another in July 1992. Pahl also maintained ties with the couple between interviews (Pahl 1984: 300), so that even in the later interviews we hear him apologising for having to ask them questions about things they have already told him privately.

5 Pahl Notebook, 'Sheppey, January 1978–' (private collection).

We also know that he had a video recording of their daughter's wedding from 1984, that he helped the vicar compose the eulogy for Linda's funeral after her tragic early death (Pahl Interview 2009: 25), and that to his own death he kept a letter from Linda which he treasured. Linda and Jim were much more than a sociological case study to Pahl.

We are fortunate that transcripts and/or recordings survive for Pahl's nine formal interviews with Linda and Jim between 1978 and 1992.[6] Taken together they represent an unusually rich longitudinal source for understanding how two people experienced, and made sense of, life at the sharp end of the economic restructuring that took place across those decades. This is a theme we explore in an earlier essay based on transcripts from the first seven interviews (Elliott and Lawrence 2016).[7] But these interviews also shed light on the social science encounter itself; on the ways in which intimacy influences the encounter, shaping what can and cannot be said. Pahl was well aware that long-term engagement altered the nature of the interaction; that in some ways later interviews would be less 'pure'. But he was surely right to suggest that if this meant Linda and Jim became more reflexive, more conscious of 'what they would prefer to have recorded', this was something to be respected (Pahl 1984: 280).

In the discussion that follows we adopt this position to explore the final interview from 1992 in greater depth. We treat Linda and Jim's words as considered testimony about their lives, and how they wished those lives to be understood both by Pahl and by those who they imagined would read his work. The 1992 interview allows us not only to extend the rich case study that Pahl provided in *Divisions of Labour*, but also to examine how Linda and Jim used narrative to construct an identity for themselves a decade after the interviews that informed Pahl's book. These later interviews also demonstrate how Pahl felt drawn to return to Sheppey by the powerful connections that are so often generated by community studies (Pahl 1995; Crow 2012).

However, first it is necessary to say a little more about the context of this final interview. In *Divisions of Labour* Pahl devotes twenty-four pages to Linda and Jim's story up to February 1983. As we have seen, the narrative centres on the devastating impact of Jim losing his job in late 1980, and his subsequent fruitless struggle to find paid employment. By 1982 'Kim', their eldest child, is also unemployed and Linda has been forced to give up work because her employment made them worse off after deductions from other benefits. The family was at a low ebb in 1982, but they had not given up. Instead, they were looking into the

6 R. Pahl, 'Social and political implications of household work strategies, 1978–1983' SN: 4876, UKDS, University of Essex, Box 5 and 6. Much of this material has now been digitised. See also the digitised interview in R. Pahl, 'Changing sociological construct of the family, 1930–1986'. SN: 4872, UKDS, QualiBank, University of Essex (interview 009).

7 Interviews 8 and 9 appear not to have been transcribed and the tapes have only recently come to light.

possibility of setting up a business delivering meals to the elderly. The idea was that all three would work in the business, freeing them from dependency on state benefits. A year later they were still trying to get support for this idea (with Pahl's continued support and encouragement), though Linda was also pursuing other schemes which might allow her to become the family's main provider. In a footnote inserted as *Divisions of Labour* went to press, Pahl tells us that Jim's meals-on-wheels scheme finally gained council approval in February 1984; 'Their story is continuing', he writes (Pahl 1984: 304).

Pahl's footnote strikes an upbeat note, ending: 'They are both eager that I follow their story into the better life that they can now see opening up in front of them.' But this 'better life' was not to be. Instead, as the later interviews chronicle, the couple's plans gradually unravelled as debts mounted and trading margins shrank. The next formal interview took place in March 1989. Most of the interview is concerned with the recent activities of relatives interviewed in Wilson and Pahl's mid-1980s kinship study, but we also get an update on Linda and Jim. Their meals-on-wheels business had been trading since 1984, delivering 300 meals per week to elderly people on the island, and at various points also involving Linda and friends running a day-time café from the firm's kitchen. There are signs that all is not well. There is talk of bills left unpaid, including mortgage arrears (the couple had bought their council house in 1985). By 1989 Linda had left the business and was working in a factory to try and earn enough cash to keep the family afloat. Although supplying cooked meals was far from lucrative, people were trying to move in on their trade (including an in-law who had worked closely with Jim in the past). Linda mentioned that they were thinking of selling up both business and house in order to buy a local pub.

This never happened. When Pahl interviewed them again, apparently for the last time, in July 1992, he found them back at the sharp end of the macroeconomic cycle. By 1990 their mortgage arrears had mounted to the point where the building society was beginning to threaten repossession. Then Linda, still in her 40s, had a heart attack, effectively scuppering their latest escape plan: to sell up and buy a chip shop. Jim sold the business for barely half what he had been offered two years earlier, and the couple lived off the proceeds while they tried to sell their home in a falling market. When the money ran out they reluctantly resumed claiming benefits. With the house finally sold and their debts cleared they had enough left over to buy and refurbish a chalet on a nearby holiday park. Theoretically, they were not allowed to live here through winter, but Jim planned to buy a generator to cover the times when the power was switched off. They had expected to be able to resume claiming welfare benefits in their new home, but when Pahl visited these had been suspended. Local benefit officers alleged that they had misused the proceeds from the sale of their house. With no income, Linda and Jim were quickly eroding the meagre savings they had set aside. But both still spoke animatedly about plans for the future. Jim hoped to be able to make money crafting wooden furniture and toys in a workshop he would build in his daughter's garden, while Linda wanted to teach herself to type and possibly even write a book.

In the final interview Pahl indicates that he feels government policies such as the Enterprise Allowance scheme, which encouraged Linda and Jim to set up their failed business, and the 'right-to-buy' policy for council tenants, had done much to shape their fate. Having heard how their mortgage payments spiralled upwards in the late 1980s he comments: 'never in a month of Sundays would you have paid that same amount you paid to the bank, would you?' Linda blames the government for encouraging them, and Pahl strongly affirms her analysis (and arguably shapes her response with his emphasis on powers of persuasion):

> *Pahl*: If you think back, what really persuaded you it was a good idea to buy the house?
> *Linda*: Well investment really. And always thinking that you've got something be'ind you, and you know, something for the kids, you know, at the end of the day they would have something. And, you know, it wasn't too expensive at the time, and they were saying buy yer house now and, you know, you'll reap the rewards later. Well it didn't work out that way. I blame Margaret Thatcher – Tory governments [laughs]. But it *was* them at the time, wasn't it?
> *Pahl*: Oh yes, they were telling people to do that … that's right, that's right, and of course a lot of people have been repossessed. (ends 37m 12s)

Of course there was a sense in which Pahl had *also* encouraged their bold plan to escape the benefits system by setting up in business, but neither he, nor they, was indelicate enough to mention this. The fault lay with 'the system', which, as he had argued in *Divisions of Labour*, Pahl saw as stacked against those who lacked resources and a strong position in the labour market, regardless of their personal qualities. At one point, apparently determined to affirm their self-identity as decent, hard-working people, Pahl commented: 'No you're not afraid of hard work, and it's a shame that by your willingness you've made it more difficult for yourselves' (60m 48s). Linda appreciated Pahl's empathy, replying: 'Yes, that's right … yeah. Cos you could have just been like a lot of people and just sat back, you know' (Linda regularly switched pronouns when talking about herself).

Linda and Jim's plight in 1992 underscored many of the central aspects of Pahl's analysis in *Divisions of Labour*: the polarisation of society into work-rich and work-poor households, the disincentives to work embedded in the welfare system, and above all, the arbitrariness of economic success and failure in the context of rapid deindustrialisation and the liberalisation of labour markets. But the long, free-flowing interviews Pahl conducted over fourteen years do more than chronicle the hardships of 'getting by' in Thatcher's Britain, they offer unusually rich insights into what it *felt like* to be at the sharp end of economic 'restructuring', including how their experiences shaped their identity and sense of self. As we have argued in a previous essay, the earlier interviews tell us much about what work (and the lack of it) meant to Linda and Jim, here the focus shifts more to the meaning of 'home', and the importance of home ownership for establishing identity (Elliott and Lawrence 2016).

In the remainder of this chapter we offer a detailed analysis of Pahl's final formal interview with the couple in July 1992. The recording of this interview has only recently come to light, and has not, to our knowledge, been analysed before. A focus on this last interview with Linda and Jim enables us to extend the longitudinal analysis that Pahl had started in the six interviews reported in *Divisions of Labour*. It allows for an examination of how work, in the broadest sense, is discussed now that Linda and Jim's children have all left home. A new recurrent theme is the importance of housing as an investment and a resource for establishing and maintaining identity. But our focus is not only on the *content* of this final interview, we also pay close attention to the dynamics of the interview encounter itself, exploring things left unsaid, or handled tangentially out of respect for a long-term friendship (Cotterill 1992; Poland and Pederson 1998; Charmaz 2002; Lawrence 2014).

Pahl conducted his ninth formal interview with Linda and Jim shortly after they had moved into their refurbished chalet on a Sheppey holiday park. It was two months after John Major had won the Conservatives' fourth general election in a row; a victory achieved despite the fact that economic recession was still biting hard in places like Sheppey. Linda registered the irony, telling Pahl that '[Labour] did pretty well on the Island in the election – but not well enough' (73m 50s).

In many respects the 1992 interview necessarily covered familiar ground. After seven years running their own business, Linda and Jim were now once again enmeshed in the complexities of the social welfare system. Retelling how they had been refused benefits after moving into the chalet, Linda deeply resented the inspector's assumption that she and Jim were habitual claimants. But what angered her most was that he claimed the right to tell them how they could spend their own money.

> *Linda*: We ended up with 7,000 exactly, after we bought this.
> *Jim*: 7,900.
> *Linda*: We've never had new. Cos we were going to live here we thought we'll try and make it as comfortable as we can. But he's saying 'you're not allowed to do that'. You know, I've got to make do. He's saying 'Why did you have to have a new bed? You didn't – you must have had a bed.'
> *Jim*: Well our bed wouldn't have fitted in there anyway.
> *Linda*: Well I said, 'I did have a bed', I said, 'but I'd had it nearly 32 years', you know. I said 'you have a bed for 32 years and see if you want a new one.' But it wouldn't have fitted in there. He said: 'Well you can't just go around buying all new stuff', he said, 'and expect the state to keep you.' Well I said: 'I don't expect the state to keep me, I paid a full stamp when I was at [factory name] and I was entitled to sickness benefit.' (19m 15s)

At least as retold to Pahl, there was evidently a total clash of expectations between Linda and the inspector. When Pahl commented, 'he seems a bit of a tough case', Linda replied,

> Oh he is, yeah, and he sounds, you know, he sounds young and, you know, he's sort of 'you're down there and I'm telling you, you can't have all this new stuff'. He said, he said, 'you're joking aren't you? You can't go buying double glazed doors and things'. (21m 38s)

Throughout the interviews Linda strongly identified herself as a breadwinner who always did whatever she could to put food on the table, even when benefit rules meant that it was barely worthwhile going out to work. Now, rendered unfit for work by heart disease, she bridled at this man's haughty manner.

A few minutes later Linda returned to the subject, this time spelling out that she had never actually met the inspector – their 'nasty' exchanges had all been over the telephone. In this telling of her story the clash of expectations was even starker. Linda and Jim saw themselves as doing what they could to mitigate the disaster of being forced to swap their home of thirty-plus years for a run-down holiday home. It was obvious to them that they had a right to spend their own money to make this new home as habitable as possible; but the inspector had a very different view of the moral economy of welfare benefits.

> *Pahl*: And what do they say, do they say they're going to start it [their benefits claim] again sometime?
> *Linda*: No, he said that they probably won't give me any money, 'ee said, 'because you've 'ad this money', and 'ee said I 'at to prove what I'd done with it. Which I did. I collected all the receipts and I wrote a covering letter and I told 'im everything and sent all the receipts off and in the end I got fed up with 'im because he kept being nasty on the phone and in the end I thought well, bugger it, I'll put it all in an envelope and I'll send the whole lot. And of course then he phoned and he said 'You can't have this, you can't buy that,' you know. 'You can't do this, and 'ave that' he said. 'You can't just go and have all new carpets and furniture.' So I said, 'Well, why can't I?' [laughs]. He said, 'Cos you can't do that and expect the state to keep you', 'ee said.
> *Jim*: But there wasn't any carpets in here.
> *Linda*: But there wasn't any carpets anyway. It was tiles. And you know, you think to yourself, well out of all that you're gonna, we did, I thought, well at least I'll have a decent home round me, and, you know, I won't want anything else. It'll do us now for the rest of our time. (25m 33s)

By their reckoning it was obvious that they had done the state a favour by cutting their losses and selling up. Twice they indignantly pointed out the irony that the authorities were now refusing to pay them anything whereas before they had happily found not just their welfare benefits but also an additional £47 per week to cover their mortgage interest payments (19m 05s; 43m 40s). In many ways their sense of outrage was rooted in this clash of moralities: they insisted they had saved public money by displaying initiative; officials insisted that they had broken the rules by spending their capital without permission. In essence, they were being punished for failing to display the dependence and servility expected of welfare claimants; and they knew it.

This tone of righteous indignation is a recurrent theme throughout the 1992 interview. Indeed, Pahl's interview style is to ask quite abrupt questions and to check carefully with Linda and Jim that he has fully understood the details of what they are recounting. Arguably, it is by mirroring their intonation, and echoing their sense of injustice, that he builds and maintains a rapport within the interview.

But though Linda still appeared to relish recounting her clashes with 'the Social', when Pahl asked, 'So how are you going to manage? Because they've just got to give you money', her answer underscored how the events of recent years, including her ill-health, had taken their toll.

> *Linda*: I don't know, I just honestly don't know. If it 'ad 'appened maybe two or three years ago I'd have really fought it and argued with it, but now, when 'ee was like that with me I just come off the phone and I just end up in tears then, you know. And I think: 'Don't let them get you like that'. But before I would have gone back there and bounced back. But now I just don't, I can't do that. (26m 55s)

This passage is striking in terms of how Linda constructs an identity through her narrative. Poor health and financial hardship have taken their toll, and she feels resigned to the change in her levels of resilience. This specific incident is used as an exemplar and Linda provides a resolution to the vignette which makes a more general point, 'but now I just don't [bounce back]'. Indeed, there are a number of places in the 1992 interview where we see signs of a more general 'narrative foreclosure' – a sense that for Linda and Jim future options are declining; that there are no more chapters of life to look forward to and a gradual decline towards an end point is already determined (Bohlmeijer *et al.* 2011; Freeman 2011). Hence Linda's comment that their chalet would 'do us now for the rest of our time'. In these cases Linda's reflexiveness was spontaneous, but at other times Pahl actively encouraged both Linda and Jim to reflect on their current situation and how things had gone wrong. It was a line of questioning which began when Pahl asked Linda, 'If you look back on it all, would you have done anything different?',

> *Linda*: I think I would have done, yeah.
> *Pahl*: What would you have done?
> *Linda*: Well, I think, some ways I regret that we sold the business, even though we were strugglin'. And, you know, I think it took that heart attack to make me realise that. And you know, I think like with the 'ouse, like lots of people are getting repossessed and that, but when you think that's all your years of 'ard work you've put into it, and you come out and you end up, you know, in somewhere like this. (28m 16s)

Again we see that, above all, it is the loss of her house which haunts Linda. Hence her comments about owning a house being 'an investment', and 'something for the kids', but, above all, a way to feel 'you've got something be'ind you' (37m 12s); that is a source of security and independence. It was meant to be the concrete embodiment of years of hard work. And though they were pleased to own the chalet outright they acknowledged that moving there had been an unhappy compromise.

Despite their comments about saving the state money, or their hopes of buying a chip shop, it was the fear that they too could end up being repossessed that ultimately persuaded Linda and Jim to sell up in a depressed market. As Linda explained, although 'the Social' told them they should have sat tight and waited to be rehoused, they knew better.

> *Linda*: They say if you stay there and you're repossessed the council will rehouse you, but they don't because the council say even though you're repossessed you're intentionally homeless, because you haven't paid your way.
> *Pahl*: Hmm.
> *Linda*: Because we know lots of people it's happened to, and the council promised to 'ouse 'em and they're still in bed and breakfast. And you know, you've got loads of families living and sharing toilets and bathrooms. Well, I'd sooner go and sleep in a tent. (29m 24s)

Here we see how Linda weighed personal experience, and the information gleaned from informal networks, more highly than the supposedly 'expert' advice of professionals (probably with good reason). We also see how important it was to her to maintain her sense of privacy and independence. The idea of sharing facilities with strangers might not have been enough to persuade her to live in a tent, but it did make imaginable the only apparent alternative – buying a holiday home intended only for seasonal use. Linda was equally clear that buying the chalet was preferable to moving in with close relatives. She explained,

> *Linda*: 'Beryl' [sister], she'd already said to me 'Don't worry about it. I've got two rooms.' But you know it's … at our age you don't want to go and live with, you know, your sisters.
> *Pahl*: Hmm, no.
> *Linda*: We could have gone in 'Kim's' [daughter], but I don't think I could have … I mean three weeks was enough with the three kids [laughs]. And you know, you just – at our age you just shouldn't have to end up like that. (29m 50s)

Again concerns about privacy and convenience may have been at play here, but Linda also signalled a strong sense that it was somehow wrong 'at our age' (i.e. late 40s and mid-50s) to have to turn to relatives for a roof. That was not how the narrative of her life should end.

The imperative to be independent and self-providing ran deep for Jim as well as Linda. Asked what he would do differently, Jim focused on his regret at losing the business, and failing to buy the chippie. These reverses, he was clear, represented his last chance to be a provider: 'there's no chance of me getting a job [hollow laugh]' (31m 40s). It was a theme he returned to later in the interview, when he made it clear that despite being proud to have run his own business, he had only done it because, in 1980s Britain, age had barred him from securing paid employment (when he lost his coveted job on the water in the recession of 1980 he'd been in his early 40s).

> *Jim*: I think it was better to try, at least I can say I've had a go …
> *Pahl*: Yeah, but that's alright for your pride, but in a sense, you know, you've suffered because of, um, them really being against you.
> *Jim*: Yeah, well I think actually what was against me, right from being made redundant, was me age.
> *Pahl*: Yeah.
> *Jim*: I'd have been straight back in employment if it hadn't been for me age. That's been against me really. I started doing things too late [hollow laugh]. (39m 08s)

But if Pahl seems to chide Jim in this exchange, suggesting that his sense of personal pride is no substitute for earning a good living, at other times, as we have seen, he sought to boost the couple's self-respect by praising their refusal to give up. When he commented 'you're not afraid of hard work', he knew he was playing to their strong sense of being grafters who disliked the need to claim benefits. It's striking that when he made this comment Linda latched on to the implication that others *were* afraid of hard work, replying: 'Yes, that's right, yeah. Cos you could have just been like a lot of people and just sat back, you know' (60m 46s). In an earlier interview Linda had spoken harshly about 'people that don't want to work anyway – they've never worked' (Interview 7: 26), and here too she sought to draw a clear line of distinction between herself and those who 'just sat back'. It was also why she bridled when the haughty welfare official assumed that her ignorance of National Insurance rules marked her as someone unused to work, rather than unused to benefits.

Despite her comments about having lost the will to fight tenaciously for her rights, Linda still liked to present herself as determined to make the best of things. At one point, when Pahl commented: 'It's almost as if you're being penalised for trying', she responded by declaring: 'Yeah, this is right, yeah [pause]. So you sort of think, you don't wanna give up, you've gotta keep – you gotta …' (43m 24s – Linda trailed off here, unable to find a suitable verb). Later, during the discussion about her plans to take up writing, Linda returned to the theme, making it clear that part of the appeal of writing was that it offered a new way of keeping active:

> *Linda*: Cos I said I can't do any sort of physical work anymore, I mean the doctor told me that – 'you'll never be able to go an' work again', you know, to do a physical, you know, job where you've got to do a lot.
> *Pahl*: Hmm.

Linda: And, um, so I thought, well, you know, I'm not gonna sit here – and I think well, I don't know, I'm 48, I'm not gonna sit here till I'm sort of – till my time's come, doing nothing.
Pahl: No, no.
Linda: You know, I just don't wanna do that, I wanna, I still wanna do something with my life, you know.
Pahl: Hmm, hmm – I think you're onto a good line of thought there … (69m 14s)

Linda's urge to 'do something with my life' was not new, but it took on a new meaning in the context of her premature heart attack. This was the only time that Linda herself alluded to death, but Jim let slip, during the discussion about being refused welfare benefits, that the savings they were now having to dip into had been set aside to meet funeral costs (so that their children would not have to meet them) (46m 34s). Linda, in particular, had always prided herself on her ability to look to the future and to plan. In 1981 she had told Pahl 'other people I talk to, they say you don't want to worry about, you've just got to live from day to day, but you don't just live from day to day, you've still got to be next week or next month all the time' (Interview 4: 10). Contemplating mortality, and planning for it, was an extension of this outlook, but it brought a new, foreboding sensibility to the exchange.

By 1992 most of the plans Linda and Jim had shared with Pahl in the 1980s had been dashed. They had lost both their home and their business, but they continued to think up new ways to keep busy and possibly make money. Linda insisted that in planning to write she was determined it should be something 'worth reading' – something drawn from her own experiences (perhaps partly inspired not just by Pahl's continued interest in her life, but also by the example of his rendition of that life in *Divisions of Labour*) (67m 50s). Jim had plans to build a workshop to make pine dressers and traditional children's wooden toys. As they explained to Pahl, the idea came to them at a car boot sale when they were bombarded by people wanting to buy a pine dresser top that Jim had made: 'we could have sold it ten times over' (40m 57s).

At the close of the interview the discussion returned to Jim's new business plans. Jim acknowledged that it would cost him £600 just to get started. The workshop would have to be built solidly from breeze-blocks 'cos of the way they get broke into nowadays', and he would also need to buy equipment, including a band saw (75m 15s). He confessed that he had no idea how many hours had gone into making the original pine dresser. This prompted Pahl to comment: 'I've known you for years – you always under-price your stuff don't you?' Jim's response was to explain how buying the band saw would allow him to speed up production. He estimated that he would be able to turn out four dressers in a day using templates on a machine. But he didn't discuss how he would get them to market, or what he would need to charge to make the whole thing worthwhile. In fact, there is a sense that the whole project existed partly for the sake of having a project – or perhaps for constructing, within the interview, some fragile sense of hope. But when Pahl mentioned that he had a friend who owned a toy shop and that he might be keen to sell Jim's wooden forts and doll's cradles, the response was underwhelming. Linda said 'yeah', but she sounded doubtful and unenthusiastic (77m 14s). Jim's response was also downbeat – he finally acknowledged that when he had sold the original dresser he had 'priced it up for just buying the wood … and to buy the wood was more than what I sold it for'. It's impossible to know why he said this, but there is a sense in which he seems to be saying 'let's not kid ourselves, we both know this won't happen, we're not like that'.

When one recalls the active role Pahl had played in helping Linda and Jim bring their earlier business to fruition, this moment could be read as Jim saying 'not again'. Except he didn't have to say it: indeed the understanding between them was now so developed that many things could be left unsaid, or said implicitly. We see something similar when Pahl asks questions about Linda's extended family, many of whom had been interviewed for earlier research. When Linda is discussing which relatives had come to see her since the move, Pahl registers that she has not mentioned her youngest brother, 'Peter', who had recently been promoted into management. We can hear him faltering as he tries to find a delicate way to ask about this: 'You don't see … cos "Peter" used to be like a neighbour didn't he?' (53m 10s). Linda confirms he hasn't visited and the matter is dropped. But a few minutes later Pahl asks, 'So, who's doing well on the Island?', and sure enough the conversation returns to Peter:

> *Linda*: Umm, in my family I think Peter, innit?
> *Jim*: Yeah.
> *Pahl*: Cos he's gone into management.
> *Linda*: Yeah, I think Peter.
> *Pahl*: How much does he get then?
> *Linda*: I don't know, I haven't got a clue, but, you know, it's gotta be quite a bit [laughs]. (54m 30s)

But neither Pahl nor Linda chose to label the fact that Peter had prospered while they had struggled, let alone the potentially related fact that they now saw much less of him. These things were left unsaid – arguably the proximity of the two discussions was enough.

We are not suggesting that the social and cultural differences between Pahl and his interviewees had ceased to matter after fourteen years of friendship, and at least nine lengthy interviews. Pahl was still 'my professor' to Linda; they were still a sociological case to him. But in both cases they were also *more* than this. The intimacy and trust that had developed between them allowed their conversation to flow with a natural rhythm. Pahl's empathy – his determination to encourage and affirm them – runs through the interview. He evidently shares their outrage that the council would not support their meals business, and their incredulity that the state should now refuse them benefits. But intimacy has its disadvantages. Pahl may have felt able to probe Linda's feelings about her brother's success (and about his failure to visit them), if he had not known her (and Peter) for fourteen years. Similarly, it is striking that he asks few questions about Linda and Jim's two youngest children, both still young and single, beyond establishing that they are living in rented flats elsewhere on the Island. Again, perhaps this reticence may reflect his sensitivity to their situation, and to the possibility that their children may have had little choice but to move out once repossession loomed. He does raise the issue of 'Marilyn's' impending wedding, evidently fearful that it might impose another heavy financial burden. Towards the end of the interview he tentatively asks: 'But what would happen come [Marilyn's] wedding? That would be a bit of money, wouldn't it?' (70m 24s). Linda picks up the cue, replying frankly about their situation and how it will preclude them treating the younger daughter as they had treated Kim in 1984.

> 'Well it is, yeah. Well I've said to her and "David", I said, we haven't got anything now, and I know, you know, in the next two years' time, unless somebody up there's good to us, we're not going to have that sort of money to pay out for a – a wedding.' (70m 29s)

In later life Pahl was clear that this series of interviews had affected him deeply. Speaking in 1998, a year before Linda's death, he spoke of their story as 'tragic' and lambasted the agencies of the local and national state for how they had treated them: 'they broke him, even though they knew that he was far more efficient, cheaper, and effective than the other statutory services' (Pahl Interview 1998: 106). Arguably, in these comments he could still be said to be talking about Linda and Jim as a tragic case – as victims of 'the system' – but in the 2000s he was more open about the deep personal tensions thrown up by 'being involved with people over a long period' (Pahl Interview 2006: 8). He talked about feeling guilty that the professional ethics which led him to use pseudonyms in *Divisions of Labour* had denied 'Linda' the recognition she craved for *her* story. He recalled how she had confronted him on the issue, saying 'did I ask to be called Linda?' and asking why he hadn't used her proper name 'so I could show my friends? (Pahl Interview 2009: 42–3). Pahl continued to believe he had had no choice given some of her revelations, but he regretted not having found a way to give her recognition later, perhaps by writing a piece attacking the council for undermining the business venture that finally got them off benefits in 1984,

> everyone would have known then in public that [XXX] was Linda. I could have done that and I think it is a bit of a feeble excuse to say I was too busy, but at least I was aware that I should have done that and I should have gone and seen [Jim] after the – after she died. Didn't get down to the funeral – I feel bad about that and that's not because I think I did anything wrong in the research terms, but just

> on the personal friendship. I think I let them down and they were very trusting, very trusting of me, um, and always very open and you know it was interesting that we got on just so well. 'My professor,' she would say. (Pahl Interview 2009: 44)

In the same interview he also discussed how Linda came to rely on him, 'she would phone me up and say I've got this friend, or I've got this problem with my daughter what shall I do?' (*Ibid.*: 42). Pahl clearly valued their friendship. Speaking of Linda he recalled how 'she would give this cackle and she would really laugh and we got really fond of each other and *we* got completely screwed by the county council who wouldn't let them do their meals on wheels … and I was pleased to try and help them.' (*Ibid.*: 25, emphasis added). Pahl's use of 'we' here is suggestive – showing how strongly he identified with their scheme to escape from the benefits system (a scheme he did much to help facilitate).

Though adamant that he had done nothing wrong in research terms in helping to make their plans possible – what else were friends for? – Pahl was evidently troubled by the perceived asymmetry of their friendship, and especially by the fact that he had let the connection slip after moving from Kent in 1994. Immediately after his comments about missing Linda's funeral Pahl commented,

> you leave some bruises behind and those bruises, I think – emotional bruises – are the price that we really unreasonably extract from our respondents who have built up loyalties to us that we don't always —. Some people are better at doing it than me, we don't play our part in accepting and, what's the word, acknowledging. There is a kind of emotional commitment that we build up which we then, rather then, brutally break because of career, circumstances, geography and posts at the University of Essex. (*Ibid.*: 45)

But from the way he spoke about the couple a decade after Linda's death it seems clear that both researcher and researched had paid the price of intimacy, and there were emotional bruises on both sides.

Excerpts from *Divisions of Labour*, chapter 12

'All Forms of Work towards the Year 2000' (excerpts from pp. 334–6)

I have shown how a new focus on all forms of work in the household tends to blur the distinction between the conventionally separate middle and working classes. Examination of home ownership, multiple earners and stage in the life cycle has shown how households are the essential units of production and reproduction, as they always have been. Some domestic units at certain stages of the domestic cycle can neatly intermesh with employers' labour requirements. Inevitably, however, certain households do not fit in so well; as a result, they suffer.

One new element for the future may be the growth in ownership of domestic property among a wider section of the population. The majority of people born after 1970 are likely to inherit a house, or a portion of one, from their parents or grandparents. This seems to be a situation without precedent. Those not owning their dwellings in the year 2000 are likely to be a small, poor and politically ineffective minority.

Of all the forms of work, the one that has the most political significance for the middle mass is self-provisioning. This political fact has been slow to find expression in party terms. Strikingly little creative political thinking took place in Britain between 1964 and 1984; these were twenty years of uncertain drifting after the British colonial empire was dispersed and the process of de-industrialization began to accelerate. The fact that most people during this period were extremely busy expanding and developing all forms of work was barely noticed. But there are signs that some intellectuals are rediscovering the practical politics of ordinary people. The rediscovery of Gramsci, and (for example) the work of Rudolph Bahro in Germany and Sebastiano Timpanaro in Italy, are helping to put the individual back into socialism. The reaction against oppressive bureaucracies can be found throughout the political spectrum: it simply had further to go on the Left.

Centralization and nationalization have been undermined by microtechnology and automation as much as by the recognition of the evils and dangers of bureaucratization. More now can be produced by fewer people, and this leads not just to the renegotiation of the social division of labour but also to the declining centrality of employment, one form of work, as the basis for social and political consciousness. New forms of consciousness have only very recently been recognized and articulated. Raymond Williams points to such a new change of mind:

> when we have replaced the concept of 'society as production' with the broader concept of a form of human relationships within a physical world: in the full sense a way of life. ... It can then make a difference that this alternative is being classified theoretically. The central element is the shift from 'production' to 'livelihood': from an alienated generality to direct and practical ways of life. These are the real bases from which co-operative relationships can grow, and the rooted forms which are wholly compatible with, rather than contradictory to, other major energies and interests. They are also at this historical stage, in the very development of the means of production, the shifts that most people will in any case have to make.[1]

Williams has consistently refused to be bemused by the self-images of the age and has recognized the centrality of what he calls 'the reproduction of a restricted everyday reality', which, he goes on to say, 'we have temporarily bypassed, or ideally superseded but which is there and settled and is what we have really to believe'.[2]

It is this reproduction of a restricted everyday reality that I have been documenting and analysing on the Isle of Sheppey over the past six years. My understanding from that experience is that the ideas of Gershuny, Mingione and Gorz, with which I began this chapter, are all partially correct. Social innovation, survival strategies and personal political liberation are all part of what is involved in creating a contemporary sociology to understand work and society towards the year 2000. The nature and pattern of employment is evidently changing very fast. In 1983, for the first time in two hundred years, Britain recorded a deficit in trade with the rest of the world in manufactured goods. The nation that pioneered the Industrial Revolution came to the point when it had to import more manufactured goods than it exported. The international division of labour is also clearly changing. Between 1960 and 1980, the number of part-time workers doubled to about 4.4 million, whereas the number of full-time workers fell by over 2 million. Of the 4.4 million part-time workers, 3.8 million were female. This, again, is a substantial shift in the division of labour in employment. Most of the increase in part-time work is in the service sector; most of the decline in full-time work is in manufacturing. All this is well-known, and serves to demonstrate the impossibility of clinging to old concepts associated with an earlier stage in the development of capitalism.

1 R. Williams, *Towards 2000*, Chatto & Windus, London, 1983, pp. 226–7.
2 *Ibid.*, p. 268.

I conclude with a warning. However much I have stressed the importance of all forms of work in this book, it is clear that only the work of employment or self-employment generates income. And money is necessary to do all the other forms of work. In general, I can report that the work ethic is alive and well: people enjoy working and there is plenty to do. Often they may not particularly enjoy their employment, but they do enjoy and need the money that it brings. If there were a national minimum wage instead of the present system of benefits and allowances, the total amount of work done would almost certainly increase. With more money, people could do more work– whether or not it was paid. The contrast between the households with money being productive and busy and the households without money being unproductive and idle is the overwhelming conclusion of the empirical part of this book. This may be paradoxical, but it is true.

There is no doubt that the divisions of labour will continue to change. The old established order of whatever golden age people prefer to believe in has gone. The ways in which ordinary people struggle to organize all the work they do to get by – very often despite, not because of, well-meaning yet insensitive interventions – seem not to have been understood, even though they are going on all around us. Perhaps if the importance of all forms of work is seen, and if what ordinary women and men say about their lives is listened to and understood, we could begin to hope that out of that restricted everyday reality a more humane society will emerge.

6 *Divisions of Labour*: Sociology in search of a new jurisdiction

John Holmwood

Introduction

Divisions of Labour was written on the cusp of a period of change in British society and its political economy. The research was begun in the mid-1970s and, by the time it was published in 1984, Britain was in the midst of an aggressive wave of deindustrialisation. In addition, the first government of Mrs Thatcher took office in 1979 and had been re-elected in 1983 indicating, perhaps, that something was different in the political landscape. She is not mentioned, though the Falklands conflict of 1982 gets a vignette.

We do not get an account of the nature of these social changes and their implications for the practice of sociology set out for us in sweeping theoretical statements as would have been more characteristic of other sociological contributions at the time. Instead, the need for a new and different sociological engagement is implicit on each page in the handling of data and in reflections on the detail of life on Sheppey derived from surveys and from Pahl's familiarity with his respondents. These draw us into the texture of social relations and leave us with sharply posed puzzles about the capacity of sociology (as then constructed) to represent them. There is theory aplenty in the book – especially, around the very organising idea of divisions of labour, as, for example, is clearly set out in other chapters in this volume – but the direct address of theory, and theorists, in the conventional sense, is done more as a series of barbs and goads. It is this combination of lightness of touch and acerbic commentary on the state of the discipline along with its exhibition of the craft of sociology, what might be called its inductive theorising, that makes it such a delight to read now. It is the significance of that craft in calling forth a new 'jurisdiction' for sociology that I want to address in this chapter.[1]

I also want to suggest that this theoretical challenge has stood the test of time and it should be a goad to us today, when we might think we have already absorbed all we could learn from the book. Let me begin with the challenge that is built into its very structure. The book starts with the history of work – formal

1 Andrew Abbott (2001a) calls the constellation of concepts, objects and orientations that define a subject-field a 'jurisdiction'. As we know from writings in the history of science, the ability to delineate a 'jurisdiction' depends in part upon its demise, even if what is in the process of replacing it might be unclear.

and informal and the changing relations between them – as a prelude to the ethnographic fieldwork and survey of present-day Sheppey. But the latter is designed to return the present to the past in order to re-ground our thoughts about possible futures. The narratives of Linda and Jim, for example, would be recognisable as illustrative cases in Pahl's account of the past, while those of Beryl and George seem to live only in the present,[2] at the same time as they potentially are left 'high and dry' by the return of features of life that had seemed to be consigned to the past. They are of the present, but not deeply anchored in it. It is clear that Pahl thinks that their rootedness in the increasingly fragile 'certainties' of the post-Second-World-War settlement makes it likely that they, not Linda and Jim, may be the anomaly in the future.

But it is Beryl and George who would have fitted better into the narratives of recent British sociology, for example, that of Goldthorpe *et al.*'s (1968a, 1968b, 1969) *Affluent Worker* study and its theme of the privatised, instrumental worker. Pahl does not say much in *Divisions of Labour* about the political commitments of his respondents, but if Beryl and George appear in hindsight as the 'angels in marble' of the Thatcher project,[3] they are not viewed by Pahl as a secure basis of support for that project. At the same time, however, Linda and Jim are outside the comfortable narratives of class-based politics, which Pahl understands to motivate much sociological commentary, especially that which purported to confront Thatcherism and its sociological conditions. Beryl and George have entered the 'middle mass', but that status depends on maintaining employment, which is likely to be far from secure and subject to changes dictated from offshore.

This is one of the rare occasions in the book where he takes care to underline his point: 'the *unprecedented* period, in terms of the patterns of the last 250 years, was the boom period of full employment for men in the 1950s and 1960s. That period of rising real wages, of demand for teenage and immigrant labour and of expanding state expenditure in health, social services and education has formed the base level, the conception of what is normal, for politicians, media commentators and many academics' (Pahl 1984: 313, emphasis in original). The implication is that British sociology had unwittingly organised itself around false assumptions about the continuity of sociological conditions which were shifting even as they were being written into existence as the objects of concern.

More recently, Savage (2010) has also characterised the 1950s and 1960s as constituting British sociology's defining 'moment' in which its characteristic

2 George is a stevedore on the docks, while Beryl works part time. They have bought their own house on a 'new development' and they were in the middle of a 'military campaign' of redecoration from top to bottom (1984: 304–5).

3 The reference is to Conservative prime minister, Benjamin Disraeli's identification of the possibility of blue-collar workers voting for the Conservative Party, rather than the Liberal Party – like a sculptor able to see the angel in the marble prior to cutting. See Pahl and Wallace (1988) for an explicit discussion.

themes – community, class and social mobility – and its political orientation of reformist modernisation were established. Savage's book addresses Pahl's earlier work in his treatment of this 'moment', but does not mention *Divisions of Labour* (an omission rectified in the Afterword to this book, albeit that Savage sees Pahl's critique of class analysis as being less fundamental than do I). Pahl's *Urbs in Rure* (1965), or Hertfordshire villages study, and *Managers and their Wives* (1971), written together with Jan Pahl, perhaps fits that mould, but *Divisions of Labour* breaks it. The latter is of fundamental importance within British sociology, I shall suggest, precisely because it one of the first to challenge British sociology's post-war 'jurisdiction' (Abbott 2001a) from the inside and to begin the delineation of a new moment with which it would have to contend.

However, I shall go further to suggest that it does so more effectively than other attempts, including that of Savage himself. The latter self-consciously articulates a 'politics of method' that was operative in British sociology's early defining moment. However, he effectively depoliticises the more recent sociological undertaking and aligns it with 'knowing capitalism' (Savage 2010: 248), that is a capitalism increasingly organised as a knowledge economy. This is an argument reiterated in the Afterword to this book. Where Savage turns sociological reflection inward on to the question of how it can ensure its continuity within the academy,[4] Pahl turns it outward. For Pahl, the task always remained *how to know capitalism and its effects in order to ameliorate them*. His *presence* in the social world he studies is palpable. This is something he carried into the Archbishop of Canterbury's Commission on Urban Priority Areas which began its review in 1983 and reported – to the consternation of the Conservative government – its recommendations as a 'call to action for Church and Nation' in *Faith in the City* (1985).[5] This is something to which I will return in consideration of claims for a 'public sociology'.

Divisions of Labour's moment

Savage's outline of post-war British sociology ends just before the effects of the Robbins Report (1963) became evident. This recommended the expansion

4 At the close of his discussion of the 'politics of method', for example, Savage leaves us to a technical discourse and the bloodless politics of the academy: 'if there is a future for the social sciences, it consists in forming intellectual and technical alliances with ways of knowing – from the humanities, sciences, and informational systems – with which they are currently only weakly affiliated' (2010: 249).

5 Woodrow Wyatt reported Mrs Thatcher complaining that, 'there's nothing about self-help or doing anything for yourself in the report' (2000: 22). There is a nice irony that Pahl reports that a book on *Self Sufficiency* is on Beryl and George's shelf (1984: 304), but concludes that Linda and Jim, 'had more enterprise, initiative and determination to achieve, yet they were oppressed by circumstances they could not control' (1984: 309).

of higher education, an expansion that brought many new sociology departments into being, particularly in the newly-created universities of Essex, Sussex, Lancaster, York, Warwick, Kent and East Anglia, as well as the Open University (and, of course created and expanded provision at older universities, too). These were all departments that would quickly be seen as defining a new sociological imagination and Pahl himself spent much of his career at the University of Kent before moving to the University of Essex. This expansion also brought a new generation of students into the university, students without an experience of war or national service, and also many who were the first in their families to go to university, including increasing numbers of female students.

Between the period described by Savage and the publication of *Divisions of Labour*, lay the election in 1964 of the first Labour government since the 1945–51 Labour governments which were widely seen as the architect of the post-war welfare state. Disappointment with the 1964 government and its Labour successors culminated in the election in 1979 of a government committed to dismantling the welfare state. At the same time, influenced by the US civil rights movement, anti-colonial struggles (particularly significant in British sociology for the émigrés from South Africa who took up positions in the discipline made available by its expansion), the women's movement and the movement against the Vietnam War, a new spirit of radicalism entered the university. It was particularly influential in sociology, which moved politically in a different direction from that of the wider public (at least, as expressed in electoral support and the policies that such support facilitated).[6]

The 1970s became a period of intense criticism of existing approaches within sociology, especially of empirical sociology, and a rediscovery of Marx and Marxism, frequently in the form of highly abstruse theoretical argument. This occurred alongside the charge that existing sociologies falsely universalised the experience of men and neglected issues of gender; the mainstream of the discipline, the 'post-war jurisdiction', then, was under assault theoretically and methodologically. On the one hand, existing approaches to inequality and employment were argued to be deficient from the point of view of their conceptualisation of class and, on the other hand, they were argued to be too focused on formal, paid employment to the neglect of unpaid work and the labour of the household. By the 1980s the rising tide of Marxism had receded and a new rapprochement in class analysis was being forged around what was to all intents and purposes a Weberian form of class analysis, especially as articulated by Goldthorpe and other

6 This is something that Michael Burawoy later described as the 'scissors movement' that confronts any revived public sociology: 'the aspiration for public sociology is stronger and its realization ever more difficult, as sociology has moved left and the world has moved right' (2005: 6). The shift to the right is first discussed by Hall (1979), absent the parallel discussion of sociology's move to the left.

colleagues (Goldthorpe *et al.* 1980; Marshall *et al.* 1988). Compared with Marxist approaches, this extended the number of classes and displaced the specificity of the capital–labour relation, albeit continuing the emphasis on the centrality of the labour contract (a contract that Pahl would argue, was becoming increasingly precarious for many workers). Proponents of class analysis continued to defend vigorously the occupation of the male 'head of household' as the index to the class position of the other members of the household (Goldthorpe 1983).

The problem for class analysis was that the increase in women's employment, together with the concentration of women's employment in routine non-manual jobs, meant that the distributions of women and men in the class structure looked very different. Once the class position associated with female employment was taken into account, a significant proportion of households would be made up of members in different class positions – that is, would be 'cross-class families' (McRae 1986). Goldthorpe's (1983) response that this could be ignored because male class position did most of the explanatory work, appeared uninterested in exploring the question of why class was mediated for women but not for men, while the argument that 'cross-class' households had distinctive sociological properties constituted a reification of class. For example, why regard class as the independent variable in a series of 'determinations' – such as educational attainment, morbidity and mortality – but not in the decisions associated with people's intimate lives? Pahl's response was probably too quiet to be heard above the din – the idea of a 'cross-class' household was a reification, but its deconstruction was best addressed through empirical research not by ignoring it. Class and gender should be brought together, but not directly in theory, until after a careful consideration of their mutual constitution through detailed sociological research.

On the face of it, however, Pahl's response to all this ferment looks not so much quietly considered, but rather insouciant. After all, his class analysis of the survey data gathered for *Divisions of Labour* was based on a three-class scheme, formed from collapsing the Registrar-General's seventeen socio-economic groups, together with a fourth, residual class. There is barely a nod to the wider debate over class when he sets out his scheme. At the same time, however, his address of *divisions* of labour and the inclusion of formal and informal work, as well as self-provisioning activities, was a radical challenge to standard class analysis that showed the influence of feminist approaches and a willingness to open up the empirical analysis of work to a wider set of concerns, and as I shall suggest, a wider understanding of social consequences.

When Pahl identifies emerging 'polarisation', it is very different from a putative polarisation familiar from class analysis; put somewhat simply, it is a polarisation *within* a 'class' and not polarisation *between* classes. Indeed, the case studies of Linda and Jim and Beryl and George are precisely an illustration of the polarisation within the working class. The two couples might easily live next door to each other, but their fates are very different. As Jane Elliott and Jon Lawrence show in

Chapter 5, Linda and Jim buy their council house, but ultimately cannot keep up their mortgage and end up trying to live year round in a holiday chalet; Beryl and George had moved from council housing into the privately built owner-occupied sector. These different trajectories extend to their children. The lives of Linda and Jim's children are constrained by the straitened circumstances of their parents; Beryl and George are able to help their children, especially with doing up their own houses.

Sociological commentary on *Divisions of Labour* was comforted by a familiar word – 'polarisation' – but uncomfortable with drawing out the implications of the analysis or connecting them to contemporary politics. Linda and Jim fitted a sociological interest in the 'underdog' and Pahl provided a fine sociological account of their lives that challenged an emerging discourse on the 'underclass'. However, most readers did not wish to engage with Beryl and George and understand how their narrative exemplified a 'polarisation' that was occurring within the same 'class' (the same, that is, on the sociological criteria that Pahl was challenging).

Something of the significance of Pahl's approach can be judged in retrospect from a consideration of the context of the general field of social stratification research in Britain. The Social Science Research Council (later to become the Economic and Social Research Council) had since the 1960s funded an annual workshop on social stratification – the Social Stratification Research Seminar – which brought together all those whose research they funded, together with other invited participants. For the first time in 1984, gender was addressed as the focus of the meeting, bringing together feminist researchers and mainstream stratification researchers. Pahl presented *Divisions of Labour*.[7] Significantly, his paper was not selected for the volume of papers from the seminar that Rosemary Crompton and Michael Mann (1986) edited.

A new edition of the Crompton and Mann book was published in 1994, together with a new introduction where they comment that the relationships among gender, class and stratification continued to be unexamined. This was notwithstanding the great growth of interest in, and research on, gender, albeit focused on the, 'individual and interpersonal, rather than the collective and structural' (Crompton and Mann 1994: viii). But, in the interim, 'sociological interest and research in stratification, together with its major organizing concept, class, have not flourished over the last decade' (1994: viii). They associate this 'decline of class' with social and economic developments that displaced the traditional manual worker and the turn to consumerism (both developments registered

7 I should say at this juncture that I had been a member of the seminar since the early 1970s when a graduate student and at the 1984 meeting was discussant of the papers by Pahl and Lockwood which were presented in the same session, having been appointed to a lectureship at the University of Edinburgh in 1980. The meeting, I recall, was stormy.

by Pahl, as Strangleman notes) as well as with conceptual confusions within the discipline over the meaning of class.

Once again, they do not reference Pahl, but this is odd because, in the meantime, he had published a paper that challenged class analysis at its heart (Pahl 1989) and is a continuation of the argument of *Divisions of Labour*. Pahl called his article, 'Is the Emperor naked?' to indicate what he considered to be the rather threadbare nature of class analysis, and in this context, and mixing the metaphor, we might regard Crompton and Mann's new introduction as a discussion of Hamlet without mentioning the Prince. The omission was also odd, given that there had been a very bad-tempered and dismissive response to Pahl's paper by Goldthorpe and Marshall (1992), articulating 'the promising future of class analysis' and a further response by John Scott (1994), 'Class analysis: back to the future'. Apparently, all was well with class analysis, just when, if Crompton and Mann are to be believed (and they were writing broadly in the same tradition as Marshall, Goldthorpe and Scott), there was a 'decline of class'. This is odd. It is as if the significance of the consciousness of 'class' on the part of sociologists had trumped its relative absence in the consciousness of others. Now we get an opportunity to see Pahl's sociological imagination at work on theory and the puzzle that the public salience of class as a way of understanding the production and reproduction of inequality is declining just at the same time as those inequalities are increasing.

Rethinking class: the problem of change

The response to Pahl was rather simple and straightforward. Notwithstanding a common view of him as a Weberian,[8] Goldthorpe and Marshall's, and Scott's, judgement was that his critique applied to Marx and not to Weber. Marxist class analysis had either converged in all essentials with a revised Weberian approach, as in the case of Erik Olin Wright, or had been supplanted by it, and Weberian class analysis had a promising future as a programme for research. Yet this rather missed Pahl's point. It may be the case that the linkages between structure, consciousness and action (SCA) had been clearly specified in Marxist approaches, albeit without the expected consequences, but this could not absolve Weberian class analysis from the challenge of also addressing linkages in a way that was more consistent with social developments. Yet this seemed to be what Marshall and Goldthorpe concluded; Weberian class analysis, quite properly for them, was unconcerned with a 'theory of history', which lay outside the proper focus of a scientific research programme.

But Pahl had drawn his criticism from Lockwood (1981) and the latter's criticism of Marxism for a theory of action that constituted the 'weakest link in the

8 Crow and Takeda (2011) rather see him as Durkheimian in his orientation, which I think is correct as I shall suggest in the conclusion to this chapter.

chain'. The point for Pahl was that the links of the SCA chain were weak or missing – not that they were an irrelevant concern – and that the problem lay with the concept of class which was ceasing to do useful work. It should not have escaped the attention of Pahl's critics that a similar argument on Lockwood's part was the basis of the latter's Weberian argument at the ESRC Social Stratification Seminar that, while social stratification was gendered, gender was not itself a principle of stratification in the same way as class or status (Lockwood 1986). This was because the idea of a class society, or status society, made sense in stratification terms, and, indeed the historical transformations giving rise to capitalism might be understood as a transformation from status society to class society, but it was difficult to imagine gender as descriptive of a social formation in the same way (see also, Scott 1996).

I leave aside the consternation this argument caused at the seminar. Clearly, many feminists could imagine a society organised around the principle of gender and, indeed, they named it – patriarchy.[9] Importantly, Lockwood (and Marshall and Goldthorpe and Scott) were not making an empirical point, but a 'theoretical' point. Indeed, Lockwood thought it unlikely that capitalism empirically *would become a class society*; in other words, he did not accept Marx's account of increased social polarisation as a consequence of the contradictions intrinsic to capitalist class relations. Nonetheless, *the idea of a class society was integral to the principle of class.* Using the language of Giddens, class was integral to *structure*, but not necessarily to *structuration*.[10] As Giddens (1973) put it, it was possible for there to be class societies without classes and for classes to exist in societies – such as state socialism – that were defined analytically as not being class societies because of the absence of market exchanges based in private property.

It might be argued that all that is being said is that other factors intervene between class (as conceived analytically) and the structuring of social classes as groups – for example, factors like gender and race and ethnicity. But this is precisely to argue for a hierarchical ordering of concepts (and, perhaps, mechanisms), without a proper accounting for that 'ordering'. Essentially, Pahl suggests that the interactions among different factors – let us call them what he called them, *divisions of labour* – should be addressed without assuming priority to one factor over the others. More importantly, what counts in everyday life is that these interactions are integral to the construction of experience and they do not necessarily constitute that experience as contradictory (as is implied by a hierarchical order of intervening and countervailing factors; see Holmwood and

9 From a different perspective, Elias and Scotson (1965: 146–7) suggested that it is difficult to envisage communities without women and children, but not difficult to envisage them without men.

10 Pahl (1989: 710) expresses himself favourable to Giddens's theory of structuration, but I see the latter as being directly bound up in the same problems that Pahl otherwise acutely sets out.

Stewart 1983). Sociologists who give priority to 'class' will always be asserting the 'objectivity' of their account against the ('false', or 'mediated') subjectivity of actors and, at best, always risk talking past them (at worst, for Pahl, they invoke a 'directionality' contained in the principle of class, but which in the 'last instance' never comes).[11]

Here is the paradox that Pahl thinks he has skewered. Class analysis begins from an assumption about the direction of social change that derives from a mechanism integral to a particular understanding of the linkages of SCA. However, social changes are different from what was expected and the response is to say that the possibilities were 'real', but 'unrealised'. The consequence however, is that 'class' cannot provide an account of those changes that did occur. Social change shifts from being internal to class analysis – one of its objects – to being something that exists in the 'environment' external to it; that is social change produces effects that impinge upon class formation, but class analysis is no longer the means of accounting for social change.[12]

This, then, is the first of Pahl's summary conclusions about the weakness of class analysis: 'class as a force for social and political change is problematic since the links in the SCA chain are inadequately theorized and there is little empirical indication that the model has much relevance in practice' (Pahl 1989: 715).

Rethinking class: the problem of class structure

What Pahl thinks he has demonstrated in *Divisions of Labour* is a polarisation *within* what, from the perspective of class analysis, would be called the *same class*. That polarisation derives from an analysis of formal employment, household labour and self-provisioning and would be undiscoverable from an analysis that concentrated just on formal employment, which is, of course, the basis of defining class position within the standard approaches. In the later article, he reinforces this point about the artificiality of class analysis. It is worth setting out the different elements of the critique because, as far as I am aware, his argument has been dismissed on first principles and not by looking at the cogency of the different arguments he makes setting out the limits of class analysis. In doing so he also relies on a more familiar

11 The first criticism is directed at Weberian approaches, the second at Marxist ones. It is a criticism made explicit in the article, but which also informs the criticisms of theoretical claims about the future of work in chapter 12 of *Divisions of Labour*.

12 This is, perhaps, no more evident than in Goldthorpe's (1990) 'principled' repudiation of historical sociology, anathema to many, but especially Pahl who begins, as we have seen, from the location of his concerns in history. Goldthorpe uses the language of Lakatos's (1970) research programmes to justify the 'scientificity' of his approach. He fails to acknowledge the sting in Lakatos's argument that scientificity is better demonstrated by falsification, than 'purification' and that the restriction of scope which Goldthorpe describes as a progressive problem shift has the form of what Lakatos calls a 'degenerative problem shift', which begs the question of the status of hard core assumptions that are being defended.

idea of polarisation between 'classes', suggesting that this, too, is beyond class analysis, partly because of its emphasis on *employment*, which means a neglect of the advantaged (as well as missing the polarisation that occurs among the disadvantaged).

Following the summary conclusion with which I ended the previous section, he goes immediately into two other conclusions: 'Secondly, as a classificatory device class does little to help us to understand the lifestyles of the privileged and adds nothing to the brute facts of poverty when considering the other end of the social structure. Finally, it is apparently well-nigh impossible to operationalize the concept in order to make international comparisons' (Pahl 1989: 715).

Some of these issues have come into direct focus again for us following the publication of Thomas Piketty's (2014) *Capital in the Twenty-First Century*. Most significantly for present purposes, Piketty shows an accumulation of income in the top 10 per cent reaching its height in Europe and the USA at the turn of the nineteenth/twentieth centuries. Since then there was a secular decline in their share (with fluctuations) until the late 1970s, after which there was a reversal, with inequality rising again almost to reach its previous levels (and predicted to exceed them as the twenty-first century unfolds). The force of Piketty's argument is to challenge Kuznets's (1953) theory that the maturing of capitalism and long-term economic growth would bring about a decrease in income inequality (and, by implication, also of wealth). Kuznets presented data for the years 1913–48 and his analysis was seen to be further reinforced by post-war developments up to the mid-1970s, a period Piketty describes as the 'Trente Glorieuses' and which is broadly aligned with British sociology's moment, as set out above, namely the high point of the development of the welfare state and reducing inequalities.

The question we need to ask is whether the 'return of inequality' reinforces sociological 'business as usual' – that is, the business of mainstream class analysis – or whether it confirms Pahl's suspicion articulated at the very moment when the trend in inequality was beginning to be reversed, that the mainstream approach was already unequal to the task.

Picketty shows the inertial power of wealth to accumulate and for top incomes to convert into assets. The likely future of capitalism is to continue the present trend of widening inequalities in incomes and wealth (especially the latter) and, further, not only will the fortunes of the top 10 per cent of income earners outstrip the bottom 90 per cent, but this will be even more pronounced for the top 1 per cent and the top 0.1 per cent. In other words, the logic of capitalism is to produce a patrimonial order where inheritance increasingly triumphs over merit. It is clear from the graphs of the income shares of the top 10 per cent that Piketty presents, the two key moments in the development of post-war British sociology – the professional consensus in the immediate post-war period and the radical critique in the 1970s – were both shaped by the downward trend of reducing inequality, but each is out of step with subsequent developments of widening inequality. Of course, the political sensibilities of sociologists – 'professionals' and 'radicals' alike – are sympathetic to the goals of reducing inequality and, therefore, are unlikely to see the discipline as implicated in the great reversal of that trend.

In this context, then, the paradox of Piketty's book is that, among sociologists, the typical response has been that it is a welcome re-statement of what we already knew. Moreover, it is also seen to be dependent on weak sociological categories, namely an analysis in terms of distributional shares (proportion of income and assets accruing to the top 10 per cent and bottom 10 per cent etc.), rather than social relations (see Savage 2014). In fact, there is little substance to the latter claim. It might appear that any discussion in terms of distribution by 'shares' is concerned only with position within a distribution order, rather than with the mechanisms by which that order is produced and reproduced. Yet, most class analysis operates on the basis of class position as a proxy for a place within a distributional order and this is precisely one of Pahl's points.[13] The different classes that are identified (with the possible exception of a 'petite bourgeoisie' which appears in class classifications but is frequently elided for purposes of subsequent analysis) are represented as hierarchically ordered. Their use to demonstrate the consequences of inequality for other outcomes – such as educational attainment, mortality and morbidity, and so on – are no better than approaches which represent inequality as a continuum. Indeed, class schemes approach the explanatory power of the latter only when they multiply the number of classes, thereby, moving their schemes closer to a continuum.

One problem is that class schemes seek to identify discontinuities – boundaries – in relation to factors which are continuous in their distribution – for example, income, authority, working conditions and so on. As Prandy and Bottero (1997) comment, this is indicated by the use of terms such as 'level', 'degree' and 'chances' to describe them (see also, Bland 1979; Prandy and Blackburn 1997). This is why an increase in the number of classes improves the performance of the scheme and, presumably, lies behind Erikson and Goldthorpe's comment that the number of classes could be, 'as many as it proves empirically useful to distinguish for the analytical purpose in hand' (Erikson and Goldthorpe 1992: 46).

In this sense, social stratification moved closer to Pahl's idea that what he was observing was increasingly a middle mass of small gradations, albeit that there was a need to address the broader divisions of labour than simply those deriving from employment. Moreover, to speak simply of a 'middle mass' also misses a sense that the labour contract was becoming more precarious for many

13 See, especially, his later sally (Pahl 1993) against Goldthorpe and Marshall, where the latter present classes as 'demographic groupings' – or what Pahl calls 'lumps': 'why should readers assume that lumps or categories are anything other than proxy indicators of highly complex processes of accumulation and reproduction of advantageous characteristics? The nature of current employment relations seems to be a tiny screen on which to project central concerns of sociological analysis' (1993: 257).

workers, including those currently affluent while their employment remained. What was also becoming evident, for Pahl, was that a shared 'precarity' was also associated with the specific emergence of an underclass, even if he did not use this designation pejoratively.[14] That is, in so far as unemployment befell some, but not all, many of those who were unemployed were increasingly separated from other means of 'getting by', disadvantaged both by the operation of the labour market and by the benefits system. In fact, things have turned out rather less favourably than Pahl imagined when he wrote in the final pages of the book (excerpted ahead of this chapter) that by the year 2000 the operation of the housing market would have made owner-occupation the norm to such an extent that tenants would comprise 'a small, poor and politically ineffective minority' (1984: 334). In practice the UK has not become the nation of home owners that Saunders (1990) and others anticipated, but the return of rental tenure, rather than confounding Pahl's general analysis confirms the acuity of his perception of the new forms of polarisation and division within what others are pleased to regard as 'classes'.

What should also be evident is that Piketty has a mechanism to account for the determination of distributive shares, namely the structural tendency for the rate of return on capital to exceed the rate of growth of income and output (r>g).[15] This might be a fairly simple mechanism, although that need not undermine its power, but, in any case, as I have already suggested, sociological class analysis itself allows that any such mechanism is 'external' (i.e. is potentially a topic for 'economics', not 'sociology'). But the situation is worse. 'Capital' (income derived from assets) also lies outside sociological class analysis, which is grounded in the characteristics of employment (or the labour contract). If we regard capitalism, at its simplest, as a system in which there are three classes of income – rent, interest and earnings from employment – then sociological class analysis is focused exclusively on the last of these (with the marginal exception of self-employment and, therefore, petty-ownership of the means of production). This is the reason why Pahl argues that class analysis cannot account for the 'lifestyles of the privileged' (something called for by Savage (2014) as a 'new' topic for sociology, or an 'old' topic to which it should return).

14 Ironically, Goldthorpe and his colleagues had great difficulty in demonstrating clearly demarcated classes, but were eager to argue that there was no 'underclass'. However, it transpired that the underclass was more of a class than other groups designated as classes, while right-wing proponents of the pejorative account of the underclass could gain little from that conclusion, since it was less of a class than they were claiming and the factors of precarity associated with risk of falling into such a class were more widely distributed than they supposed, just as Pahl suggests in *Divisions of Labour*.

15 When Pahl was writing, the main concern was that of a 'profits squeeze' (Glyn and Sutcliffe 1972), but it was the context for the shift in economic policies whose impact was also being felt by Pahl's respondents.

But it is not only that class analysis fails to address different kinds of 'capital', but that it regards the distribution of kinds of employment – the occupational order that will be represented as discrete class positions with common characteristics – to be determined by processes external to sociological class analysis. This is a consequence of making social change exogenous to class analysis. Thus, while the occupational structure is argued to be a class structure, where different jobs can be aggregated together because they possess a cluster of common market-relevant characteristics (of income, job security, relation to authority, etc.), what determines the distributions of jobs with those characteristics – for example, the proportions of skilled and unskilled manual jobs, or the proportion of routine non-manual jobs, and so on – is also exogenous to class analysis, which simply takes that distribution as a given and subject to change deriving from other processes.

This is nowhere more evident than in mobility studies. One concern among class analysts (though it is not restricted to this approach, since similar demonstrations could be made within an approach that regarded inequality as a continuum) has been to distinguish between 'absolute' and 'exchange' mobility in order to indicate the openness of society. Thus, a changing distribution of class positions in terms of a decline in the number of unskilled manual positions and a relative increase in non-manual positions will produce increased intergenerational mobility. However, controlling for the changing structure, will provide better insight into the 'openness' of society by indicating the relative chances of achieving a higher occupational position by those whose social origins are outside that 'class' when compared with those who are from social origins of that higher class (Erikson and Goldthorpe 1992). However, what should be evident is that as soon as the question at hand is shifted from that of the 'openness' of society to that of class formation, which is an underlying concern of class analysis, then the nature of changes to the structure of positions will have as much impact as the degree of fluidity (see Kingston 2000).

At best, then, sociological class analysis is concerned with a different – perhaps complementary – aspect of inheritance to that set out by Piketty, that of occupational class position and the rewards of income it entails. But it excludes other forms of income, deriving from assets, and also proposes that the market processes that determine the shape of the class structure are of interest only in so far as they change the data that enter into sociological explanations and not in their own right. Thus, there might be polarisation between 'good jobs' and 'bad jobs' (Kalleberg 2013), something also flagged up by Pahl as potentially an emerging problem, but this is then argued to be a consequence of general conditions in the labour market that are external to class analysis as such. It looks as if Pahl's early objections have been reinforced.

Moreover, as Piketty's data show, while there are common trends, there are also significant differences in income inequalities and distributional shares among countries and across epochs. How do we explain those differences? Sociological class analysis would also assign epochal differences to 'economics' for explanation – this was Goldthorpe's argument, for example, and is implicit among his colleagues. Thus, for many sociologists, the trend outlined by Kuznets, as well as the explanation of it, was a feature of mature capitalism (rather than, say, of 'politics'). Piketty, for his part, sees the downward trend as a consequence of exogenous factors – namely the disruptive (and destructive) effects of war and contingent features of post-war reconstruction involving solidarities forged during those conditions. For Piketty, the 'economic' logic of capitalism is to produce widening inequalities and a fundamentally unequal society unless countered by social and political action, but for sociological class analysis that social and political action is exogenous, too.

There are other issues of a fundamental kind, too. Sweden, for example, is much more equal than the USA and remains more equal after a period of widening inequality than other countries achieved during the period of reducing inequality (see also Wilkinson and Pickett 2009). Might the social and political formations of different national distributional orders also be a relevant question for analysis? Does it mean the same to be in, say, 'Goldthorpe class' VII (semi-skilled and unskilled manual workers and farm workers) in the USA as it does in Sweden? Is the greater equality between classes in Sweden an issue of 'social relations', or are 'social relations' simply the definitional basis for determining what are to be judged the 'same' classes in the USA, Sweden and elsewhere (where differences in class structure, for example would be assigned to differences in level of industrial or post-industrial development)?[16] Would it mean the same in class terms for there to be a society in which there was inequality, but no poverty (as defined, say, by the EU definition of falling below 60 per cent of median income), compared with a society of poverty amid abundance, as Prasad (2012) describes the situation in the USA? Finally, are class positions to be judged the same over time – say, between 1920 and 1970, or 1950 and 2000 – merely differing in their proportional representation, such that there are fewer occupations judged to be 'Goldthorpe class' VII, in earlier compared to later periods, but the meaning of 'Goldthorpe class' VII, itself, remained stable across the different time periods?

What should be obvious is these differences potentially represent outcomes of social struggles for reform and amelioration, yet their success (or otherwise) cannot be represented within class analysis. The failure to address SCA, as Pahl observed, cannot be neatly insulated from other aspects of class analysis. They seem to be mutually implicated.

16 See, for example, Goldthorpe's (2010) response to Wilkinson and Pickett's (2009) argument about distributional differences that they do not understand class analysis, but it is Goldthorpe himself who wishes to deny distributional differences any significance for class analysis.

Perhaps the most telling part of Pahl's critique in this later article is where he argues that class analysis has failed to address issues of consumption, which itself reflects the increasing role of credit associated both with house purchase and consumption-led growth. Here he points to the way in which 'advertisers' and 'market researchers' have moved away from class to address markers of 'identity' and 'lifestyle'. Market-based 'class position', apparently, does not do work for the commercial 'market' in research. This argument has also been made by Savage and Burrows (2007), but the answer is clearly not, for Pahl, the replication of the problems of class analysis in the analysis of identities.

Let me conclude this section with Pahl's own solution, and, once again, it returns us to SCA as itself the basis of a new research programme designed to advance theoretical understanding: 'from informal social networks, through families, kinship links and the whole range of formal and informal associations of civil society people are engaging in voluntary solidaristic and collective activity for a variety of goals' (1992: 719). This emphasis on *association* evokes Oliver Cromwell Cox's (1948) great critique of the sociological analysis of class stratification where the sociologist defines 'objective class/occupational positions' according to some set of criteria, assigns populations to these classes (or aggregates), and then considers their 'subjective' responses to membership in these common aggregate groups. It remains the standard sociological approach, whether these aggregates are called classes (whether using neo-Marxist or neo-Weberian conceptualisations) or some other term ('occupational groups', etc). As Cox suggests, variation within supposedly discrete aggregates is potentially as considerable as that which divides groups. The real substance of class, for Cox, lies in the associations that are formed among people; that is in solidarities, constructed through action. 'Class' ('identity') is constructed in action and association, not from the a priori definitions of sociologists, or as E. P. Thompson (1963) put it in his preface to *The Making of the English Working Class*, it is a 'relationship', not a 'thing'.[17]

One nation sociology?

Ray Pahl was deeply concerned with inequality and its consequences in terms of distress and disrespect – this, after all, is the source of his empathy with Linda and

17 Pahl, in fact, cites E. P. Thompson to similar effect, though that can be a little misleading. Most commentators associate Thompson's critique of theory with the critique of Althusser and structuralist Marxism, but he is also criticising class stratification approaches: 'sociologists who have stopped the time-machine and, with a good deal of conceptual huffing and puffing have gone down into the engine room to look, tell us that nowhere at all have they been able to locate and classify a class. They can only find a multitude of people with different occupations, incomes, status-hierarchies and the rest … Of course, they are right, since class is not this or that part of the machine, but the way the machine works once it is set in motion' (cited in Pahl 1989: 717).

Jim. He showed their great resilience and resourcefulness in the face of the forces ranged against them and, if they had difficulty 'getting by', others in similar situations were likely to fare less well (we now know from his follow-up interviews, discussed by Elliott and Lawrence, just how badly things did go for them). In an early chapter of *Divisions of Labour*, Pahl refers to the period between 1945 and 1970 as the 'years of incapacitation'. He writes,

> The unions got stronger and led their members to believe that collective solidaristic action would lead to a permanent position on the rising escalator of incomes. Men were pulled out of their households and, as it were, put in the block vote with other men in an all-male fraternity. It was held to be a victory when overtime was 'won', keeping the men away from home when their wives were at their busiest feeding the children and putting them to bed. Those in these expanding and flourishing unions and factories were the affluent workers. They were also most likely to want to own their own homes – so when the factory closed or laid them off, they had little to fall back on and still had a large mortgage to pay. (1984: 56–7)

The contrast between Linda and Jim and Beryl and George points to a possible fate where economic and social change potentially spills them off the escalator of rising incomes.

This theme of incapacitation is carried into his analysis of public policy:

> Perhaps the clearest embodiment of these principles can be seen in the way New Towns were planned. Neighbourhood units were laid out some distance from the main shopping and recreational facilities in the town centre, with just a few shops within walking distance for daily needs. Men went to the industrial estates, segregated some distance from the living areas, so that earning and consuming were kept physically separated. There was no expectation that women would want to have employment close to their homes or that opportunities for part-time work might encourage women to combine the care of small children with paid employment. (1984: 79)

'Work on the side' for 'cash in hand' would help people to get by, but the benefits system increasingly regarded this as 'cheating' and encouraged jealous neighbours to inform on those working in the 'informal economy'.[18]

However, I have also suggested that Pahl regarded sociology itself as suffering 'incapacitation'. He was no radical in the sense that would have been understood by other sociologists at the time. Indeed, the nature of his engagement, whether with those in precarious positions or senior managers and others reflecting on success almost precluded the normal kind of radicalism. Anyone's 'private' troubles and their social structural causes interested him and amelioration could be

18 Although the unemployed also faced material barriers to 'working on the side', since 'they cannot afford to go to the pub in order to make essential contacts, and, they cannot afford the tools and equipment to do such jobs as decorating or car repairs' (1984: 96).

directed at all private troubles for which a social structural cause could be identified. So what was the politics of the new jurisdiction for sociology that Pahl was setting out? In this concluding section, I set out some speculations – I regret that I did not have the gumption to ask him directly while he was alive.

I think a clue lies in his involvement with the Archbishop of Canterbury's Commission on Urban Priority Areas, which coincided with his research for *Divisions of Labour* and which was deeply influenced by that research. My tag for this section – 'one nation sociology' – is not intended to evoke one nation conservatism, but an 'Anglican' conception of the nation as it was developing in concerns over rising unemployment, inequality and poverty. I suggest that Pahl was setting out a sociology that drew part of its inspiration from a particular moment in Anglicanism and its turn toward social issues that made it no longer the 'Tory party at prayer', as the familiar jibe had it. Pahl's sociology, as this chapter should suggest, indicates a strong 'dissenting' tradition, but he had an 'Anglican' faith in sociology, understanding it as a broad church made up of different positions. But I also mean something more by my reference to a new Anglican sensibility, and it turns on the figure of 'polarisation' that plays such a role in his work and in the report of the Archbishop of Canterbury's commission.

When Pahl (1992: 714) refers to metaphors of the military (class struggle) being replaced by the market (individual lifestyle), I do not believe that he regrets the passing of 'military engagements', which may also characterise some of the conflicts among sociologists at the time. What he regrets is the individualising of social responsibility and what he is seeking to articulate is the emergence of new collectivities and new responsibilities – social solidarity, rather than class war. And here the Anglican church in its declaration of faith in the city (playing on both the role of faith ministering to the city, and faith in the poor of the city) can stand as an example.

What distinguishes the Anglican ministry is that, deriving from its status as an established church, there is a formal responsibility for all members of the parish – whether those members accept that responsibility or not. Unlike other religious faiths, the responsibility is not only to the members of the congregation (temple, mosque, etc.), but to all, including those of no faith. It is this that provided the capacity for the church to intervene on social issues of the day and initiate interfaith dialogues as well as provide their capital (physical spaces) to be available to other religious groups for meetings. It has become particularly significant in British cities, especially those with significant ethnic minorities and people of different faiths. In this context, it is no accident that the then Archbishop, Robert Runcie, should accept a responsibility in relation to designated urban priority areas following riots in 1981 (and, subsequent to the Report's publication, in 1985) in Brixton (London), Handsworth (Birmingham), Chapeltown (Leeds) and Toxteth (Liverpool). The concerns were precisely those that engaged Pahl – problems of poverty, inequality and disrespect – and much of the Report draws on his research. It seems to me that Ray Pahl accepted a similar responsibility for sociology. Unlike his Isle of Sheppey study, where the ethnic minority population was tiny and remains so to this day, urban priority areas required a direct address of ethnicity and a Britain different from that described in the earlier community studies addressed by Savage (2010) as searching for an English Middletown.[19]

This was another respect in which sociology's jurisdiction was changing and changing, perhaps, through the influence of a different kind of agency than that expected by most sociologists – not government or class-based agency, but that of the church. Significantly, the studies addressed by Savage neglected race and ethnicity. The *Affluent Worker* study, for example, looked at geographically mobile workers who moved to Luton, but did not address non-white workers who were also present (see the restudy by Devine (1992)). Similarly, Coates and Silburn's (1970) study of poverty in Nottingham, *Poverty: The Forgotten Englishmen*, forgot the people from the Caribbean who were alongside them. There were studies of race and ethnic minorities – for example by Little (1948), or by Rex and Moore in Sparkbrook (1967). These are absent from Savage's account of British sociology's moment, but such issues could hardly be absent from any new jurisdiction. 'One nation sociology' would necessarily be a sociology *of* multicultural Britain and *for* multicultural Britain.

I think it is significant that Pahl should be attuned to a problem of existing approaches to social stratification in the analysis of these issues. The argument that he was beginning to articulate in *Divisions of Labour* proposes that an adequate address to social inequality would need to make its *dynamics*, and not its *categorisation*, central to a new sociological jurisdiction. It would also need to find a new language to connect the private troubles of inequality to public discourses that could generate political motivations to ameliorate them.

The final preparation of this manuscript coincided with the outcome of the UK referendum on membership of the European Union and the decision by a small majority to leave. Pahl researched *Divisions of Labour* a short time after the UK joined the European Economic Community (as it then was) in January 1973. This was a time when the UK shifted from a political economy of imperial/Commonwealth preferences (Holmwood 2000) in which Sheppey, its community and its labour markets, had been formed. One response to the vote to leave – at least when talking about voters in disadvantaged areas (it is important to recognise that prosperous middle-class Conservative voters also voted to leave) – is to refer to 'left behind Britain' and to mark it implicitly as a *white* working class. On the basis of Pahl's analysis, we might associate that not just with the experiences of Linda and Jim, but also the underlying precarity of those in the

19 As Lassiter (2012) has argued, Lynd and Lynd (1929) excluded the African-American population of Middletown in their representation of its typicality, notwithstanding that the proportion of African Americans was higher than many other US cities.

seemingly more advantaged position of Beryl and George. Yet we must remember the peculiarities of the Sheppey study. The conditions associated with being 'left behind' are shared by ethnic minorities (and by migrants). Ours is a dangerous time when a new polarisation on the basis of race and ethnicity is emerging and it is important that any new politics of inequality bears witness to all the spaces in which that inequality is reproduced and transcends the segregated experiences and spatial divisions that industrial decline has generated and which are all too readily inscribed in sociological understandings of 'community' and 'class'.

Afterword

Mike Savage

Reading *Divisions of Labour* afresh after a gap of thirty years, I was immediately struck by what an utterly remarkable and unusual book it is. It is a book which is *sui generis*, failing to conform to established formats of the research monograph. The book begins with five chapters of largely historical and synthetic discussion of the history of work and employment on a very general scale, in order to situate the study of the Isle of Sheppey in the wider historical context of the challenge of de-industrialisation. The core of the book, six chapters focused on household work strategies in Sheppey does not begin until page 141. This includes another historical study of the Sheppey context itself, before finally homing in on the empirical study of households in earnest in chapter 8, starting on page 199. And then we are exposed to a remarkable pot-pourri of analysis, especially focusing on the sample of (only?) 730 households (of which only 526 are the 'couple' households which are the focus of study). Having been led through the construction of a series of scales to measure degrees of involvement in the informal economy, the analysis changes direction in the key chapter 10 to look at the gendered division of labour with the construction and modelling of the 'DOMDIV' index (of which he was proud, though later researchers have not taken it up). And then, in the book's penultimate, perhaps best, chapter, it is the case of a single household which is held up for detailed analysis.

Any PhD student would definitely not be advised to take this as a model. I have lost count of the number of times I have told students to get to their data quickly, and certainly not wait until well over half way, and then to tread a consistent path through the analysis, not to dart around between different formats and modes of presentation. And yet Pahl renders this maverick style into what is almost certainly the greatest work of 1980s British sociology, possibly the enduring contribution to studies of de-industrialisation in post-war British society. He does this fundamentally through championing his own voice and vision, refusing to compromise and follow expected formats. And in particular, there are four great features which ring loud as a bell thirty years on, and which command our respect in 2016 as much as they did at the time.

These are, first, Pahl's emphasis that social change happens in places. It does not happen through some abstract processes, removed from everyday life, which then plonk themselves down in uniform or predictable ways across society, but it is the lived and felt experiences of living, working, loving, getting by in places which are fundamental to understanding social process. Pahl's love of Sheppey shines through in this book which is ultimately a monument to the men and women he has researched. Pahl himself makes his acknowledgements to the anthropological tradition clear here, and one gets the clear sense of pride that he feels he has found a tribe which no one has yet discovered. Yet there is much more to Pahl's use of Sheppey than this. The case study is made to elaborate sociological points – hence the long historical introduction and the selection of the place as analytically appropriate for his ends.

Second is Pahl's underlying respect and admiration for the people he studies. This is fundamentally sociology at its democratic best. Time and again he casts scorn on the arrogance of sociologists for thinking they might be able to decide what is going on better than the people concerned. This comes over beautifully in his rendering in the excerpt from chapter 7 of Marxist, Durkheimian and Weberian interpretations of social change in the lay words of the Sheppey population itself rather than in the abstract theoretical propositions which dominate academic discussion. This is a book of theory which refuses to be 'theoreticist'. And we should not underestimate the profound importance of the theoretical innovations Pahl makes. His arguments about provisioning have been very significant in the sociology of consumption, notably on Alan Warde (e.g. 1997), and in a more indirect way the 'material culture' turn. His focus on strategy allowed a distinctive way of rendering 'agency' which came to be much discussed in later years (e.g. Crow 1989). As Pahl shows very clearly, theory can emerge powerfully through this inductive mode.

Methodologically, third, this concern also reveals itself in Pahl turning to Jim, Linda, Beryl and George for the last word, even after the wonders of the DOMDIV index have been revealed. This sensitivity is fundamentally borne out in his central argument that we need to understand work and employment not from the perspective of corporate players or the state, but in terms of the myriad strategies, compromises and lives of ordinary people. A key aspect of his work here is a concern to make women's lives visible. Rather than women being seen as marginal workers, his focus on household work strategies, and his rendering of formal employment, informal work and domestic labour as analytically equivalent allowed women's work, as much as men's, to be fully part of his investigations.

Finally comes Pahl's insistence that research methods are tools for inquiry, not objects of reverence in their own right. Pahl uses historical, ethnographic, survey and qualitative interview analysis side by side, without privileging any of these, and without letting methodological nit-picking get in the way of telling the story as he wants to convey it. In the context of the scaling up of methodological sophistication in recent decades, Pahl's almost wilful irreverence is remarkably refreshing and an encouragement to researchers not to lose their own voice.

Fundamentally, what marks out great work in social science is the vision, urgency and originality which underpins it. We are so often distracted by disciplinary, theoretical or methodological debates and the 'gate-keeping' which goes along with this, that we can lose sight of this fundamental point. Pahl's great book reminds us of the need to insist on the power of our own voice – as modulated and refined by the voices of others we talk to as we go about our research.

Divisions of Labour as a community study

In my book *Identities and Social Change: The Politics of Method* (2010), I argued that the rise of the 'social science assemblage' has been a key feature of post-war society – as indeed it has been throughout the entire world. In place of the 'amateurish' investigations of social life based on 'gentlemanly observation' which preceded the Second World War, a battery of new devices – especially the social survey and interview – allowed social scientists to define the social world in new and powerful ways which were taken up by powerful institutions and agents. As they did this, they lifted social life out of specific locations into the world of abstract categories – class, gender, ethnicity and suchlike – leading to the social sciences themselves becoming implicated in the operations of what Nigel Thrift (2005) has termed 'knowing capitalism', and the proliferation of new kinds of technical expertise.

Ray Pahl is a fascinating figure to engage within the context of my argument, and indeed his role in championing the new interview method played a significant element in my account. He did not always welcome my interventions, especially pertaining to the way that I claimed that interview methods allowed a new group of young academic men to gain prominence by revealing ordinary lives. He and I engaged in vigorous debate, both over the phone and then later distilled (more politely!) in the review he wrote in *Sociological Review* (Pahl 2011). Recently, I have been shown his marked-up copy of my book (which I had sent him) where, alongside the occasional approving tick, he wrote angrily that my analysis of his own contribution is 'all bollocks'.

I am enough of an ethnographer to know that when someone gets seriously riled it is often a sign that you have touched a telling nerve, so I see Ray's reaction as informative in its own right. And reflecting on this now, I think that Ray's reaction is associated with his ambivalent Janus-faced position, to the extent that he felt uncertain about his own place in the canon of British sociology. His work looked backwards to older models of social science at the same time that he was a pioneer of new methods. In one key respect, he was (and remained) rooted in old 'landscaped' conceptions of social change. He refused social abstractions and rooted social change in places – as much in the 1960s when he was interested in suburbanisation as a process of social and spatial change as in *Divisions of Labour* twenty years later. In some respects this marked him out as one of the last of the gentlemanly phase of researchers that I have identified (Savage 2010). My first memory of him, dating from the time that the fieldwork for this study was being done and I was studying for my doctorate at Lancaster University, was in his role as University Grants Committee visitor. I was one of the PhD students who had been chosen to meet him as he conducted his investigations into the Sociology Department. After half an hour or so of fairly casual banter, the Head of Department, John Urry entered the room to be told by a smiling Ray, 'Don't worry, well done, I couldn't crack them.' Pahl enjoyed being an old-fashioned broker at the same time that he cocked a snoop at the very operations of the audit culture. Thus, as Jay Gershuny also relates, at the very same time that Pahl was writing his magnum opus, he was also involved (albeit humorously and with tongue in cheek) in the early operations of the academic audit culture which has become so pervasive today.

Yet just as Pahl was rooted in the gentlemanly tradition he was also a pioneer – especially methodologically with his use of qualitative household interviews to probe community relations and household dynamics – though also with survey methods as we see in this book. And in fact he was a central protagonist in the powerful attempt to mainstream the 'community study' within post-war sociology. Pahl's was perhaps the last major work in a key tradition of British social science which flowered in the 1950s and 1960s, and which sought to make 'community' the focus of sociological investigation. Thus, Pahl's work has echoes of Young and Willmott (1957) going to East London in the 1950s to consider how housing and family life was being transformed in the post-war years, or Margaret Stacey (1960) going to Banbury (also in the 1950s) to consider how new industry had transformed a traditional Midlands town, or John Goldthorpe and David Lockwood (1969) considering how new affluent workers in assembly line industries were transforming working-class culture.

Some of the parallels are uncanny, such as Pahl's decision to buy a house for his research team in Sheppey, in a similar way to Margaret Stacey in Banbury, or Ronald Frankenberg in Silverdale (see Hunt 1980). As Elliott and Lawrence show, this is also an era before principles of informed consent had been formalised. Just as Elizabeth Bott (1957) wondered how to deal with friendship relationships among her respondents in 1950s London, so Pahl got fully engaged in his community, especially the lives of Linda and Jim. Such a close relationship with respondents would be almost unimaginable now, in the era of consent forms, ethical committees and risk assessments. And in fact the brilliance of Pahl's work indicates just what has been lost by this formalisation of community research and how a sense of passion, justice and engagement matters so much.

In this respect, Pahl was sensitive to the way that by the 1970s, and certainly the 1980s, the 'community studies' tradition had fallen from grace, in part due to the problems of conceptualising community, and also as nationally representative sample surveys became increasingly used. Interestingly, Pahl avoids the concept of community altogether in *Divisions of Labour*, seeking to render it as a study of work and employment and hence avoiding the problematic baggage of the community studies tradition. And it was this sensitivity to the fact that 'his' tradition of community research had become side-lined that perhaps explains his sensitivity to the arguments in my book, and the feeling that his role in the development of sociology was being called into question.

In fact Pahl's study did encourage the revival of 'locality' research which boomed in British social science. Yet the idea that economic restructuring needed to be studied in local context was driven less by Pahl's work and more by the radical geographer Doreen Massey, whose *Spatial Divisions of Labour* (also published in 1984) came to have emblematic status and provoked major interest in understanding social change across a range of British localities. From this impetus came two major programmes of study, the *Social Change and Economic Life* initiative led by Duncan Gallie, and the *Localities* programme led by Phil Cooke (see e.g. Cooke 1987). The former broke new ground by conducting representative surveys in all its sites whereas the latter preferred a more idiographic case study approach. In both cases, Pahl's work was important (especially with respect to the use of survey elements in the SCELI programme) but not the fundamental underpinning due to the focus on employment and economic restructuring which both these programmes deployed.

Despite his enormous success, therefore, Pahl also felt undervalued and unappreciated. *Divisions of Labour* was meant to be the answer to what he saw as the devaluing of community studies. Yet, though hugely successful and significant in its own terms, it conveyed a Canute-like quality in the context of its attempts to still the methodological incoming tide and the claims of radical geographers to offer more powerful ways of rendering place and locality.

And yet, as Gershuny relates, Pahl had the last laugh. His insistence on the value of emerging ways of grasping social change fed into the currents that gathered pace through the 1980s to support the use of longitudinal panel data sets. Until the formation of the British Household Panel Study (BHPS) in 1991, surveys had been entirely cross-sectional and hence not necessarily best placed to reveal the nuances of change which a sensitive community study might bring out, especially one for which the fieldwork lasted some six years. Pahl's work in *Divisions of Labour* as well as his subsequent work at Essex University helped to establish the BHPS, and therefore to launch one of the UK's major research instruments. Indeed, Nick Buck, who has for many years been central to the BHPS cut his teeth as a PhD student on the Sheppey study.

This ability to look in two directions perhaps describes *Divisions of Labour* most accurately, as an amazing work which marked the turning point of a great tradition of community-based sociology, while at the same time pointing to the brave new world of large-scale panel data.

Class analysis

There is another side of Pahl's work which I also want to bring out, which emphasises his prescience and originality in detecting new and emerging social class divisions. This sensibility was amply evident in his work in the 1960s, where he showed a pioneering interest in the new suburban middle classes and in the phenomenon of 'spiralist' managers who moved geographically in the context of the internal labour markets of their company. This fascination with emerging class divisions put Pahl very much alongside other sociologists of his generation. However, and in keeping with my remarks above, Pahl refused the theoretical and methodological purisms which came to dominate class analysis and instead championed a more inductive and intuitive style of analysis. This approach to class is one which I continue to find very powerful, and indeed which I see myself as following. The point of studying class is to unravel the fractures and cleavages evident around us, not to obsess over a specialist sub-discipline of sociology: this is a view which Pahl's work exemplifies perfectly.

Pahl was indeed a pioneer who went against the grain of conventional analysis of class, especially that elaborated by John Goldthorpe, and which emphasised the difference between the 'middle' (or 'service') and 'working' classes. Although he used classifications which approximated to this approach (e.g. Pahl 1984: 203), Pahl looked back to his own view from 1969 that the main class divisions distinguished a 'senior salariat', a 'middle mass', and an 'underclass'. He thus detected the erosion of clear class boundaries and saw the emergence of a 'middle mass' which brought together lower middle and upper working-class households. This went against the grain of much sociological thinking, and was indeed to be disputed in the major national study by Gordon Marshall and colleagues (Marshall *et al.* 1988), but looking back now, it is highly pertinent to the arguments which I and my colleagues put forward in *Social Class in the 21st Century* (Savage 2015). Here, we see a fundamental divide between a wealthy elite and a 'precariat', with a more fragmented group of classes in the middle. This is not a million miles from Pahl's own prescient account.

Pahl's book failed to win the arguments in the short term. His claims about class were critiqued by Gordon Marshall, leaving Pahl (1989) to question the value of the class concept, only then to be subject to a roasting by Goldthorpe and Marshall (1992). And yet, in the longer term, it is Pahl's 'feel' for understanding class on the ground which seems far more perceptive for recognising the power and meaning of class today. Perhaps it is a shame that Pahl never felt any common cause with Bourdieu's sociology. Many of the issues posed by Pahl could be amply illuminated by Bourdieu's thinking, including the fundamental interest in 'strategies' which the translation of Bourdieu's early Bearn studies have brought out. A move in this direction would have aligned Pahl with the emerging current of work which was beginning to redefine class analysis in Britain from the 1990s. There are some striking parallels between Pahl and Bourdieu in their use of mixed methods (including photographs), in their critique of positivist methods, and in their attention to personal and everyday life (manifest in Bourdieu's case especially in *The Weight of the World* (1999)). Of course, it is easy to see why Pahl might have resisted this comparison – Bourdieu can appear to be a French theoreticist, of a kind which would have been highly uncongenial to Pahl's quintessential English empiricism. Nonetheless, it is an intriguing thought to consider whether Pahl was – or could have been – Britain's home-grown version of Bourdieu.

Conclusion

Pahl is an enigmatic figure in British sociology. He championed a vision of the discipline as engaged, democratic and attuned to the urgencies of its time. His prescience and capacity to render social change as located in specific places is clear and manifest. It is important for us to see him not simply as a commentator on prior times, but as embodying a vision of the sociological imagination which remains live today. This book shows the contemporary urgency of Pahl's vision of sociology.

References

Abbott, A. (2001a) *Chaos of Disciplines* (Chicago: University of Chicago Press).

Abbott, A. (2001b) *Time Matters: On Theory and Method* (Chicago: University of Chicago Press).

Abbott, P. and C. Wallace (2007) 'Talking about health and well-being in post-Soviet Ukraine and Russia', *Journal of Communist Studies and Transition Politics*, 23, 181–202.

Abbott, P., C. Nativiel and C. Wallace (2013) 'Dual earner parents' strategies for reconciling work and care in seven European countries', *Observatoire de la Societe Britannique*, 14, 73–97.

Abrams, P., R. Deem, J. Finch and P. Rock (eds) (1981) *Practice and Progress: British Sociology 1950–1980* (London: George Allen & Unwin).

Ahmed, S. (2006) *Queer Phenomenology: Orientations, Objects, Others* (Durham and London: Duke University Press).

Anderson, M., F. Bechhofer and J. Gershuny (eds) (1993) *The Social and Political Economy of the Household* (Oxford: Oxford University Press).

Archbishop of Canterbury's Commission on Urban Priority Areas (1985) *Faith in the City: A Call for Action by Church and Nation* (London: Church House Publishing).

Archer, M. (2007) *Making Our Way Through the World* (Cambridge: Cambridge University Press).

Arnold, E. *et al.* (1982) 'Microelectronics and women's employment', *Department of Employment Gazette* (September), 377–84.

Barrett, M. and M. McIntosh (1982) *The Anti-Social Family* (London: Verso).

Beck, U. and E. Beck-Gernsheim (1995) *The Normal Chaos of Love* (Cambridge: Polity).

Becker, G. S. (1965) 'A theory of the allocation of time', *Economic Journal*, 75, 493–517.

Bell C. and H. Newby (eds) (1977) *Doing Sociological Research* (London: George Allen & Unwin).

Bell, D. (1973) *The Coming of Post-Industrial Society: A Venture in Social Forecasting* (London: Peregrine).

Bell, D. and G. Graubard (eds) (1997 [1967]) *Toward the Year 2000: Work in Progress* (Cambridge, MA: MIT Press).

Bensman, D. and R. Lynch (1987) *Rusted Dreams: Hard Times in a Steel Community* (New York: McGraw-Hill).

Berk, R. and S. Berk (1983) 'Supply side sociology of the family: the challenge of the New Home Economics', *Annual Review of Sociology*, 9, 375–95.

Blackaby, F. (ed.) (1979) *De-Industrialisation* (London: Heinemann).

Bland, R. (1979) 'Measuring "social class"', *Sociology*, 13, 283–91.

Bluestone, B. and B. Harrison (1982) *The Deindustrialization of America: Plant Closing, Community Abandonment, and the Dismantling of Basic Industry* (New York: Basic Books).

Blyth, M. (2002) *Great Transformations: Economic Ideas and Institutional Change in the Twentieth Century* (Cambridge: Cambridge University Press).

Bohlmeijer, E. T., G. J. Westerhof, W. Randall, T. Tromp and G. Kenyon (2011) 'Narrative foreclosure in later life: Preliminary considerations for a new sensitizing concept', *Journal of Aging Studies*, 25:4, 364–70.

Böhme, G. (1993) 'Atmosphere as the fundamental concept of a new aesthetics', *Thesis Eleven*, 36, 113–26.

Bott, E. (1957) *Family and Social Network* (London: Tavistock).

Bourdieu, P. (1999) *The Weight of the World: Social Suffering in Contemporary Society* (Cambridge: Polity).

Brannen, J. and A. Nilsen (2002) 'Young people's time perspectives: From youth to adulthood', *Sociology*, 36:3, 513–37.

Brown, W. H. (no date) *Co-operative Centenary 1816–1916: A Century of Co-operation at Sheerness: Being a Chronicle of the Oldest Co-operative Society in Existence in the United Kingdom* (Manchester: Co-operative Wholesale Society).

Bryant, J. and J. Ellard (2015) 'Hope as a form of agency in the future thinking of disenfranchised young people', *Journal of Youth Studies*, 18:4, 485–99.

Buck, N. (1981) *An Admiralty Dockyard in the Mid-Nineteenth Century: Aspects of the Social and Economic History of Sheerness* (Urban and Regional Studies Unit, University of Kent).

Bulbeck, C. (2005) 'Schemes and dreams: Young Australians imagine their future', *Hecate*, 31:1, 73–84.

Burawoy, M. (2005) 'For public sociology', *American Sociological Review*, 70, 4–28.

Búriková, Z. and D. Miller (2010) *Au Pair* (Cambridge: Polity).

Burns, S. (1977) *The Household Economy* (Boston: Beacon Press).

Byrne, D. (1989) *Beyond the Inner City* (Milton Keynes: Open University Press).

Byrne, D. (2002) 'Industrial culture in a post-industrial world: The case of the North East of England', *City*, 6:3, 279–89.

Byrne, D. and A. Doyle (2004) 'The visual and the verbal', in C. Knowles and P. Sweetman (eds), *Picturing the Social Landscape: Visual Methods and the Sociological Imagination* (London: Routledge).

Carabelli, G. and D. Lyon (2016) 'Young people's orientations to the future: navigating the present and imagining the future', *Journal of Youth Studies*, 19:8, 1110–27.

Castells, M. and A. Portes (1989) 'World underneath: The origins, dynamics and effects of the informal economy', in A. Portes, M. Castells and L. Benton (eds), *The Informal Economy: Studies in Advanced and Less Developed Societies* (Baltimore: Johns Hopkins University Press), pp. 11–37.

Central Statistical Office (1981) *Social Trends* (London: HMSO).

Chaney, J. (1981) *Social Networks and Job Information: The Situation of Women Who Return to Work* (Manchester: Equal Opportunities Commission, SSRC/EOC).

Charmaz, K. (2002) 'Stories and silences: disclosures and self in chronic illness', *Qualitative Inquiry*, 8, 302–28.

Clemens, P. (2011) *Punching Out: One Year in a Closing Auto Plant* (New York: Doubleday).

Coates, K. and R. Silburn (1970) *Poverty: The Forgotten Englishmen* (Harmondsworth: Penguin).

Coleman, R. (2008) '"Things That Stay": Feminist theory, duration and the future', *Time and Society*, 17:1, 85–102.

Cooke, P. (1987) *Localities: The Changing Face of Urban Britain* (London: Unwin Hyman).

Cooke, P. *et al.* (1983) 'New technology and regional development in austerity Britain: The case of the semiconductor industry', paper prepared for SSRC Conference on Urban Change and Conflict, Department of Town Planning, UWIST (mimeo).

Cornford, J. (1978) *Policing the Hidden Economy* (London: Outer Circle Policy Unit).

Corrin, C. (ed.) (1992) *Superwomen and the Double Burden* (London: Scarlet Press).

Corti, L., V. Van den Eynden, L. Bishop and M. Woollard (2014) *Managing and Sharing Research Data* (London: Sage).

Cotterill, P. (1992) 'Interviewing women: Issues of friendship, vulnerability and power', *Women's Studies International Forum*, 15:5–6, 593–606.

Cowie, J. and J. Heathcott (eds) (2003) *Beyond the Ruins: the Meanings of Deindustrialisation* (Ithaca: Cornell University Press).

Cox, O. C. (1948) *Caste, Class and Race* (New York: Monthly Review Press).

Creswell, T. (2004) *Place: A Short Introduction* (Oxford: Blackwell).

Crompton, R. (2006) *Employment and the Family* (Cambridge: Cambridge University Press).

Crompton, R. and M. Mann (eds) (1986) *Gender and Stratification* (Cambridge: Polity Press).

Crompton, R. and M. Mann (1994) 'A new introduction', in R. Crompton and M. Mann (eds) *Gender and Stratification* (Cambridge: Polity Press).

Crompton, R., D. Gallie and K. Purcell (eds) (1996) *Changing Forms of Employment: Organisations, Skills, Gender* (London: Routledge).

Crow, G. (1989) 'The use of the concept of "strategy" in recent sociological literature', *Sociology*, 23:1, 1–24.

Crow, G. (1997) *Comparative Sociology and Social Theory: Beyond the Three Worlds* (Basingstoke: Macmillan).

Crow, G. (2012) 'Community re-studies: lessons and prospects', *Sociological Review*, 60:3, 405–20.

Crow, G., P. Hatton, D. Lyon and T. Strangleman (2009) 'New divisions of labour?: Comparative thoughts on the current recession', *Sociological Research Online*, 14:2/3, www.socresonlline.org.uk/14/2/10.html.

Crow, G. and D. Lyon (2011) 'Turning points in work and family lives in the imagined futures of young people on Sheppey in 1978', Young Lives and Imagined Futures: Insights from Archived Data, *Timescapes Working Paper Series*, No. 6, 12–26.

Crow, G. and N. Takeda (2011) 'Ray Pahl's sociological career: Fifty years of impact', *Sociological Research Online*, 16:3, www.socresonline.org.uk/16/3/11.html.

Daly, A. A. (1904) *History of the Isle of Sheppey* (London: Simpkin, Marshall, Hamilton, Kent and Co.).

Davis, M. (2000) *Aphoristics: How 'Interesting Ideas' Turn the World Inside Out* (Bridgewater, NJ.: Superior Books).

Day, A. and K. Lunn (eds) (1999) *History of Work and Labour Relations in the Royal Dockyards* (London: Mansell).

Department of Employment (1979) 'Changing composition of the labour force, 1976–1991', *Employment Gazette*, 546–50.

Department of Employment (1983) 'A changing labour force: Constants and variables', *Employment Gazette*, 91:2, 49–54.

Devine, F. (1992) *Affluent Workers Revisited: Privatism and the Working Class* (Edinburgh: Edinburgh University Press).

Devine, F. and S. Heath (1999) *Sociological Research Methods in Context* (Basingstoke: Macmillan).

Ditton, J. (1977a) *Part Time Crime: An Ethnography of Fiddling and Pilferage* (London: Macmillan).

Ditton, J. (1977b) 'Perks, pilferage and the fiddle: the historical structure of invisible wages', *Theory and Society*, 4:1, 39–71.

Edgell, S. (2006) *The Sociology of Work* (London: Sage).

Ehrenreich, B. and A. Hochschild (eds) (2003) *Global Woman: Nannies, Maids and Sex Workers in the New Economy* (New York: Metropolitan Books).

Elias, N. and J. Scotson (1965) *The Established and the Outsiders* (London: Frank Cass).

Elliott, J. (2010) 'Imagining a gendered future: Children's essays from the National Child Development Study in 1969', *Sociology*, 44:6, 1073–90.

Elliott, J. and J. Lawrence (2016) 'The emotional economy of unemployment: a re-analysis of testimony from a Sheppey family, 1978–1983', Special Edition on 'Developments in Secondary Data Analysis', *Sage Open*.

Erikson, R. and J. Goldthorpe (1992) *The Constant Flux: A Study of Class Mobility in Industrial Societies* (Oxford, Clarendon Press).

Esping-Andersen, G. (1999) *Social Foundations of Postindustrial Economics* (Oxford: Oxford University Press).

Fineman, S. (ed.) (1987) *Unemployment: Personal and Social Consequences* (London: Tavistock).

Freeman, M. (2011) 'Narrative foreclosure in later life: Possibilities and limits', in G. Kenyon, E. Bohlmeijer and W.L. Randall (eds), *Storying Later Life: Issues, Investigations, and Interventions in Narrative Gerontology* (New York: Oxford University Press), pp. 3–19.

Gallie, D. (ed.) (1988) *Employment in Britain* (Oxford: Blackwell).

Gershuny, J. (1978) *After Industrial Society? The Emerging Self-service Economy* (London: Macmillan).

Gershuny, J. (1979) 'The Informal Economy', *Futures*, 11:1, 3–15.

Gershuny, J. (1983) *Social Innovation and the Division of Labour* (Oxford: Oxford University Press).

Gershuny, J. (1992) 'Change in the Domestic Division of Labour in the UK, 1975–1987: Dependent Labour vs Adaptive Partnership', in N. Abercrombie and A. Warde (eds), *Social Change in Contemporary Britain* (Cambridge: Polity Press).

Gershuny, J. (1982) 'Livelihood IV: Household tasks and the use of time', in S. Wallman and associates, *Living in South London* (Aldershot: Gower), pp. 149–81.

Gershuny, J. I. and I. D. Miles (1983) The New Service Economy: The Transformation of Employment in Industrial Societies London: Frances Pinter).
Gershuny, J. I. and R. E. Pahl (1979) 'Work outside employment: Some preliminary speculations', *New Universities Quarterly*, 34:1, 120–35.
Gershuny, J. I. and R. E. Pahl (1980) 'Britain in the decade of the three economies', *New Society*, 3 (January), 7–9.
Gershuny, J. I. and R. E. Pahl (1981) 'Work Outside Employment: Some Preliminary Speculations', in S. Henry (ed.) *Can I Have It in Cash? A study of informal institutions and unorthodox ways of doing things* (London: Astragal Books), pp. 73–88.
Gershuny, J., I. Miles, S. Jones, C. Mullings, G. Thomas and S. Wyatt (1986) 'Time budgets: preliminary analysis of a national survey', *Quarterly Journal of Social Affairs*, 2:1.
Gershuny, J., M. Bittman and J. Brice (2005) 'Exit, voice and suffering: Do couples adapt to changing employment patterns?', *Journal of Marriage and the Family*, 67:3, 656–65.
Gershuny, J., M. Godwin and S. Jones (1994) 'The domestic labour revolution: a Process of Lagged Adaptation', in M. Anderson, F. Bechhofer and J. Gershuny (eds), *The Social and Political Economy of the Household* (Oxford: Oxford University Press).
Giddens, A. (1973) *The Class Structure of the Advanced Societies* (London: Hutchinson).
Giddens, A. (1991) *Modernity and Self-Identity* (Cambridge: Polity Press).
Giddens, A. (1996) *In Defence of Sociology: Essays, Interpretations and Rejoinders* (Cambridge: Polity Press).
Glucksman, M. (1995) 'Why Work? Gender and the "Total social organisation of labour"', *Gender, Work and Organisations*, 2:2, 63–75.
Glucksmann, M. (2009) 'Formations, connections and the division of labour', *Sociology*, 43:5, 878–95.
Glyn, A. and B. Sutcliffe (1972) *British Capitalism, Workers and the Profits Squeeze* (Harmondsworth: Penguin).
Goch, S. (2002) 'Betterment without airs: Social, cultural, and political consequences of de-industrialization in the Ruhr', *International Review of Social History*, 47, 87–111.
Goldthorpe, J. (1983) 'Women and class analysis: in defence of the conventional view', *Sociology*, 18, 465–88.
Goldthorpe, J. (1990) 'The uses of history in sociology: Reflections on some recent tendencies', *British Journal of Sociology*, 42, 211–30.
Goldthorpe, J. (2010) 'Analysing social inequality: A critique of two recent contributions from economics and epidemiology', *European Sociological Review*, 26, 731–44.
Goldthorpe, J. and G. Marshall (1992) 'The promising future of class analysis: A response to recent critiques', *Sociology*, 26:3, 381–400.
Goldthorpe, J., C. Llewellyn and G. Payne (1980) *Social Mobility and Class Structure in Modern Britain* (Oxford: Clarendon Press).
Goldthorpe, J., D. Lockwood, F. Bechhofer and J. Platt (1968a) *The Affluent Worker: Industrial Attitudes and Behaviour* (Cambridge: Cambridge University Press).
Goldthorpe, J., D. Lockwood, F. Bechhofer and J. Platt (1968b) *The Affluent Worker: Political Attitudes and Behaviour* (Cambridge: Cambridge University Press).
Goldthorpe, J., D. Lockwood, F. Bechhofer and J. Platt (1969) *The Affluent Worker in the Class Structure* (Cambridge: Cambridge University Press).

Goodwin, J. and H. O'Connor (2015) *Norbert Elias's Lost Research: Revisiting the Young Worker Project* (Farnham: Ashgate).
Gregson, N. and M. Lowe (1994) *Servicing the Middle Classes: Class, Gender and Waged Domestic Work in Contemporary Britain* (London: Routledge).
Gstrein, M., L. Mateeva, P. Rodige-Lassning, P. Abbott and C. Wallace (2014) *Quality of Life in Europe: Quality of Society and Public Services* (Dublin: European Foundation for the Improvement of Living and Working Conditions).
Guttman, P. (1977) 'The Subterranean Economy', *Financial Analysts Journal* (November/December).
Haerpfer, C., C. Wallace and P. Abbott (2013) 'Health problems and the transition from communism in the former Soviet Union: towards and explanation', *Perspectives on European Politics and Society*, 14:4, 460–79.
Hall, S. (1979) 'The great moving right show', *Marxism Today*, January, 14–20.
Halsey, A. H. (2004) *A History of Sociology in Britain* (Oxford: Oxford University Press).
Hamermesh, D., M. Burda and P. Weil (2013) 'Total Work and Gender: Facts and Possible Explanations', *Journal of Population Economics*, 26:1, 239–61.
Hareven, T. (1982) *Family Time and Industrial Time* (Cambridge: Cambridge University Press).
Harloe, M. (1985) review of Divisions of Labour in *Cities* 2:3, 272–4.
Harloe, M. (2011) entry for R. Pahl in *Oxford Dictionary of National Biography*, www.oxforddnb.com/view/article/103967.
Harris, C. C. (1987) *Redundancy and Recession* (Oxford: Basil Blackwell).
Hart, K. (1973) 'Informal income opportunities and urban employment in Ghana', *The Journal of Modern African Studies* 11:1, 61–89.
Henderson, S., J. Holland, S. McGrellis, S. Sharpe and R. Thomson (2007) *Inventing Adulthoods* (London: Sage).
Henry, S. (1978) *The Hidden Economy* (London: Martin Robertson).
Henry, S. and G. Mars (1978) 'Crime at work: the social construction of amateur property theft', *Sociology*, 12:2, 245–63.
Himmelweit, H. *et al.* (1952) 'The views of adolescents on some aspects of the social class structure', *British Journal of Sociology*, 3:2, 148–72.
Hirschman, A. (1970) *Exit, Voice and Loyalty: Responses to Decline in Firms, Organizations and States* (Harvard, MA: Harvard University Press).
Hobsbawm, E. (1994) *The Age of Extremes: The Short Twentieth century, 1914–1991* (London: Michael Joseph).
Hochschild, A. (1989) *The Second Shift. Working Parents and the Revolution at Home* (New York: Viking Press).
Hockey, J. (2009) 'The life course anticipated: gender and chronologisation among young people', *Journal of Youth Studies*, 12:2, 227–41.
Holmwood, J. (2000) 'Europe and the 'Americanization' of British social policy', European Societies, 2:4, 453–82.
Holmwood, J. and A. Stewart (1983) 'The role of contradictions in modern theories of social stratification', *Sociology*, 17, 235–54.
Hunt, P. (1980) *Gender and Class Consciousness* (London: Macmillan).
Hurstfield, J. (1980) 'Part-time pittance', *Low Pay Review*, 1.

Ingold, T. (2007) *Lines: A Brief History* (London: Routledge).

Jahoda, M., P. Lazarsfeld and H. Zeisel (2002 [1932]) *Marienthal: Sociography of an Unemployed Community* (New York: Transaction Publishers).

Jamieson, L. (1998) *Intimacy: Personal Relationships in Modern Societies* (Cambridge: Polity).

Johnson, C. H. (1995) *The Life and Death of Industrial Languedoc 1700–1920* (Oxford: Oxford University Press).

Kalleberg, A. (2013) *Good Jobs, Bad Jobs: The Rise of Polarized and Precarious Employment Systems in the United States, 1970s to 2000s* (New York: Russell Sage Foundation).

Kingston, P. (2000) *The Classless Society* (Stanford: Stanford University Press).

Klein, V. (1965) *Britain's Married Women Workers* (London: Routledge & Kegan Paul).

Koistinen, D. (2013) *Confronting Decline: The Political Economy of Deindustrialization in Twentieth-Century New England* (Tallahassee: University Press of Florida).

Kuznets, S. (1953) *Shares of Upper Income Groups in Income and Savings* (Cambridge, MA: National Bureau of Economic Research).

Lakatos, I. (1970) 'Falsification and the methodology of scientific research programmes', in I. Lakatos, A. Musgrave (eds), *Criticism and the Growth of Knowledge* (Cambridge: Cambridge University Press).

Lamont, M. (2009) *How Professors Think* (Cambridge, MA: Harvard University Press).

Lassiter, L. E. (2012) '"To fill in the missing piece of the Middletown puzzle": lessons from re-studying Middletown', *Sociological Review*, 60, 421–37.

Laughland-Booÿ, J., M. Mayall, and Z. Skrbiš (2014) 'Whose choice? Young people, career choices and reflexivity re-examined', *Current Sociology*, OnlineFirst.

Lawrence, J. (2014) 'Social-science encounters and the negotiation of difference in early 1960s England', *History Workshop Journal*, 77, 215–39.

Leccardi, C. (2006) 'Facing uncertainty: Temporality and biographies in the new century', in C. Leccardi and E. Ruspini (eds), *A New Youth? Young People, Generations and Family Life* (Aldershot, UK and Burlington, VT: Ashgate).

Leeds Trade Union and Community Resource and Information Centre (1982) *New Technology and Women's Employment* (London: Equal Opportunities Commission).

Leicester, C. (1982) 'Towards a fully part-time Britain', *Personnel Management*, 14:6 (June), 28–31.

Lewis, J. (1992) 'Gender and the development of welfare regimes', *European Journal of Social Policy*, 2:3, 159–73.

Lewis, J. (2001) 'The decline of the male breadwinner model: The implications for work and care', *Social Politics*, 8:2, 152–70.

Linkon, S. (2014) 'The half-life of deindustrialisation: Twenty-first century narratives of work, place and identity', unpublished presentation to Deindustrialization and Its Aftermath: Class, Culture and Resistance, Centre for Oral History and Digital Storytelling / Scottish Oral History Centre, 1–4 May, Montreal, Quebec.

Little, K. L. (1948) *Negroes in Britain: A Study of Racial Relations in English Society* (London: Routledge & Kegan Paul).

Lloyds Bank (1982) *Economic Bulletin*, 42 (June).

Lockwood, D. (1981) 'The weakest link in the chain: Some comments on the Marxist theory of action', *Research in the Sociology of Work*, 1, 435–81.

Lockwood, D. (1986) 'Class, status and gender', in R. Crompton and M. Mann (eds), *Gender and Stratification* (Cambridge: Polity).

Lynd, R. and H. Lynd (1929) *Middletown: A Study in Contemporary American Culture* (New York: Harcourt Brace).

Lynd, S. (1982) *The Fight Against the Shutdowns: Youngstown's Steel Mill Closings* (San Pedro, CA: Steeplejack Books).

Lyon, D. and G. Carabelli (2015) 'Researching young people's orientations to the future: The methodological challenges of using arts practice', *Qualitative Research*, OnlineFirst.

Lyon, D. and G. Crow (2012) 'The challenges and opportunities of re-studying community on Sheppey: Young people's imagined futures', *Sociological Review*, 60:3, 498–517.

Lyon, D., B. Morgan Brett and G. Crow (2012) 'Working with material from the Sheppey archive', *International Journal of Social Research Methodology*, 15:4, 301–9.

MacInnes, J. (1987) *Thatcherism at Work: Industrial Relations and Economic Change* (Milton Keynes: Open University Press).

Madge, J. (1970) *The Origins of Scientific Sociology* (London: Tavistock).

Mah, A. (2012) *Industrial Ruination, Community, and Place: Landscapes and legacies of Urban Decline* (Toronto: Toronto University Press).

Marsden, D. (1982) *Workless: An Exploration of the Social Contract Between Society and the Worker* (London: Croom Helm).

Marshall, G. (1985) 'Review of *Divisions of Labour*', *International Journal of Urban and Regional Research*, 9:3, 449–50.

Marshall, G. (1990) *In Praise of Sociology* (London: Unwin Hyman).

Marshall, G., D. Rose, H. Newby and C. Vogler (1988) *Social Class in Modern Britain* (London, Unwin Hyman).

Marx, K. (1954) *Capital, volume I* (London: Lawrence & Wishart).

Massey, D. B. (1984) *Spatial divisions of labour: Social structures and the geography of production* (London: Macmillan).

Massey, D. and R. Meegan (1982) *The Anatomy of Job Loss: The How, Why and Where of Employment Decline* (London: Methuen).

McDonald, P., B. Pini, J. Bailey, and R. Price (2011) 'Young people's aspirations for education, work, family and leisure', *Work, Employment and Society*, 25:1, 68–84.

McDowell, L. (1986) 'Review of *Divisions of Labour*', *Economic Geography*, 62:2, 182–3.

McEwan Scott, A. (1994) *Gender Segregation and Social Change* (Oxford: Oxford University Press).

McLeod, J. and R. Thomson (2009) *Researching Social Change: Qualitative Approaches* (London: Sage).

McRae, S. (1986) *Cross-Class Families: A Study of Wives' Occupational Superiority* (Oxford: Clarendon Press).

Meissner, M., E. Humphries, S. Meis and W. Scheu (1975) "No Exit for Wives", *Canadian Review of Sociology and Anthropology*, 12, 424–39.

Mills, C. W. (1970) *The Sociological Imagination* (Harmondsworth: Penguin).

Mische, A. (2009) 'Projects and possibilities: Researching futures in action', *Sociological Forum*, 24:3, 694–704.

Morgan, D. (1985) 'Review of *Divisions of Labour*', *Sociological Review*, 33:3, 615–17.

Morris, L. (1990) *The Workings of the Household* (Cambridge: Cambridge University Press).

Murray, C. (1984) *Losing Ground. American Social Policy 1950–1980* (New York: Basic Books).

Neal, S. and K. Murji (2015) 'Sociologies of Everyday Life: Editors' Introduction to the Special Issue', *Sociology*, 49:5, 811–19.

Newman, K. (1985) 'Urban Anthropology and the Deindustrialization Paradigm', *Urban Anthropology and Studies of Cultural Systems and World Economic Development*, 14:1/3, 5–19.

O'Reilly, J., J. Roche, T. Nazio and J. MacInnes (2008) *Labour Market Transitions and Households' Capabilities Around Time, Care and Employment*, www.abdn.ac.uk/socsci/research/nec/workcare/: Workcare Report no.7. Social Quality in Work, Care and Welfare Across Europe.

Pahl, J. (1989) *Money and Marriage* (Basingstoke: Macmillan).

Pahl, J. M. and R. E. Pahl (1971) *Managers and Their Wives: A Study of Career and Family Relationships in the Middle Class* (London: Allen Lane).

Pahl, R. E. (1965) *Urbs in Rure* (London: LSE Geographical Papers).

Pahl, R. E. (1968) 'The rural-urban continuum', in R. Pahl (ed.), *Readings in Urban Sociology* (Oxford: Pergamon), pp. 263–97.

Pahl, R. E. (1970) *Patterns of Urban Life* (Harlow: Longmans).

Pahl, R. E. (1973) 'The self and social order: Thoughts on reading Erving Goffman', BBC Radio 3, 10 January.

Pahl, R. E. (1975) *Whose City?* (Harmondsworth: Penguin).

Pahl, R. E. (1977) 'Playing the rationality game', in C. Bell and H. Newby (eds), *Doing Sociological Research* (London: George Allen & Unwin).

Pahl, R. E. (1978) 'Living without a job: How school leavers see the future', *New Society* (2 November), 259–62.

Pahl, R. E. (1980) 'Employment, work and the domestic division of labour', *International Journal of Urban and Regional Research*, 4, 1–19.

Pahl, R. E. (1982) 'Family, community and unemployment', *New Society* (21 January), 91–3.

Pahl, R. E. (1984) *Divisions of Labour* (Oxford: Basil Blackwell).

Pahl, R. E. (ed.) (1988a) *On Work: Historical, Comparative and Theoretical Approaches* (Oxford: Basil Blackwell).

Pahl, R. E. (1988b) 'Some remarks on informal work, social polarisation and social structure' *International Journal of Urban and Regional Research*, 12:2, 247–67.

Pahl, R. E. (1989) 'Is the Emperor naked? Some questions on the adequacy of sociological theory in urban and regional research', *International Journal of Urban and Regional Research*, 13:4, 709–20.

Pahl, R. E. (1993) 'Does class analysis without class theory have a promising future? A reply to Goldthorpe and Marshall', *Sociology*, 27:2, 253–58.

Pahl, R. E. (1995) *After Success: Fin-de-Siècle Anxiety and Identity* (Cambridge: Polity Press).

Pahl, R. E. (1998) Interview with Michele Abendstern, in Paul Thompson, Pioneers of qualitative research, 1996–2007, Interview 26, UKDA, Essex, 10.5255/UKDA-SN-6226-2.

Pahl, R. E. (2000) *On Friendship* (Cambridge: Polity).

Pahl, R. E. (2006) Interview with Iain Wilkinson, Network, 93, 6–9, British Sociological Association.
Pahl, R. E. (2009) Interview with Libby Bishop and Dimitris Vonofakos, Bishop's Castle, UK Data Service, Essex.
Pahl, R. E. (2011) Review of Savage (2010), *The Sociological Review*, 59:1, 165–76.
Pahl, R. E. with J. H. Dennett (1981) *Industry and Employment on the Isle of Sheppey*, HWS project report, University of Kent. First annual report to SSRC.
Pahl, R. E. and P. Thompson (1994) 'Meaning, myths and mystifications: The social construction of life stories in Russia', in C. Hann (ed.), *When History Accelerates: Essays on rapid social change, complexity and creativity* (London: Athlone Press).
Pahl, R. E. and C. Wallace (1988) 'Neither angels in marble nor rebels in red: Privatisation and working-class consciousness', in D. Rose (ed.), *Social Stratification and Economic Change* (London: Hutchinson Education).
Picketty, T. (2014) *Capital in the Twenty-First Century* (Cambridge: Belknap Press of Harvard University Press).
Poland, B. and Pederson, A. (1998) 'Reading between the lines: Interpreting silences in qualitative research', *Qualitative Inquiry*, 4:2 (1998), 293–312.
Porter, M. (1993) *Place and Persistence in the Lives of Newfoundland Women* (Aldershot: Avebury).
Portes, A. (2010) *Economic Sociology: A Systematic Inquiry* (Princeton: Princeton University Press).
Prandy, K. and R. M. Blackburn (1997) 'Putting men and women into classes: But is that where they belong? A comment on Evans', *Sociology*, 31, 143–52.
Prandy, K. and W. Bottero (1997) 'The social analysis of stratification and mobility', Cambridge: Sociological Research Group Working Paper No. 18.
Prasad, M. (2012) *The Land of Too Much: American Abundance and the Paradox of Poverty* (Cambridge, MA: Harvard University Press).
Redclift, N. and E. Mingione (eds) (1985) *Beyond Employment: Household, Gender and Subsistence* (Oxford: Basil Blackwell).
Rex, J. and R. Moore (1967) *Race, Community and Conflict: A Study of Sparkbrook* (Oxford: Oxford University Press).
Robbins Report (1963) *Higher Education: Report of the Committee appointed by the Prime Minister under the Chairmanship of Lord Robbins* (HMSO Cmnd. 2154).
Rose, D. (1986) 'Review of *Divisions of Labour*', *Journal of Historical Geography*, 12:3, 334–6.
Rose, R. (1983) *Getting By in Three Economies: The Resources of the Official Unofficial and Domestic Economies* (Centre for the Study of Public Policy, University of Strathclyde).
Runciman, W. G. (1989) *Confessions of a Reluctant Theorist* (London: Harvester Wheatsheaf).
Runciman, W. G. (1997) *A Treatise on Social Theory, volume III: Applied Social Theory* (Cambridge: Cambridge University Press).
Runciman, W. G. (2010) *Great Books, Bad Arguments: Republic, Leviathan and The Communist Manifesto* (Princeton, NJ: Princeton University Press).
Salaman, G. (1986) *Working* (London: Tavistock).
Sanders, J. and R. Munford (2008) 'Losing self to the future? Young women's strategic responses to adulthood transitions', *Journal of Youth Studies*, 11:3, 331–46.

Saunders, P. (1985) 'Review of *Divisions of Labour*', *Sociology*, 19:4, 645–6.

Saunders, P. (1990) *A Nation of Home Owners* (London: Unwin Hyman).

Savage, M. (2010) *Identities and Social Change in Britain Since 1940: The Politics of Method* (Oxford: Oxford University Press).

Savage, M. (2014) 'Piketty's challenge for sociology', *British Journal of Sociology*, 65, 591–606.

Savage, M. (2015) *Social Class in the 21st Century* (Harmondsworth: Penguin UK).

Savage, M. and R. Burrows (2007) 'The coming crisis of empirical sociology', *Sociology*, 41, 885–99.

Scase, R. and R. Goffee (1982) *The Entrepreneurial Middle Class* (London: Croom Helm).

Scott, J. (1985) *Corporations, Classes and Capitalism* (London: Hutchinson).

Scott, J. (1994) 'Class analysis: Back to the future', *Sociology*, 28, 933–42.

Scott, J. (1996) *Stratification and Power: Structures of Class, Status and Command* (Cambridge: Polity).

Sennett, R. (1998) *The Corrosion of Character: The Personal Consequences of Work in the New Capitalism* (London: W. W. Norton).

Sennett, R. (2000) 'Work and its narratives', in J. Eldridge, J. MacInnes, S. Scott, C. Warhurst and A. Witz (eds), *For Sociology: Legacies and Prospects* (Durham: Sociology Press), pp.119–30.

Spencer, L. and R. E. Pahl (2006) *Rethinking Friendship: Hidden Solidarities Today* (Princeton, NJ: Princeton University Press).

Stacey, M. (1960) *Tradition and Change: A Study of Banbury* (Oxford: Oxford University Press).

Standing, G. (2014) *The Precariat: The New Dangerous Class* (London: Bloomsbury).

Strangleman, T. (2005) 'Sociological futures and the sociology of work', *Sociological Research Online*, 10:4, www.socresonline.org.uk/10/4/strangleman.html

Strangleman, T. (2007) 'The nostalgia for permanence at work?: The end of work and its commentators', *Sociological Review*, 55:1, 81–103.

Strangleman, T. (2013) '"Smokestack nostalgia", "Ruin porn" or working class obituary?: The role and meaning of de-industrial representation', *International Labor and Working-Class History*, 84, 23–37.

Strangleman, T. (2016) 'Deindustrialisation and the historical sociological imagination: Making sense of work and industrial change', *Sociology*. Online first. Available at http://dx.doi.org/10.1177/0038038515622906

Strangleman, T. and J. Rhodes (2014) 'The 'new' sociology of deindustrialisation?: Understanding industrial change', *Sociology Compass*, 8:4, 411–21.

Strangleman, T., J. Rhodes and S. Linkon (2013) 'Introduction to crumbling cultures: deindustrialisation, class and memory', *International Labor and Working-Class History*, 84, 7–22.

Szelenyi, I. (1988) *Socialist Entrepreneurs* (Wisconsin: University of Wisconsin Press).

Thatcher, A. R. (1979) 'Labour supply and employment trends', in F. Blackaby (ed.), *De-industrialization* (London: Heinemann Educational Books).

Therborn, G. (1995) *European Modernity and Beyond: The Trajectory of European Societies, 1945–2000* (London: Sage).

Thompson, E. P. (1963) *The Making of the English Working Class* (London: Victor Gollancz).

Thomson, R. and J. Holland (2002) 'Imagined adulthood: resources, plans and contradictions', *Gender and Education*, 14:4, 337–50.
Thrift, N. (2005) *Knowing Capitalism* (London, Sage).
Turner, A. (2008) *Crisis? What Crisis? Britain in the 1970s* (London: Aurum Press).
Veness, T. (1962) *School Leavers: Their Aspirations and Expectations* (London: Methuen).
Wallace, C. (1987) *For Richer, for Poorer: Growing Up in and Out of Work* (London: Tavistock).
Wallace, C. (1993) 'Reflections on the concept of "strategy"', in D. Morgan and L. Stanley (eds), *Debates in Sociology* (Manchester: Manchester University Press).
Wallace, C. (2000) 'Misunderstandings and misleading stereotypes: A western feminist goes east', *Soundings*, 16, 144–67.
Wallace, C. (2002) 'Household strategies: Their conceptual relevance and analytical scope in social research', *Sociology*, 36:2, 275–92.
Wallace, C. (2011) Ray Pahl obituary, *Guardian*, www.theguardian.com/theguardian/2011/jul/26/ray-pahl-obituary.
Wallace, C. with R. E. Pahl and J. H. Dennett (1981) *Housing and Residential Areas on the Isle of Sheppey*, University of Kent at Canterbury, part of the Final Report to the SSRC of project no. G00230036.
Walley, C. (2013) *Exit Zero: Family and Class in Postindustrial Chicago* (Chicago: Chicago University Press).
Wallman, S. (ed.) (1982) *Living in South London: Perspectives on Battersea, 1871–1981* (London: Gower for the London School of Economics).
Warde, A. (1997) *Consumption, Food and Taste* (London: Sage).
Warde, A. and K. Hetherington (1993) 'A changing domestic division of labour?: Issues of measurement and interpretation', *Work, Employment and Society*, 7:1, 23–45.
Waters, M. (1979) 'The social history of the Chatham Dockyard workforce 1860–1906', unpublished PhD thesis, University of Essex, 1979.
Westergaard, J. (1995) *Who Gets What? The Hardening of Class Inequality in the Late Twentieth Century* (Oxford: Blackwell).
Westergaard, J., I. Noble and A. Walker (1989) *After Redundancy: The Experience of Economic Insecurity* (Cambridge: Polity).
Wiener, M. (1981) *English Culture and the Decline of the Industrial Spirit, 1850–1980* (Cambridge: Cambridge University Press).
Wilkinson, R. and K. Pickett (2009) *The Spirit Level: Why Equality is Better for Everyone* (London: Allen Lane).
Williams, G. (1945) *Women and Work* (London: Nicholson and Watson).
Williams, R. (1983) *Towards 2000* (London: Chatto & Windus).
Wilson, P. and Pahl, R. E. (1988) 'The changing sociological construct of the family', *Sociological Review*, 36:2, 233–66.
Wyatt, W. (2000) *The Journals of Woodrow Wyatt, volume 2: Thatcher's Fall and Major's Rise* (edited by Sarah Curtis) (London: Macmillan).
Young, M. and P. Willmott (1957) *Family and Kinship in East London* (London: Routledge and Kegan Paul).
Young, M. and P. Willmott (1973) *The Symmetrical Family: A Study of Work and Leisure in the London Region* (London: Routledge & Kegan Paul).

Index